The Anthropologists' Cookbook

The Anthropologists'
Cookbook

edited by Jessica Kuper

illustrated by Joan Koster

Universe Books

New York

First published in 1977
by Universe Books
381 Park Avenue South
New York, N.Y. 10016
Copyright The Royal Anthropological Institute 1977
No part of this book may be reproduced in
any form without permission from the
publisher, except for the quotation of brief
passages in criticism

Library of Congress Catalog Card Number: 77–80179
Cloth edition: ISBN 0–87663–301–7
Paperback edition: ISBN 0–87663–971–6

Printed in Great Britain

I told [Burke], I had found out a perfect definition of human nature, as distinguished from the animal. An ancient philosopher said, Man was 'a two-legged animal without feathers,' upon which his rival Sage had a cock plucked bare, and set him down in the school before all the disciples, as a 'Philosophick Man.' Dr. Franklin said, Man was 'a tool-making animal,' which is very well; for no animal but man makes a thing, by means of which he can make another thing. But this applies to very few of the species. My definition of *Man* is, 'a Cooking Animal.' The beasts have memory, judgement, and all the faculties and passions of our mind, in a certain degree; but no beast is a cook. The trick of the monkey using the cat's paw to roast a chestnut, is only a piece of shrewd malice in that *turpissima bestia*, which humbles us so sadly by its similarity to us. Man alone can dress a good dish; and every man whatever is more or less a cook, in seasoning what he himself eats. – Your definition is good, said Mr. Burke, and I now see the full force of the common proverb, 'There is *reason* in roasting of eggs.' (James Boswell, *The Journal of a Tour to the Hebrides with Samuel Johnson, LL.D.*)

Ploughing in southern Europe

Contents

Introduction   *Mary Douglas*   1
Preface   *Jessica Kuper*   8
Weights and Measures   14
Acknowledgments   16

SECTION 1: Europe

Le Stockfish   *Julian Pitt-Rivers*   19
Serve it Forth: Food and Feasting in
    Late Medieval England   *Lorna J. Sass*   22
From the Flocks of Greece: *Galopita*   *Joan Bouza Koster*   27
From the Fields of Greece: *Hortopita*   *Mari H. Clark Forbes* 31
Melitera: Greek Island Cheese-Cakes   *Margaret Kenna*   34
The Spanish Pig Preserved: the *Olla*
    and the Ham   *Susan Tax Freeman*   37
Salt and Sugar in Portugal   *Susan Plant Dos Santos* 45
Faroese Fare   *Anthony Jackson*   48
Bosnian Coffee   *Eugene Hammel*   52
On Strata in the Kitchen, or the
    Archaeology of Tasting   *Joseph Rykwert*   53

SECTION 2: The Middle East

Meydiha's *Kısır*: a Wheat Dish from
    Southern Turkey   *Marianne and Jerry Leach* 61
Israeli Food   *Elaine Baldwin*   69

SECTION 3: Africa

Cooking in the Garden of Ensete   *William and Dorothy Shack*   77
Some Yoruba Ways with Yams   *William Bascom*   82
Cameroon Koki: a Bean Pudding from Bangwa   *Robert Brain*   86
An Adaptation of Tiv Sesame Chicken   *Laura Bohannan*   87
Ghanaian Groundnut Stew   *Esther Goody*   89
Groundnut Stew from Sierra Leone   *Gay Cohen*   91
Snacks and Stew from Ghana   *Lynn Brydon*   93
A Sauce from Sierra Leone   *Carol P. MacCormack*   98
Social Aspects of Iteso Cookery   *Ivan and Patricia Karp*   101
Food and Recipes in Padhola   *Anne Sharman*   107
Malagasy Cooking   *Bakoly Domenichini Ramiaramanana*   111
Two Recipes from Southern
    Morocco   *Allan R. and Anne R. Meyers*   116
Tasty Little Dishes of the Cape   *Sheila Patterson*   121

SECTION 4: The Americas and the West Indies

A Mexican Fish for Easter   *Eva Hunt*   131
Rice and Old Clothes   *Stephen and Roxane Gudeman*   134
Peruvian *Cebiche*   *Eugene Hammel*   139
Maroon Jerk Pork and other
    Jamaican Cooking   *Barbara Klamon Kopytoff*   141
Fish Chowder with the Chugach Eskimos   *Frederica de Laguna*   147
Amazonian Smoked Fish and Meat:
    a Colombian Indian Technique   *Stephen Hugh-Jones*   149
Three Recipes from the Trumai Indians
    of Brazil   *Aurore Monod-Becquelin*   151
Cooking and Eating among the Siriono
    of Bolivia   *Allan R. Holmberg*   156

SECTION 5: South-East Asia, Ceylon and Japan: 'Rice with Everything'

Time and Menu   *Jacques Dournes*   161
Fish in Laos   *Alan Davidson*   165
Kammu Dishes   *Kristina Lindell and Damrong Tayanin*   171
Food with the Yao   *Annie Hubert-Schoumann*   175
Some Recipes from Northern Thailand   *Merete Aagard Henriksen*   180
Cooking in a Kelantan Fishing Village, Malaya   *Rosemary Firth*   183
Foods of Bali   *Ingela Gerdin*   191

Pukkai   *Dennis McGilvray*   194
Oyakodonburi from Japan   *Naomichi Ishige*   198

SECTION 6: The Pacific and Australia

Roasting Dog in an Earth Oven (Ponape)   *Naomichi Ishige*   203
The Earth Oven: From the Highlands
    of Papua New Guinea   *Paul Sillitoe*   206
Pacific Island Recipes   *Lindsay Verrier*   214
'The Natives Live Well'   *Isobel White*   216
The Roast and the Boiled   *Claude Lévi-Strauss*   221

Mary Douglas

Introduction

These recipes will draw some wider attention to the anthropologist's interest in food. It was clever of the editor to choose this well-established form, the cookery book. Just as rightly, she has used the form in the free, inventive way of the great exemplars. From Culpeper to Beeton and Elizabeth David, from Brillat-Savarin to the *Larousse Gastronomique*, the recipe is seldom left to speak for itself. Her contributors have been asked to describe something about the ingredients and the context in which the food is prepared and eaten. Sometimes this means describing a hunt, a dance, a ceremony, even a swim. But it is not for the sake of nostalgic bedside reading. She has also asked contributors to deal with foods that can be procured in most Western capitals, so she clearly expects us to try them out at home, even if it means raiding the zoo or the tropical house at Kew. So far, a charming gesture to international gastronomy and help to the Royal Anthropological Institute which will benefit from any profits. But there is much more in this idea.

Perhaps Jessica Kuper's *Anthropologists' Cookbook* will be the first of a series, followed by one on beverages and then others homing in on herbs and flavourings, stimulants and sedatives. I hope that such a series might also expand in the other direction, with, say, a book on menus through the week, or something on people's ideas of how long they can go without food at all, their concepts of infant feeding and invalid cookery, of good cooking and bad, their general idea of the importance of the culinary arts among other cultural forms. Food-taking is often an occasion for prayer, not merely for grace, but a communion rite in itself. The idea of food underlies the idea of sacrifice. When the themes of blood-shed and life-giving are counterpointed in elaborate harmony at the high point of religion, the meanings of food could never be exhausted. In such cultures food would surely rank above music, above theatre, above dance and poetry. But the gastronomic arts are hardly likely to be developed there – perhaps rather the opposite. Perhaps gastronomy flourishes best where food carries the lightest load of spiritual meanings.

1

One reason why the anthropologists are so interested in food is that it is such an apt medium for purely social symbolism, from private hospitality to great ceremonial dramas. This cook book, because of the structure chosen for it, emphasizes the intimate end of the scale and probably the other end, which sees stupendous waste and prodigal display, is much better known.

The peoples of the world are becoming conscious in this era that the work of feeding their numbers is a common problem. While millions starve, other millions waste food in sheer destructive splendour, while other millions quietly gorge on more than their physical capacity can stand. One would suppose that the twenty-or-so rich countries of the world, whose conscience is politically alert in this respect, would damp the home demand for food so that the impact of demand from the needy on growers could be more effective. But no: in rich countries we find the paradox of general subsidizing of food. Subsidies going direct into the pockets and larders of those in want is obviously above reproach and not what I am referring to. But it is important to ascertain whether food is really what they want. There is always a lobby for distributing free food, but a case against it when the initial emergency is over needs to be explained. Here it is in a nutshell put by the Director of the Wisconsin Institute of Research on Poverty arguing against the use of food stamps (Watts, 1969):

> The first issue here is whether, aside from the public passion for feeding the poor, there is any lasting reason for dealing with food separately from the general and varied needs of people with low incomes. There is ample empirical evidence that people spend a substantial part of any increase in income on food. This is particularly true of the poor . . . If . . . we try to make people spend substantially more on food (and correspondingly less on clothing, housing, transportation, education, etc.) than they would with an all cash benefit, we shall be facing a serious enforcement problem in preventing families from re-selling the stamps on food.

Even when food stamps are issued, it is not clear that those who are entitled to cash them will not prefer to sell them to those who are not. A general all-round subsidy on food solves this administrative puzzle. But what a strange enactment it is in a rich country, where slimming bread and slimming biscuits sell like hot cakes proverbially used to, and where mass media compete to propagate methods of eating less of the superabundance on offer.

Here people would evidently like to eat less, but find it hard – why so? And what deep emotions stir to a political outcry when the price of bread or meat or potatoes rises? Why do our elected representatives, when they think of hardship and poverty, jump to the idea of relieving it by handing out food? – a suitable anthropological problem, for historical answers take us nowhere. It could be argued, and often is, that historically poverty here meant hunger, as it does still in those starving places abroad, and that alms in food, once it has taken possession of the symbolic apparatus of our culture, has simply stayed on as the top priority, the most self-evidently valuable form of alms. But this will not do. That argument would require us to adopt an unworkable model of human thought. The mind does not adopt an idea historically once and for all and remain subject to its dominion ever after. Such arguing is self-contradictory, for it cannot say how the first upsurging thought got a foothold in minds defined to be by nature rather firmly closed to circumstances. The anthropological approach allows a more flexible view of the mind's activity. People would like to eat less, but they eat more: why? Because food is being forced upon them under pressure of social institutions which use food as a medium of relationship. To refuse the proffered food may mean refusing the relationship, potentially a more harmful course than putting on weight. People think the poor are hungry: why? Giving food is the easiest and cheapest form of charity and it pleases the producers. But that would hardly explain its prestige as the noblest form of almsgiving. What about the undoubted fact that it is the least radical solution to problems of poverty: it is harder by far to reorganize society so that those who are excluded can be brought back into the system of reciprocal exchanges which is the basis of friendship and support. Voting to give food from public money is of its essence a non-reciprocal gesture. The recipient can only stay outside the mesh of personal transactions which would normally result in himself and his family getting social support and moving out of poverty. To translate a social loss into a physiological lack and then to remedy the latter is mere evasion. It ensures the poor will always be there, on the outside, a reproach to feasters and merry-makers, clearly left out, though not necessarily needing to be fed.

To explain how food draws such distracting, crooked, symbolic arguments to itself, one good illustration will make these uncomfortable thoughts clear.

The Gurage inhabit the fertile plateaux of south-west Ethiopia, west of the Rift Valley lake chain. (What follows is taken from the essay by William Shack, 1971.) They cultivate a hardy crop, Ensete, the 'false banana plant', which provides a constant and abundant food supply; until the Great Ethiopian Drought of 1970, famine and starvation were unknown in Gurage history. Ensete is stored in deep earth pits. Most homesteads grow far more than year to year family requirements. Stored crops provide an almost inexhaustible food supply, with plenty for daily food, barter, ceremonial feastings and the occasional emergency when other crops have been damaged by weather.

Although supplied with plenty, the Gurage seem to be obsessed about food. They have two eating patterns, one public, when food is dispensed as a normal part of social intercourse; small, frequent meals, as suffused with etiquette and about as filling as our afternoon tea. The other is private; after the daily round of visiting is over, late at night the family starts to eat again in the secrecy of the dimly lit hut. This way the norms of kinship and generosity to strangers and neighbours can be circumvented, without fear of gossip. The ridicule of neighbours could be damaging, for dispensing food unsparingly is one of the few socially acceptable ways of displaying power and prestige. The best food-providers are the men who enjoy most prestige and authority in all spheres of life. These successful men, and those who try to copy them with more restricted means, both seem so anxious to keep enough to give away later that they restrict the quantity taken in their three meals a day to somewhere between handfuls and mere nibbles. But Shack also mentions that some Gurage cannot afford to engage in hospitality, pared down though it always is.

Here we have a well described case of a people who grow enough food for their year's needs and more, every year, but who are obsessed with anxiety about it. They lavish far more labour and far more complex methods of farming upon this easy crop than anyone else in the same cultivating complex; they hoard supplies from year to year and they hoard their cooked food in the day so as to eat it secretly at night. They are understandably anxious about food, because it is the symbol of success in a society that is strongly competitive but which does not allow competition to be open. The only conspicuous display permitted to the successful person is the gesture of lavish food-giving. Every other sign has to be muted, secret influence in dim corners. When they eat, personal restraint is the approved style. Over eating is regarded as coarse and vulgar, and they always leave something on the dish (for 'Mr. Manners', as it were).

Dr Shack presents them as if suffering from a culturally induced hunger. Everything they do focuses their anxieties onto food and encourages them to worry, hoard and wait for it. They could easily be more generous, give up secret feeding, make their public meals more satisfying, have fewer of them, use up the year's harvest and wait together for the next crop. But in context after context they clearly choose to compete with one another, individually and secretly, and to show off the results by these thin acts of visible hospitality. In such a society, and in such a culture, what does it feel like to be unsuccessful? It certainly must feel like not having enough food to dispense to all-comers. And what comes to the mind of the fortunate when the miseries of their less successful brethren are forced upon their attention? The thought comes that hunger is the cause of their troubles (even if the symptom is lack of appetite), and the further thought, that this can be cured by a dollop of food, is soon translated into action (1971, pp. 35–6):

Now, when a man complains of loss of appetite, nausea, and
intermittent attacks of severe stomach pains, immediately suspicion
is awakened that any of several potentially harmful spirits has
'touched' him. (Evil spirits are believed to dwell in the dense forests
and alongside the streams which demarcate village settlements,

forming spatial and social boundaries between areas of habitation.) Discomforts of this nature are culturally stereotyped 'signs' of supernatural affliction. If such nagging symptoms of illness persist and his condition deteriorates, the patient usually sinks into a semi-stupor, and although he may occasionally become conscious, is seldom able to take food or water. In this torpid or trance-like state the victim's breathing becomes difficult; the slow regular pace of breathing is interrupted momentarily by loud, hoarse, wheezing, not unlike an asthmatic patient, and those attending him respond by reciting a short word of prayer. Violent seizures of body trembling often overcome the patient, compelling his attendants to use force in holding him down on the sleeping mat; and in severe cases, partial paralysis of the extremities may set in. If there are no signs of a 'natural' recovery of health, as indicated by a recovery of appetite, a 'wizard' (*sägwära*) is summoned to divine the causes of the illness – that is, to ascertain the type of spirit believed to have taken temporary possession of the victim. After consulting oracles to reveal the spirit's name, in this case *awre*, the wizard prescribes a routine formula for exorcising the spirit, a conventional recipe which belongs to the common repertoire of adult Gurage knowledge about supernatural matters.

The rite of exorcism consists in feeding to the sick man an enormous dishful of Ensete-food. Kinsmen and neighbours arrive at nightfall to take part in the ceremony, the hut is darkened, they chant to the hungry spirit which has seized their friend. The brimming dish is set before the patient, he lowers his head over it, a long shawl is draped to conceal him and the dish of food. Using both hands, he ravenously stuffs his mouth, eating as the company chants in time to his stertorous breathing. This goes on for twelve hours or more, till 'the spirit, speaking through the possessed person, utters with a sigh, several times – "*täfwahum*" – "I am satisfied".'

Anthropologists' interpretations of strange beliefs fall roughly into two kinds. One is the interest theory, the other the tangled web of culture. According to the interest theory, the explanation of an extraordinary belief depends on tracing the beneficiary. So the beliefs in the divinity of the king would be explained by the support they lend to the king's precarious authority. Spirit-possession likewise tends to be explained by showing what the possessed person gets in the way of moral support, sympathy, food and clothes (see I. M. Lewis, 1971, for a bird's-eye view of the subject). These approaches accord well with psychoanalytical theories of response to anxiety. But, like the latter, they tend to assume that the problems of credulousness and delusion arise most critically where the person who is possessed by an evil spirit is concerned. If this were all, the anthropologist merely interprets possession as a way of remedying a hard position. It suggests that the victim is rectifying his troubles by a confidence trick. However, the real problems of belief arise in the case of the person who is exploited by it, not the one who benefits. Here the second approach helps, the tangled web of culture. If we ask how the king's extravagant claims to obedience are made credible to the populace, the answer lies in the complex countering of one confidence trick by another, each with claims which only reflect the pattern of comparative advantage: the total belief system ends by representing the total of separate interests. In the case of invasive spirits demanding to be feasted, clothed and enriched, we ask why the husbands of possessed women give them any credence at all. Faced with speedy ruin, why do they not become violently sceptical of their wives' claims to be harbouring spendthrift covetous spirits? Why do they tamely fork out as required? The Gurage belief in seizure by a hungry spirit may be plausible to the victim who stands to gain a good meal. What makes it plausible to everyone else, especially to those who then have to give generously what they prefer to hoard?

The full explanation of the plausibility to the Gurage of the belief in affliction by hungry spirits is in the elaborately interwoven cultural themes of private competition, public restraint, fasts and tantalizing nibbles, and in the impossible reckoning of who is in control, except by assessing their capacity to distribute food. Dr Shack follows out the threads of culturally induced hunger and institutionalized deprivation of food to draw an extraordinary and convincing picture. But I am still more impressed by the solid reasons he gives for being anxious about food in a society in which a man's role can only be performed if he can distribute as well as receive it. He reports that all the cases of possessed victims were, by Gurage standards, poor men (1971):

> [They] owned small plots of land with few ensete plants, and they were encumbered by long-standing debts arising out of borrowing cattle and money. I lack sufficient evidence to substantiate local hear-say that these victims of *awre*-possession had all recently undergone some personal crisis. Even so, in the strictest sense, such men of lowly means were not destitute, nor did they constitute a social category equivalent to the depressed occupational pariah groups and ritual outcasts found in Gurage society. But land, ensete and cattle are the principal economic resources that determine the extent to which Gurage men are able to achieve recognisable status and prestige by generously dispensing food. At the same time, prestigious men also enjoy the added nutritional rewards of participating in the monthly feast exchanges organised by members of the *mwakyarite* association.

The select list of members, who regale each other in turn in feasting-clubs where they gorge on raw meat, ensete and beer, includes all the important men in Gurage society. Questioned, no one could recall such a man ever being possessed by a hungry spirit. This is a society where the theory of equality is contradicted by big differences of wealth and where selection is made by secret paths of influence. Even the rule of primogeniture may not guarantee land to the eldest son if his father does not assess him as an 'ideal' son. Brother rivals brother. The lineage and community are strong, but within the corporate groupings each homestead is on its own. Not to be on the upward path is to be on the downward slope. Below the poor Gurage, however much encumbered by debt, are other lower levels of outcastes, landless and categories of ritually inferior status. The poor man loaded with debts has certainly got something to worry about. Nothing but a complete overhaul of Gurage political institutions would solve his problems. But those who have a good hand to play are not keen on stopping the game. Much easier for the rich Gurage to believe that loss of appetite, listlessness and nausea are symptoms that can be relieved by a ritual gift of food.

I tell this tale not to shock and discomfort, but because food is a blinding fetish in our culture, as among the Gurage. We cannot formulate a consistent policy about it, we cannot control our own uses of food, we tolerate cant and contradiction in respect of it. We simply do not know the uses of food, and our ignorance is explosively dangerous. It is more convenient for us to take a veterinary surgeon's view of food as animal feed, to think of it as mere bodily input, than to recognize its great symbolic force. Only reading casually through the pages that follow we feel a glow of enchantment that has little to do with physical needs. Food is not feed. Let this be a beginning to a systematic anthropology of food.

REFERENCES

Lewis, I. M., *Ecstatic Religion: an Anthropological Study of Spirit Possession and Shamamism*, Penguin, 1971.
Shack, William, *The Gurage: a People of Ensete Culture*, Oxford University Press, 1966.
Shack, William, 'Hunger, anxiety and ritual: deprivation and spirit possession among the Gurage of Ethiopia', *Man*, 6 (1), 30–43, 1971.
Watts, Harold, 'The Family Assistance Plan: an analysis and evaluation', *Public Policy*, 19 (2), 323–53, quotes Watts's Testimony to the House Ways and Means Committee on the subject of Social Security and Welfare Proposals (91st Congress, 1st session, 15, 16 October 1969, pp. 2456–67), 1971.

Jessica Kuper

Preface

Almost all the recipes which I have included in *The Anthropologists' Cookbook* can be used outside their particular cultural area. Indeed this was my main stipulation when I invited anthropologists to contribute to this book. There are, however, a few dishes, novel cooking techniques and descriptions which I included more for their exotic flavour (after all, this is an anthropologists' cookbook). But this is not only a cookbook. I have aimed to produce a sourcebook for a variety of different dishes, and to see food in its cultural setting, to add to the growing body of culinary anthropological literature. The more theoretical aspects of this branch of anthropology are discussed in Professor Mary Douglas's Introduction, and in the extract from Professor Lévi-Strauss's *L'Origine des manières de table*.

I have derived enormous pleasure from testing the recipes in my own kitchen. I could not get hold of a puffin or a kangaroo in London – those recipes are included mainly for the benefit of the Scottish, Welsh and Australian reader respectively – but, for the rest, I had no difficulty in finding ingredients in various specialist food shops – the 'West Indian and Continental' groceries, Indian, Chinese, Japanese, Greek and health-food stores which are to be found in vast numbers in London, and elsewhere in the UK where immigrants have settled. For people outside such centres there are mail-order stores (see below). Similar, specialist food stores also exist in the main cities of Europe and North America.

Many of the recipes were previously undocumented, at least in English, and the contributors have often standardized the quantities called for on the basis of their own experience of eating the food and of observing its preparation. The reader should not be daunted by the occasional vagueness for there are seldom hard and fast rules, and often quite wide variation in modes of preparation, depending on individual preferences and the current availability of ingredients, a problem which is magnified in the absence of well-stocked stores, typical of most parts of the world from which these recipes are derived. Since taste and availability are such variable factors, one should adjust (within limits, of course), and rest content that this is a fully authentic procedure.

There were social anthropologists who felt unable to contribute to this book, despite their loyalties to the Royal Anthropological Institute. The few Chinese and Indian specialists whom I approached declined on the grounds that the cuisine of these areas was already fully documented. Other anthropologists, particularly those who worked in Oceania, faced the problem that there were no adequate substitutes for fundamental ingredients and cooking techniques. Some talked of the virtual absence of so-called recipes. I shall quote from some of my correspondence to elaborate these points.

For Marilyn Strathern, writing from New Guinea, the cooking in Mount Hagen, and most of Melanesia, could not be transferred from its ecological setting:

> What makes this cooking distinctive are environmental factors which are essentially non-exportable. First is the matter of ingredients – special kinds of cooking bananas, green vegetables, tubers; second is the matter of utensils – 'special' meals in Hagen are invariably produced in earth ovens (the food is cooked along with leaves and heated stones),* such food having a distinctive delightful and most delicate but unreproducible flavour; third, the social occasion – formal meals are prepared by certain people, the food being distributed to others, and judgement as to the quality of cooking takes into account the social requirements of the occasion, but in a pretty invariant way . . .
>
> [Then] there are no special dishes; no idea of a meal in the sense of a structure with different courses, no idea in short of a 'menu', and although people differ in the skill with which they build earth ovens and pack in the food, no real idea of a 'recipe', only of idiosyncratic touches.

Professor Lévi-Strauss likewise touched on the absence of recipes. 'The [South America Indian] tribes I worked with had very coarse cooking habits which could not be called recipes, as these were practically limited to the raw materials for which, in most cases, no substitute could be found outside tropical America.'

Professor Sir Raymond Firth also questioned the suitability of substitute ingredients and the absence of cultural contextual factors in presenting recipes from certain foreign cultures, such as those of the Pacific. He suggested that one would have to make a basic choice:

---

* I have met this challenge in part, and include instructions for making earth ovens!

Either you can go for 'cookable' recipes which bear some vague resemblance to local types, but for which data about ceremonial, etc. would be largely meaningless, or you can go for authenticity of description with much material on ceremonial treatment but with no pretences that many of the types would be cookable in a Western setting.

I have sometimes had to compromise, and to omit 'uncookable' recipes, but in general my contributors have escaped from Sir Raymond's dilemma. In any case, cultural diffusion always involves compromise. One can observe this process among immigrant communities. Despite the widespread availability of many foreign foodstuffs in London, these are often too expensive for everyday consumption. Immigrant communities are substituting all the time, and in the process a new cuisine is emerging, but one still firmly based on the old. There are none the less a few cases in which I have included descriptions of food preparation, mainly in an attempt to elucidate cultural variability.

Finally, there were the anthropologists who reacted so strongly against the local diet that they could not be persuaded to propagate its diffusion. Nancy Howell Lee, who worked among Bushmen in the Kalahari Desert, wrote:

Not everybody in the world is into gourmet cooking. We used to joke about giving a Bushmen feast when we got home – a grotesque practical joke in which we forced our friends to hike miles across sand dunes at Cape Cod to be given sandy and tough grilled meat and a couple of cracking stones and all the *mongongos* (a kind of nut) they could want (not many).

My husband, who worked elsewhere in the Kalahari, commented morosely that his main memory was of hunger.

For really desperate occasions I was hoping to include some cannibal recipes. I followed up various leads and finally contacted a distinguished historian of the Pacific, Professor H. E. Maude, but alas he had never heard of any anthropophagous recipes in the strict sense, though he had a few useful tips on dissection. He did warn that human meat was almost totally lacking in vitamin B, 'hence the prevalence of beri-beri among addicts like King Cakabou'. According to Garn and Block, in a paper entitled 'The limited nutritional value of cannibalism' (*American Anthropologist*, 1970, p. 106),

the nutritional value of cannibalism may . . . be regarded as questionable, unless a group is in a position to consume its own number in a year. While human flesh may serve as an emergency source of both protein and calories, it is doubtful that regular people-eating ever had much nutritional meaning.

My brief to contributors was general and open-ended, to present in whatever form they wished a short article about food in its cultural setting, together with one or more recipes detailing the preparation of certain dishes. The collection is, in consequence, somewhat varied: in the degree of seriousness, in the range and aspects of food in society which the contributors have chosen to emphasize and in length. It is quite as exotic and experimental as any meal prepared from its pages.

I should like in particular to thank Professor Mary Douglas; Professor Lévi-Strauss, his translators, Professor and Mrs Weightman, and his publishers, Jonathan Cape and Harper & Row; Joan Koster, who did the illustrations; Harriet Fishman, a superb typist; and all the other anthropologists who participated so enthusiastically in this project. Jonathan Benthall dealt with the copyrights and other business aspects, and with his wife translated two contributions from the French. I am very grateful to them both, to my husband for endless assistance, and to Maurice Bloch, who also helped with the translation.

Some Shops where Unusual Ingredients can be Bought

Shops catering for immigrant communities have proliferated in London in the past decade, so that it should not be at all difficult to obtain locally the unusual ingredients demanded by some of the recipes. There are also health-food shops and specialist herb stores (e.g., the Culpeper chain) from which any number of herbs, spices, lentils and wheat products are available. For those readers who live beyond the range of these exotic stores, a mail-order firm may be the answer. R. M. Jones & Co., 11 Brandon Road, Brandon, Suffolk, has a comprehensive list, covering Chinese, Indonesian and Indian commodities and a wide variety of spices, herbs, seasonings and lentils. One Greek store, which also has mail-order facilities, is the Hellenic Provision Stores, 25 Charlotte Street, London, W1. Other Greek provision stores which are well stocked include the Greek Food Centre, 12 Inverness Street, London, NW1, and John and Cascalis, 35 Grafton Way, London, W1. Oriental food can be obtained at Tokyo-ya, which has two branches in London, one at 241 Camden High Street, NW1, the other at 234 West End Lane, NW6. Japanese foodstuffs are available at Mikadoya, 250 Upper Richmond Road, Putney, and 529 Finchley Road, NW3. Among the large Chinese supermarkets in London, which cater for South-East Asian ingredients generally, are the Hong Kong Emporium Ltd, 53 Rupert Street, W1, and the Chinese Emporium, 22 Rupert Street, W1.

Shops specializing in foreign foods and ingredients have existed in large American cities almost as long as immigrants have been coming to the United States; and anthropologists and other lovers of unusual foods in Ann Arbor, Berkeley, Iowa City, Madison, and even smaller college and university towns now have access to ingredients that a decade ago would have been regarded as exotic. The growth of the organic food movement and a wider interest in the use of herbs and spices have caused a proliferation of shops and stores that stock grains, condiments and other food supplies that formerly were unheard-of or unobtainable. Some of these firms supply exotic foods by mail order. Others, in New York, Boston, Chicago, Los Angeles, San Francisco and other metropolitan centres, may be found listed in the Yellow Pages under 'Food Products – Manufacturers and Distributors', 'Gourmet Shops', and 'Importers', or in the Chinatowns, Little Italys, and sections containing concentrations of immigrants from Greece, Spain, Scandinavia, Eastern and Central Europe, the Middle East, China, Japan, South-East Asia and various Latin American countries.

Some Unusual Ingredients and Possible Substitutes

Blachan or *terasi*: Shrimp flavouring. This is a strong-smelling paste, for which anchovy or shrimp paste may be substituted.
Chillies: These are green and red, and are available in both fresh and powdered form. 2 chillies = approx. 1 teaspoon chilli powder.
Coconut cream: Fresh coconut contains a milk or cream. Authentic coconut cream, used in a number of South-East Asian and Caribbean recipes included in this book, is prepared by soaking freshly grated coconut flesh in water or in the liquid contained within the coconut, and squeezing it. The best substitute is a commercial coconut cream, obtainable under a variety of brand names. This must be soaked in hot water, the ratio depending on whether the recipes call for thick or thin cream. $2\frac{1}{2}$–3 oz. of creamed coconut in a cup of hot water will produce about half a pint of thick coconut cream, while 1 oz. in a cup of hot water produces the same quantity of thin coconut cream. After soaking for about 15 minutes strain the liquid and, if it is too sweet, add a pinch of salt.
  If this commercial preparation is not available it is necessary to resort to desiccated coconut. Soak 8 oz. in a pint of hot water for approximately 20 minutes and strain the mixture, making sure that the coconut pulp has been well squeezed out. Alternatively, liquidize the desiccated pulp in the water and then strain.
Fish sauce or nampla: This has a dark colour. If necessary, use light soy.
Green ginger: The best alternative to fresh ginger is the kind preserved in salt. If using ground ginger, $\frac{1}{2}$ teaspoon is equivalent to one or two thinly sliced preserved gingers.
Laos *or galingale*: This is a root which looks like ginger, and can be bought in powdered form. 1 teaspoon *Laos* powder = two slices.
Lemon grass: An aromatic grass, difficult to buy in England. It is equivalent to 1 teaspoon powdered lemon grass (citronella or 'Sereh' powder). If the powder is unobtainable, use lemon peel.

Scallions: Used in Caribbean and South-East Asian cookery, they closely
   resemble shallots.
Tamarind: This is a brown pod fruit which has seeds, and is very sour. By
   soaking the pod in water, a thick brown juice is obtained, and this may
   be added to curry to give a slightly sour flavour. It is also obtainable in
   pulp form. Lemon juice or vinegar can be substituted. To make tamarind
   water, soak a piece of tamarind pulp, about the size of a marble, in half
   a cup of water. Allow to soften, and then squeeze out the liquid from the
   pulp. Discard the pulp.

Weights and Measures

I have included both ounce and gram weights in the recipes, and have made liberal use of the cup as a measure. This is the British standard cup, which holds 10 fl.oz. (BSI) as opposed to the smaller American cup with a capacity of 8 fl.oz. Likewise teaspoon and tablespoon measures are British standard, which again are larger than the American.

Liquid Measures

1 US cup = 8 fl.oz. = $\frac{5}{6}$ English breakfast cup
1 English cup = 10 fl.oz.
$1\frac{1}{4}$ US teaspoons = 1 English teaspoon (tsp)
$1\frac{1}{4}$ US tablespoons = 1 English tablespoon (tbsp)
1 English tablespoon = 4 English teaspoons

$\frac{1}{4}$ pint = 5 fl.oz. = 142 millilitres (ml)
$\frac{1}{2}$ pint = 285 ml
$\frac{3}{4}$ pint = 425 ml
1 pint = 20 fl.oz. = 567 ml
$1\frac{3}{4}$ pints = 1 litre

1 US pint = 16 fl.oz. = $\frac{4}{5}$ English pint (approx. 453 ml)

Solid Measures

1 oz. = 28 grams
2 oz. = 57 grams
3 oz. = 85 grams
4 oz. = 113 grams

8 oz. = 227 grams
1 lb = 454 grams (0·5 kilogram)
2 lb = 1000 grams (1 kilogram)

Rather than worry about awkward conversions (e.g. 1 oz. = 28·5 grams) use a more convenient approximate equivalent – e.g., 1 oz. = 30 grams. The conversion of ounces to grams is done by multiplying by 28·35, and of grams to ounces by multiplying by 0·0352. It is advisable to hang a conversion table in a convenient place in your kitchen.

Oven Temperatures

°F	225	250	275	300	325	350	375	400	425	450
°C	107	121	136	150	164	178	191	205	219	233

Acknowledgments

The following items have been previously published, and acknowledgment is made for permission to use them here:

'Serve it Forth: Food and Feasting in Medieval England', by Lorna J. Sass. The recipes contained in the article are from The Metropolitan Museum of Art, copyright 1975, *To the King's Taste*, by Lorna J. Sass, and are reprinted by permission.

'Some Yoruba Ways with Yams', extracts from W. Bascom, 'Yoruba Food', *Africa*, vol. 21, no. 1, 1951, by permission of the author and the International African Institute.

'Cooking and Eating among the Siriono of Bolivia', from *Nomads of the Long Bow*, by Allan R. Holmberg, Institute of Social Anthropology Publication no. 10, 1950, by permission of the Smithsonian Institution Press, Washington, and the author's executors.

'The Roast and the Boiled', extracts from the English translation of *L'Origine des manières de table*, by Claude Lévi-Strauss. The English translation by John and Doreen Weightman is to be published by Jonathan Cape (Great Britain) and Harper & Row (USA). Reprinted by permission of the author and publishers.

The recipe for *Bacalhau à Gomes de Sá* from *Portuguese Cookery*, by Ursula Bourne, 1973, by permission of Penguin Books Ltd.

SECTION 1

Europe

Man holding salt cod

Julian Pitt-Rivers

Le Stockfish

The stockfish is a dish especially associated with the Rouergue and eastern Quercy regions of France, and local historians believe that its appearance and development in the region was associated with the international network of the wool trade in the later middle ages, when the towns of Villefranche de Rouergue and Figeac were important commercial centres. It is thought that this variety of dried cod was brought from Norway by merchants who came to buy wool. It is seldom mentioned in French cookery books on account of its very local character, but it is none the less known in other parts of Languedoc and in Provence, though it does not seem to enjoy there the esteem it has in Figeac (from which my recipe comes), where it is regarded as a supreme delicacy.

The fish itself is slightly salted only, which distinguishes it from the ordinary dried cod used to make *brandade de morue*. It may, in fact, be classed as the gourmet's version of *brandade*.

To make the dish, the dried stockfish has first of all to be soaked for ten days, during which time it gives off a most unsavoury odour. The water must be changed frequently if it is not running water, but rainwater is said to be best for this purpose, so that it was once the custom to leave it to soak in the barrels into which the drainpipes from the roof emptied in the courtyards of Figeac. In former times the dank streets stank of stockfish during late November and December. After a few days the stockfish is cut through, leaving one side intact to hold it together. It soaks more thoroughly that way.

When the time comes to prepare the dish, it is placed in cold water and brought to the boil; the potatoes to be mixed with it (three times the weight of the stockfish dry, to be calculated at 100 grams per person) are boiled apart. The stockfish is then drained and mixed in with the potatoes, making a purée, which is seasoned with salt, pepper, garlic and parsley and one egg per person stirred in slowly, and those with powerful digestions sometimes like to mix in butter and lots of cream, though this is not necessary, according to others, and makes it too rich. It must be kept very hot, and then oil –

preferably walnut oil – heated to steaming point is stirred in slowly – nearly a pint (just over 500 ml) of oil for 4 lb (2 kilos) of potatoes. Corn oil can be used as an economy, but it's a pity, for the fragrance of walnut oil, pithy as the smell of an old carpenter's workshop and sweet in after-taste, gives the fish that earthy tang that is called *graveleux* in wine. I imagine they make it with olive oil in Provence, which is surely much less exciting.

Stockfish is a meal in itself and nothing is served either before or after. But it must be kept piping hot throughout and returned to the stove between servings, though it must never be browned. It is accompanied by the *vin nouveau* which is one reason why it is eaten at the beginning of winter. But it is also the custom to eat it in Holy Week.

The late Dr Solignac was particularly fond of it but complained, '*C'est un plat cher. Il est gourmand d'huile*', and this financial preoccupation was perhaps in part responsible for the lasting quality of Dr Solignac's digestion. For, through a happy balance of two of the Seven Deadly Sins, he was able to attain moderation in both and sailed past the age of eighty with a digestion any young man might have envied.

The British reader, if his digestion conforms only to national standards, is advised to proceed with caution when doing battle with the stockfish and perhaps to equip himself in advance with a tube of Dr Bourget's 'Inositol' or such other traditional line of retreat as an experienced pharmacist of the south-west of France may recommend.

It may be worth pointing out, for the sake of those who may wish first of all to taste stockfish in its native setting, that a certain quite logical symbiosis commonly exists in the south-west of France between the chemist and the best restaurant of the town, and the former is therefore the most reliable source of information regarding the latter. But do not expect to find stock-fish on menus. It is always ordered in advance, for its preparation requires care and a certain inconvenience (including the smell while it is soaking). For this reason Madame Lacoste, the grocer's wife, says, 'The preparation of stockfish is a disgusting job. When I've got it ready myself I can hardly look at it on the table. I eat it, mind you, but not with the same appetite that I have when someone else has cooked it.'

Those who have eaten good stockfish will eagerly concede that it is worth the trouble and a certain inconvenience, but perhaps the mysterious prestige that it possesses is due to more than purely culinary considerations. It is 'in-group food', not served during the tourist season nor advertised to outsiders, but a festal delicacy of the home, eaten with only a spoon at family gatherings when the fact that it is inelegant by Parisian standards and does not conform to the canons of fashion magazines only increases its value as a rite of intimate commensality. Perhaps its mystery is ultimately due to its anomalous position within Lévi-Strauss's culinary triangle: it is dried and salted when raw; when soaked it smells rotten. It is cooked by boiling and mixed with the humblest tubercule, yet it is at the same time fried inside by the addition of boiling oil, and virtually roasted after that, though it must never be browned. It is made of humble ingredients: dried cod, the fish of the poor, potatoes and garlic and the local oil that peasants made for themselves from their own walnuts because they couldn't afford olive oil. But stockfish costs much more than ordinary cod, and nut oil now costs a fortune if you buy it in Paris and it needs a great deal of it – '*un plat cher . . . gourmand d'huile*', repeats Madame Lacoste, not knowing perhaps that this was Dr Solignac's dictum. Humble and autochthonous at first sight, it is really a great luxury. It dates from the days when Figeac was immensely wealthy and the streets were lined with gothic arcades and, like all that is most holy, it comes from far away – Norway – and bears a name as strange-sounding as 'abracadabra' when rolled round a southern tongue: '*le stoque-fishe*'. It is also called more simply '*stofish*' and, in Languedoc, '*estoufinade*', and there is a most disobliging but picturesque expression current in Marseilles which describes a person as '*maigre comme un estoquefishe*': that is to say, very scrawny indeed.

Lorna J. Sass

Serve it Forth:
Food and Feasting in
Late Medieval England

The Forme of Cury, a manuscript recipe roll from the household of King Richard II dated about 1391, reveals the late medieval preoccupation with ritual, exoticism and grandeur. Like the architects of the Gothic cathedral, Richard's cooks manifest the impulse to transcend the mundane by casting edible ingredients into aesthetic form through the manipulation of colour and shape.

Richard's chefs were culinary artists. Some were sculptors, shaping enormous *sotelties* of coloured marzipan to depict guests being honoured at the feast. These *sotelties* would be served and eaten with pomp and ceremony at the end of each of the three courses of the feast. Other cooks were builders, erecting towering castles of dough whose crenellated walls were the crusts of deep, stuffed pies:

> Take and make a foyle [leaf] of gode past with a roller, of a foot brode, and lynger by cumpas [in proportion]. Make foure coffyngs [pie-crusts] of the self [same] past upon the rolleres, the gretnesse of the smale of thyn arme, of six ynche deepnesse. Make the gretust in the myddel. Fasten the foile in the mouth upwarde, and fasten thee other foure in every side. Kerve out kyntlich [quaintly] kyrnels [crenellations] above in the manner of bataiwyng [embattlements] and drye hem harde in an ovene, other [or] in the sune. In the myddle coffyn do a fars [stuffing] of pork, with gode pork and ayren [eggs] rawe with salt, and color it with safron, and do in another creme of almandes, and helde [cast] it in another creme of cowe mylke with ayren. Color it with sandres [sandalwood] . . .

A few cooks became godlike creators, giving tangible form to the beasts of mythology. To make *cokentrice*, half capon and half pig, they instruct us:

> Take a capoun, and skald hym, and draw hem clene, and smyte hem a-to [in two] in the waste overthwart [across the waist]. Take a pigge

22

and skald hym, and draw hym in the same maner and smyte hem also in the waste. Take a nedyl and threde, and sewe the fore partye of the capoun to the after parti of the pygge and the fore partye of the pigge to the hynder party of the capoun, and than stuffe hem as thou stuffest a pigge. Putte hem on a spete and roste hym, and whan he is y-now [done], dore [make golden] hem with yolkys of eyroun [eggs] and pouder gynger and safroun, thenne wyth the ius [juice] of percely with-owte [on the outside], and than serve it forth for a ryal mete [royal food].

The cooks particularly enjoyed colouring food, not to enhance its natural beauty (as we colour an orange more orange), but to disguise it. All the colouring agents were organic. The most popular was saffron, used to transform food to gold, the colour traditionally associated with nobility and wealth. For green they used parsley and spinach juice; for red, sandalwood; for purple, turnesole; for black, blood.

Spices such as saffron and sandalwood and the very popular cinnamon, mace, nutmeg, cubeb (a pepper-like berry from Java) and galingale root (a pungent member of the ginger family) were imported at high costs from the East. The Arabs monopolized the spice trade during the middle ages and guarded their secret sources so carefully that western merchants did not discover them until the late fifteenth century. Fascinating myths grew to explain the mysterious origins of spices. Here is one told by Joinville, a chronicler of the Crusades:

Before the river [Nile] enters into Egypt, people who are accustomed so to do, cast their nets out-spread into the river at night and when morning comes, they find in their nets such goods as are sold by weight and brought into the land: ginger, rhubarb, wood of aloes, and cinnamon. And it is said that these things come from the earthly paradise, just as the wind blows down the dry wood in the forests of our own land. The dry wood of the trees in paradise that thus falls into the river is sold to us by the merchants.

Precisely because spices were such exotic luxury items, and brought with them a sense of the conquest of foreign lands, King Richard insisted that they be presented in abundance on his feast tables.

On a practical political level, Richard's desire for ostentation is understandable. In the late fourteenth century, the competition for power among the king and his wealthy barons was extremely keen. Clearly, a lavish display of wealth through a sumptuous and visually exotic feast would do much to attract followers to the king's side. In fact, the chroniclers of the period report that Richard dined with ten thousand daily and employed three hundred cooks.

But despite the seeming largesse and grandeur of the court, the four-teenth century was an epoch wrought with famine, plague and great social unrest. It has been argued that a traditional response to instability and the sense of perpetual danger is to 'colour life with fancy, to enter upon the quest of oblivion, sought in the delusion of ideal harmony'.[1] In certain respects, the medieval feast, with its precise division of labour and strict rules of decorum, presents a façade of peace and harmony in a world chaotic to its roots. The intense concentration on ritual and ceremony draws the participants into a kind of game, the rules of which must be rigidly observed. 'In the very nature of things the relationship between feast and play is very close. Both proclaim a standstill to ordinary life . . . Both are limited as to time and place; both combine strict rules with genuine freedom.'[2]

During a feast, the entire staff of the household, as well as the guests, are involved in the game. About half an hour before the dinner is to be served, the marshal raises his rod, the symbol of his authority, and commands the ewerer to set three linen cloths on the dais table. These are stretched and folded according to elaborate instructions. When the king arrives to the blasts of clarion trumpets and is seated, the pantner drapes a towel around his own neck and over his shoulders in such a way that he holds an end in each of his hands. On an outstretched left arm, the pantner balances the sovereign's napkin, seven loaves of fine quality bread for eating, and four trencher loaves; in the left hand he carries the principal salt cellar for the king's table. He then approaches the table, and with the help of the ewerer and butler, places the salt to the king's right and the trenchers to his left. He sets two carving knives, haft outwards for the carver, and sets a third down, haft inwards, before the king. The pantner then takes his own three special knives and prepares bread plates from the round trencher loaves by cutting off the top crust, squaring the edges of the bottom and smoothing the surface down with care. The pantner then kneels before the king, and the carver cuts him a slice of bread from a high quality wheaten loaf to be assayed.

After an elaborate hand-washing ceremony, a Latin grace is chanted in unison as a procession of trusted servants emerges from the kitchen with fanciful delicacies on golden platters. Before the king eats the dishes of his choice, each is tasted by the assayer to guard against poisoning. On this day, Richard will sample:

The first course: Venison in furmenty (sliced venison in a sauce of boiled, hulled wheat); Viaundbruse (a broth made of choice meats); Heads of Boars; Great Flesh (roasted haunches of meat); Roasted Swans and Pigs; Crustade Lumbard (custard with dried fruit, parsley, and, bone marrow); a Sotelte.
The seconde course: Gele (a consommé); Blandesore (capon cooked in a broth of almond milk); Roasted pigs, cranes, pheasants, herons, and chickens; Bream; Tarts; a Sotelte.

The thirde course: Almond Soup; Lombardy Stew; Roasted Venison, Chickens, Rabbits, Quails, and Larks; Payne Puff (egg yolks, bone-marrow and dried fruits baked in a crust); Longe Frutours (curds, eggs and flour fried); a Sotelte.

The feast lasts as long as the daylight. Just as the sun begins to fade, the cupbearer serves goblets of hot spiced wine and platters of wafers. The pantner places trays of whole spices in confection on each table. After a few moments King Richard rises and bids farewell to his guests. Healthful digestion and a good night's rest are now the primary concerns.

Sweet Measure: Capon in Milk and Honey

The capon is a cocke made as it were female by kervynge away of his gendringe stones. (Bartholomaeus Anglicus, *De proprietatibus rerum*, translated into Middle English by Trevisa, 1398)

Douce Ame Take gode cowe mylke and do it in a pot. Take parsel, sawge, ysope, savray and oother gode herbes. Hewe hem, and do hem in the mylke and seeth hem. Take capons half yrosted and smyte hem on pecys and do thereto pynes and hony clarified. Salt it and color it with safron and serve it forth.

This golden dish is resplendent and served to best advantage over plain white rice. Different types of honey will produce interesting variations in flavour. (To serve 4–6)

1 3–4 lb (1·5–2 kilos) capon (or chicken) cut into serving pieces	2 small leaves fresh sage, minced, or ¼ tsp dried sage
½ cup flour mixed with ½ tsp salt and ⅛ tsp freshly ground pepper	¾ tsp hyssop
2 tbsp oil	½ tsp savory
2¼ cups milk	¼–½ tsp saffron
¼ cup honey	½ tsp salt
2 tbsp minced fresh parsley	⅛ tsp freshly ground pepper
	¼ cup pine nuts (kernels)

Dredge fowl in flour mixture. Brown the pieces in oil in a large, heavy saucepan until golden on both sides. Combine milk, honey, herbs, salt and pepper in a bowl. Pour liquid over browned fowl in saucepan, stirring to combine drippings with the sauce. Cover and simmer about 20 minutes or until fowl is tender. Check seasoning. Stir in pine nuts just before serving.

Lombardy Custard

> *Crustade Lombarde* Take gode creme, and levys of Percely, and
> Eyroun, the yokys and the whyte, and breke hem there-to, and
> strayne thorwe a straynoure tyl it be so styf that it wol bere hym-self.
> Than take fayre Marwe and Datyes y-cutte in ij or iij and Prunes and
> putte the Datys an the Prunes and Marwe on a fayre Cofynne y-mad
> of fayre past and put the cofyn on the oven tyl it be a lytel hard.
> Thanne draw hem out of the oven. Take the lycour and putte
> ther-on and fylle it uyppe and caste Sugre y-now on, and if it be in
> lente, let the Eyroun and the Marwe out and thanne serve it forth.

This recipe for *Crustade Lombarde* is from the Harleian Manuscript 4016.
The spicy fruited custard was served at King Richard's feast given with the
Duke of Lancaster on 23 September 1387. It is one of my favourite medieval
dishes and always makes a hit with guests. The marrow adds a rich and
delicate flavour, and the sweetness of the dried fruits is contrasted in an
unusual way with fresh parsley. (To serve 8)

9–inch diameter uncooked pie pastry
  (4 oz. butter, 8 oz. flour)
10 each of prunes, dates and dried figs,
  cut into small pieces
1½ tbsp raw bone-marrow, crumbled*
2 tbsp finely minced parsley
8 oz. (220 grams) double heavy cream

1½ tbsp brown sugar
2 eggs, lightly beaten
pinch salt
½ tsp dried orange peel
1 tsp cinnamon
pinch mace

Bake pie pastry at 425° (gas Mk 7) for 10 minutes. Let cool. Line pie-crust with
dried fruits. Distribute marrow and parsley evenly over fruit. Combine remaining
ingredients in a bowl. Beat until thoroughly blended. Pour over fruits in crust.
Bake at 375° (Mk 5) for about 40 minutes or until custard is set and top is brown.
Let the *crustade* cool about 5 minutes before serving.

REFERENCES

1 Johan Huizinga, *The Waning of the Middle Ages*, New York, 1954, p. 39.
2 Johan Huizinga, *Homo Ludens*, Boston, 1970, p. 22.

* Ask your butcher to hack open a beef-bone so that you can easily get at the
marrow.

Joan Bouza Koster

From the Flocks of Greece:
Galopita (Milk Pie)*

'Galopita! Yaourti!' Panos shouted in anticipation as he urged his donkey up the steep mountain slope to his sheep fold where the month-old lambs were kept. Waiting in the village below was the butcher who would slaughter the lambs for the Christmas and New Year festivities. With the sale of the excess lambs, shepherds begin the daily chore of milking the lactating ewes morning and evening. Meat plays a minor role in the diet of rural Greeks, being eaten only on the major feast days of the year. The flocks of sheep and goats that roam Greece's stony mountainsides are principally kept for their milk, which may be sold to village cheese merchants, or made into butter, yoghurt, cheese and other dairy products by shepherds and their wives. Dairy products regularly supplement the staple heavy sourdough bread, beans and oil. When the cheese factories close in late May, the last of the milk production of the flock is made into *tirovoli*, a salty, semi-soft cheese that is stored in a goatskin bag (*touloumi*) for the family's use throughout the summer and autumn. By November the remaining cheese, now pungent and liquid, is baked into omelettes and cheese pies. Everyone looks forward to the fresh milk products that will follow the November lambing. As the lambs are born, colostrum, the first milk of the ewe, is occasionally collected from a particularly productive ewe, to be enjoyed boiled, the warm curds eaten lightly sprinkled with salt. But this is a rare treat because colostrum is needed for the proper development of the lambs, whose growth is anxiously watched by the shepherd.

In December the village comes alive as shepherds discuss meat prices and await the arrival of the butchers. Eyes shine as people describe the rich yoghurt and the sweet milk pies (*galopita*) that are traditionally made for the

* The following recipes for Greek *pites* (pasties or pies) were gathered during co-operative ethnographic field studies in two villages in the northern Peloponnese. These studies form a part of a larger interdisciplinary 'Argolid Exploration Project' designed to document human settlement in the southern Argolid from the Paleolithic to the present.

Milking ewes

New Year's celebration. The huge milk pies with a crust of *filo* pastry each requires 3 litres of milk and are baked in *tapsia*, or flat copper pans, roughly 50 cm in diameter. On New Year's morning, shepherds are busy delivering pails of milk to their friends, neighbours and patrons who do not have flocks of their own. *Galopita* is baked in the round stone ovens beside the roast lamb or kid, and is made again for *Apokreas* or Carnival, the two weeks of festivities preceding the beginning of Lent. Goatherds, whose kids are born later than the lambs, join in the distribution of milk throughout the village at this time. The rich, heavy pies with their complementary proteins of milk and wheat suffice for a meal. *Galopita* is easily packed for a dinner in the fields or at the fold. Wrapped in cloths and carefully boxed, *galopita* provides a convenient way to send a gift of milk by local bus to city relatives in Athens.

The recipe that follows has been adapted to British and American kitchens, but retains the simplicity and consistency of the original. It makes a pie about 10 or 12 inches across, which can be cut into twelve good-size pieces, although the author claims that in her house it is sufficient to serve only three! [ed.]

Milk Pie (*Galopita*)

For the filo *pastry:*

7 oz. (approx.) (200 grams) flour   ⅓ pt (175 ml) water

Sprinkle water into flour and knead until dough is elastic (about 5 minutes). Divide dough in half. Place one piece on floured surface. Cover remainder. Flatten dough into a circle 1·5 cm thick. Flour the dough heavily. With a broomstick or dowel (1·5 cm thick and 1 metre long) roll dough into a circle approximately 15 cm in diameter. Flour dough. Starting at edge, roll dough onto broomstick. As you roll, apply pressure from the centre out with the palms of

Rolling out filo *pastry*

the hands, slowly stretching the dough. With dough on broomstick rotate 90 degrees, unroll and roll again, applying pressure as above. Continue, turning dough one quarter-turn each time until dough is thin enough to read black writing on white paper through the pastry. The pastry is approximately 30 cm in diameter.

Oil and grease a circular pan (25 cm across) or a rectangular pan (25 x 30 cm). Place the first layer of *filo* in the pan. Brush 2 tbsp olive oil and sprinkle 1 tsp ground cinnamon on top of the *filo*. Prepare the second *filo* layer and place on top (if using commercial *filo*, use five or six layers).[1]

For the custard filling:
scant 1¼ pts (750 ml) milk   3½ oz. (100 grams) sugar
approx. 7 oz. (200 grams) flour

Heat the milk and stir in sugar to melt. Slowly sift in the flour, stirring constantly. Stir until mixture thickens and begins to boil. Remove from heat and let cool. When cool, pour into pan lined with *filo*. Fold overhanging edges of *filo* – which extends about 2 inches around the edges – over custard (there is no covering *filo*). One can spread a little custard over the overhanging *filo* as it tends to get crunchy when baked. Top with 2 more tbsp oil and another tsp ground cinnamon. Bake 5 minutes at 400°. Reduce to 350° and bake 40 minutes more (gas Mk 6, then Mk 4).

To achieve proper consistency, *galopita* must be cooled to room temperature before cutting. Cut into diamond-shaped pieces and serve.[2]

Kali Oreksi – Good Appetite!

NOTES

1   Those familiar with Greek cuisine will note that village-style *filo* is
    thicker than commercial *filo* and only two layers are used, instead of
    the multiple layers found in other Greek sweets.
2   *Galopita* never contains eggs. However, another milk pie called
    galactoboureko does, and it is generally considered more of a city
    version, as it is sold in sweetshops, and is the milk pie most often
    found in cookbooks of Greek foods.

Mari H. Clark Forbes

From the Fields of Greece: *Hortopita* (Wild Greens Pie)

Amidst a great range of colourful fruits and vegetables in the many open street markets of Athens, one invariably finds an old widow dressed all in black, selling a pile of wild *horta* (dandelion-like greens). Collecting wild greens at the edges of cultivated fields and vineyards is a popular pastime for many urban Greek women and these are an important source of winter vegetables in the countryside. Wild greens such as dandelion, chicory, sow's thistle and mustard add vitamins and variety to a village diet based primarily on the caloric staples: bread, beans and olive oil. Throughout Greece, urban or rural, wild greens are valued for their health-giving qualities. Wild food sources have traditionally been a mainstay and an economic resource for the poor, such as the widows who market them. While gathering wild greens for oneself or for gifts to urban relatives is an acceptable pastime, the collection of *horta* for sale in the market bears the stigma of poverty of one who has nothing else to trade.

The varied landscape, rainfall and temperatures across Greece influence the diversity in types of wild greens growing in different areas and the availability of wood for the preparation of *hortopita*. In areas where wood is more plentiful, *hortopita* is prepared in a round stone oven. The oven is heated by burning wood on its floor until the walls of the oven are hot enough to maintain the heat for baking bread and pies. Where wood is scarce, this pie is more frequently deep-fried in olive oil, heated over the fire of the family hearth. Within any area in Greece, each household has its own formula for the ingredients, preparation and serving. *Hortopita* is only one of the many ways that wild greens are prepared in rural and urban Greece.

Preparation

Horta are cut in the fields by severing the whole leaf rosette at the root. Back in the village, the wilted leaves and bits of root are trimmed off. The leaf

31

rosettes, still whole, are washed several times to remove all traces of soil and grit. The leaves are chopped and placed in a large wooden bread-kneading trough, or other large vessel, raised at one end to allow the excess liquid to drain off.

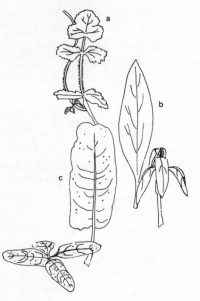

Wild greens used in hortopita*:*
(*a*) *wild parsely,* (*b*) *bladder campion,*
(*c*) *dock*

In the Mani of the south-western Peloponnese, aromatic onion-like grasses are gathered for the preparation of a popular local variation of *hortopita*. On the high upland plain of Lasithi in east-central Crete, wild fennel, wild lettuce, bladder campion and other wild greens are combined with leeks from the garden for *hortopita*. On the peninsula of Methana on the Saronic Gulf, campion, wild parsley, dock and local dandelion-like greens are used with home-grown spinach and spring onions. On Methana, *hortopita* is baked in large round pans, 15–20 inches (40–50 cm) in diameter, in the stone ovens. In the Mani and on the Lasithi plain, where wood is scarce, the pastry (*filo*) is prepared in thicker layers and cut in circles roughly 3 in. (7·5 cm) across. A good dollop (approximately 2 tbsp) of chopped sautéd greens is placed on one half of the circle of pastry. Fold the other half over, and press the edges down to seal them. Fry it in hot olive oil until lightly golden brown (roughly 5 minutes).

On Methana the preparation of *hortopita* is a social occasion when women gather to roll out *filo* pastry, to gossip and to prepare the oven for baking. Gifts of fresh *hortopita* are carried, hidden in the folds of a woman's apron, to the house of neighbours and relatives. On the streets of Athens one finds vendors selling baked *pites* filled with cheese, chicken or spinach, to be enjoyed for a quick snack as one would eat a Cornish pasty or a sandwich.

Wild Greens Pie (*Hortopita*)
This is a modified recipe for English and American *pita*-bakers, which makes
8 generous portions or 16 appetizers.

1 lb (454 grams) tender leafy greens (spinach, Swiss chard, lettuce). Note:
  rocket, nettle, chicory, cress, or chopped young red poppy leaves, or other
  small tender wild edible leafy greens of your choice, may be used for part
  of the greens for a sharper taste that more closely resembles the village
  dish.
2 oz. (60 grams) finely chopped fresh parsley
6 sprigs (approx. 1 oz. or 30 grams) chopped fresh dill (or mint may be substituted)
½ lb (227 grams) chopped leeks or spring onions
2½ tbsp (15 grams) pre-cooked white rice
salt to taste (½–1 tsp)
⅝–¾ cup (150–180 ml) olive oil

As in the village, the selection of particular leafy greens and aromatic leaves
will depend on your family's taste preference.

Thoroughly wash all greens, onions, parsley, dill. Chop and place in a shallow
dish raised at one end so that excess liquid will drain off. Oil the baking pan
(25 cm diameter if round or 25 × 30 cm if rectangular), using 1–2 tsp olive oil.
Prepare the *filo* pastry (see Joan Koster's recipe for *galopita*). Line the baking
dish with pastry. Moisten the pastry with 1–2 tsp olive oil. Place a second sheet
of *filo* on top of the first. Moisten with 1 tsp olive oil.
  Pour scant ½ cup (120 ml) olive oil into a large frying-pan. Turn on the heat
moderately high. Immediately add the chopped vegetables and rice. Stir constantly
to coat all the vegetables with oil. When the vegetables wilt and reduce in volume,
reduce the heat and cook 5 minutes, stirring frequently so that the filling does
not stick. With a large spoon, place the filling in the pastry-lined baking dish,
first round the edges and then in the centre. Place a layer of *filo* pastry over the
vegetable filling and moisten it with 1 to 2 tsp olive oil. Place a second layer
of *filo* on top of the first and moisten with olive oil.
  Perforate the pastry with a fork to form diamond-shaped individual portions.
The pastry is brittle when baked and does not otherwise cut easily. Bake
hortopita in a moderate oven – 350°F or gas Mk 4 – for 40–50 minutes until the
pastry is lightly browned.
  Serve warm but not hot.

Margaret Kenna

Melitera:
Greek Island Cheese-Cakes

This recipe comes from a small island, 'Nisos',* about a day's journey from Piraeus. The island is so steep and rocky that crops are grown on narrow terraces and those slopes too steep or bleak for cultivation are used to graze sheep and goats. About a quarter of the men make their living as shepherds, the others are mainly farmers and farm labourers. The shepherds pay the rent for grazing-land not in cash but in cheese, the amount being agreed with the owner of the land. The renting year begins on 18 May, and cheese-rent for the past year must be paid by this date. As this is usually later than Easter-time, most people want the rent to be paid not only in hard cheese, which will store well in brine or oil, but also in unsalted soft cheese used in preparing special Easter treats. The soft cheese, called *vrasti* or *mizithra*, is made from the afternoon's milk boiled up with whey from the morning's milk (used to make hard cheese) and sea-water. The coagulated result is drained in rush baskets shaped like plant-pots, and is delicious eaten with island thyme-flavoured honey.

The most delicious Easter treats are little cheese-cakes, made like jam tarts in individual pastry cases. The 'Nisos' islanders call them *melitera*, but elsewhere they are called *melitinya*; in Crete they are known as *kalitsounya*. Recognizable variants are the *Siphnopitta* (Siphnos Pie) in Joyce Stubbs's *The Home Book of Greek Cookery* and *Melopita Sifnaiki* (Sifnos honey-cake) in *Cooking the Greek Way* by Maro Duncan.

One day in May I was given a soft cheese by a shepherd's wife as a return for taking her photograph for an identity card. I asked to join a neighbour's baking day so that I could learn to make my own *melitera*. The recipe I was given, using a 1-kilo cheese, produced about eighty cheese-cakes, so I have scaled it down to a quarter-kilo, about 8 oz. The pastry was made with a Greek commercial margarine, so any pie or tart pastry recipe will do for the base.

* I have deliberately not named the island on which fieldwork was carried out.
The pseudonym 'Nisos' simply means 'island'.

Melitera

For the pastry:

8 oz. (220 grams) flour   4 to 6 oz. (110–170 grams) butter
2 or 3 tbsp cold water

Rub butter into flour and add cold water. Knead gently until flour and butter are incorporated, taking care not to handle the pastry too much. Roll out on a floured board to a thickness of about 0·25 cm. Cut out tart cases with a heavy glass tumbler.

For the filling:

8 oz. (220 grams) cottage cheese or   2 eggs
  curd cheese   2 or 3 oz. (50–85 grams) plain flour
8 oz. (220 grams) sugar   pounded mastic or ½ tsp vanilla essence

Blend the cheese and sugar in a liquidizer. Add two well-beaten eggs and flour, blending as well. Finally add vanilla or pounded mastic. Place a spoonful of cheese mixture on each pastry case, which must either be pinched around the sides to prevent cheese from spilling out, or placed in jam tart tins. Sprinkle tarts with a little sugar and cinnamon. Bake for 30–40 minutes at 350° (gas Mk 4).

Putting melitera *into the oven*

As there were no jam-tart tins, the tarts were given sides by pinching the pastry together at intervals until the mixture was held in a star-shaped container. The pastry-pinching gave rise to a lot of teasing and giggling about who liked to be pinched where and by whom, and this led on to a discussion of the ethics and aesthetics of various methods of contraception practised on the island. 'Human beings should be warm together,' said my neighbour Katina. 'How can you be warm with a piece of rubber between you?' So I always associated these cheese-cakes with her practical and affectionate appraisal of the pleasures and worries of married life.

The oven was fired by thorn bushes cut from the mountain sides and olive prunings from family land. Each housewife knew when the temperature was right by the change in colour of various stones inside the oven. When the oven was at its hottest the bread was put in. While we were making the *melitera*, the dough had been rising in wooden troughs covered by the jacket of 'a quick-tempered man', said to make it rise more quickly. After the finished loaves were taken out on the end of a long paddle and the oven was cooler, the cheese-cakes were put in. How delicious they tasted when we sat and relaxed in the sunny courtyard and wished each other *Kali Anastasi* – Happy Easter!

Susan Tax Freeman

The Spanish Pig Preserved: the *Olla* and the Ham

The culinary year of the Spanish countryside begins with the *matanza*, the pig-slaughter, whose products are basic to the cuisine. Apart from a large number of Spanish cookbooks, many are available in English, and the products of the *matanza* are called for repeatedly. However, few books give directions for their preparation (see Bibliographic note). Urban Spanish cooks are told simply to procure the necessary pork products; the rural cooks who make them regularly do not use cookbooks or write them to guide others. Foreign cooks are thus left without access to these items, are uninstructed in making them, and so usually fail to reproduce the character which the *matanza* products give to the classic dishes containing them. English

Butchering a sow

or American books usually substitute *prosciutto* or Virginia ham for *jamón serrano* (lit. 'mountain ham'), bacon for *tocino* (back fat, dried and salted), and *salami* or smoked sausage for *chorizo* sausage: these substitutions seriously diminish the Spanishness of any dish.

There is a great variety of products of the *matanza*. Here I describe three of the most widely appreciated ones: the dried ham, whose fat is choice *tocino*, the sausage called *chorizo* and the preserved loin and ribs of pork. *Chorizo* and loin and ribs are preserved in what is known as the *olla*,* the pot, in which they are covered with sterilized lard or oil. These recipes are followed by three simple country dishes which contain ham, *chorizo*, and ribs from the *olla* – not to be found in most of today's books, which describe fancier fare. The recipes are all from the Sierra Ministra, in the provinces of Soria (Old Castile) and Guadalajara (New Castile), but they are similar to those found almost everywhere in Spain. Another product crucial for many traditional dishes is *morcilla*, blood-sausage, which I omit because of the difficulty of obtaining blood in large cities.† Other parts of the pig are also used: most of the head and bones are preserved for use in stews, as are the ears, feet, and back fat; an inferior sausage, *güeña*, is made from meat-trimmings; bacon is preserved for frying in thick slices, cut across the grain and called *toreznos*; and lard is rendered down to produce *chicharrones* (crackling). The offal is eaten fresh and the intestines used for encasing the various sausages. Many of these other products are relatively unsung outside rural areas and are utterly ignored in English-language sources on Spanish cookery: even the important blood-sausage is left out of most English recipes.

The *matanza* takes place between November and February. After the pig has been stuck and its blood collected, it is singed and butchered. Further cutting up of specific parts and preservation proceed on this and the following few days. The nuclear-family household is normally assisted in its *matanza* by kinsmen and friends who live near by, and the entire workforce lunches on pig's offal and *migas de matanza* 'slaughter-day crumbs'. This dish consists of breadcrumbs fried with fresh lard and *torreznos* – bacon chunks. The bread for these *migas* is cubed the night before the slaughter by the men of the work group. The group also receive the evening meal, but this does not necessarily include pork products and is equivalent to a standard holiday dinner.[1] On the following days, the workforce is smaller and predominantly female. There is no festive food-sharing other than that associated with the tasting of the *chorizo* meat and, some three weeks later, frying the sausages: these are events largely for household members only.

* The *olla* is actually several pots, their number depending upon the number of products preserved and the amount of each. This *olla* should not be confused with the legume-based stews which are also sometimes called *ollas*.

† Some Spanish *morcillas* are similar to the French *boudin noir*, which may be available.

Utensils for stuffing sausages

Many products of the *matanza*, including *tocino*, are eaten alone, with bread, and sometimes with eggs, as snacks (*meriendas*) or as first courses. They are also served in this way in taverns and in those restaurants (*mesones*) which specialize in country foods. The *merienda* is an Iberian tradition of considerable importance. In the Sierra Ministra, on a number of occasions during the year, elaborate snacks are shared by groups of unmarried girls or youths or married adults. In these, pork products figure heavily.

In the Sierra Ministra, when people put their *chorizo* mixture 'to rest' overnight before encasing it, they cut a cross in the top of the mass. Similarly, a cross is incised in the traditional round loaf of bread as it begins its final rising before baking.[2] When human effort has done its utmost, the result is blessed as it is committed to the final and crucial steps in its conversion into food.[3] Bread and pork are products of the household's year-long endeavour to make things grow well. In the Sierra Ministra, where there is a great deal of co-operative labour in every village, the fields of grain and the pigs are tended by each individual household, without assistance from the collectivity or access to common lands: arable land is never held or worked in common, nor are pigs herded together or fed on the common woodland. While people entrust their bread to a baker's oven, or even their flour to a baker's hands, they entrust their pork to no one: it is the fruit and the symbol of the household's labour and a material focus of its pride.

Recipes

Note: Spanish cured pork products are dried but not smoked. While the *chorizo*, loin and ribs are normally fried before going into the *olla*, in some regions they are not, and are sautéd only lightly before being eaten. *Olla* products are thoroughly cooked in the Sierra Ministra recipes given here. Ham, on the other hand, is everywhere eaten raw unless it enters into stews or other combined dishes. While a few Spanish traditions give both hams and sausages some exposure to smoke or place them near the hearth to dry, strong smoky taste is not a desideratum and meats are not subjected to the heat required to kill trichinae. Thus, in areas where any trichinosis is present, the *olla* products described below should be cooked through, and ham and *tocino* made by the recipe given should be used only in cooked dishes and never eaten raw. The procedures described below are carried out in winter in unheated houses. Refrigeration is not desirable, but unheated areas should be used for resting *chorizo* meat before it is encased and loin and ribs while they are still in *adobo*, and these procedures are everywhere best carried out in cool weather.

Paprika and Garlic Pork Sausage (*Chorizo*)

30 lb (14 kilos) boneless pork, mostly lean (the shoulder yields a good ratio
    of lean to fat)
7 oz. (200 grams) salt
9 oz. (250 grams) sweet Spanish or Hungarian paprika
2 heaped tbsp dried oregano
3½ oz. (100 grams) garlic, peeled, and crushed – or more or less, to taste

These optional seasonings, in amounts to taste:
2 to 4 oz. (50–100 grams) cayenne or other hot red pepper, ground
10 to 12 oz. dry anise (Spanish Cazalla or French Pernod types)
2 lb (1 kilo) sausage casings (often sold salted – wash in several waters before
    use)
14 pts (8 litres) oil, for covering (use olive oil or a cheaper oil such as corn oil)

Put meat once through coarse cutter or meat-grinder. Crushed garlic may be ground with it. Add other seasonings and knead thoroughly in a large bowl or tub; kneading may require nearly an hour. Set mixture aside in a cool place (but do not refrigerate) overnight or for as long as 24 hours. Next day, the *chorizo* meat is proven before being encased. Fry a small amount of the mixture in hot olive oil and taste to adjust seasoning if necessary: remember that flavours are stronger after drying. (The unencased, seasoned sausage meat is known as *picadillo* and is sometimes served at this stage, often with eggs or white rice.) After proving, the sausage is stuffed into the casing (best done by two people). Gently slide each entire length of casing onto stuffing attachment of grinder and grind meat into it; do not allow casing to drop away too fast before it is tightly stuffed. Allow a few centimetres of empty casing at ends of lengths; start new sausages (even short ones will do) when breakage occurs. Set a drying-frame (a clothes-drying rack does well) in a cool place with good circulation. Good drying conditions vary. In arid Spain, coolness and draught

are the chief requirements. In more humid areas, some dryness is requisite.
In zones with freezing winters, cold may be sacrificed for greater dryness.
Thus, in Chicago, I have dried sausages most successfully in a warm but dry
basement containing a furnace, and was less successful in a colder but more
humid garden shed. Prick sausages with a needle every 2 or 3 centimetres to
facilitate drying and lay or hang them on the drying-frame so that they do not
touch one another. Drying-time varies with conditions: in Spain, up to about
three weeks; in a heated Chicago basement, one to two weeks. Do not permit
excessive desiccation, hardening or shrinkage: the chief point of drying is the
achievement of a firm texture and the slightly acid flavour produced by
fermentation as the sausages hang. If a trial cut produces a piece of sausage
firm to the touch whose filling does not come out of the ends when fried, the
chorizos are probably dry enough. When sufficiently dry, cut *chorizo* into lengths
of 10–12 centimetres. Fry these gently in hot olive oil; do not overcook. Pack
fried sausages as closely as possible into large pots of glazed earthenware or,
if more available, into large tins, such as 4-litre olive-oil tins with tops removed.
For preservation, the sausages must be covered with fresh oil which has been
heated to purify it. Eight litres should cover the amount of meat dealt with here,
and the sausages should fit into three 4-litre tins. Heat oil for covering until it
smokes, then allow to cool sufficiently before covering the sausages so that
they do not cook in it. Cover tins tightly with foil, paper or plastic and store in a
cool place. Will keep for at least one year. Remove sausages with clean tongs
as needed. Fry them for use, unless they are to be used in stews. If they are
covered with excess oil other than olive oil, they may be rinsed and fried in olive
oil instead.

Marinated Pork Loin and Ribs (*Lomo y costillas en adobo*)

Adobo is a light marinade in which pork loin and ribs are frequently seasoned
before cooking. Restaurants and urban cooks saute the meats directly from the
adobo; in homes where fresh pork must be preserved until the next slaughter,
meats are removed from the *adobo*, dried briefly, fried, and put into the *olla*.

For one whole pork loin (boneless) and one slab of ribs:
up to 6 heads garlic, crushed   2 to 4 heaped tbsp dried oregano,
9 oz. (250 grams) salt   finely crushed
10 oz. (280 grams) black pepper, ground

(Remember that taste strengthens with drying for the *olla*; for drying, ingredients
may be reduced according to taste.)

In a large pot, make paste of *adobo* ingredients and add to them enough cold
water to cover the meat. Soak the meat in this mixture overnight in a cool place.

Remove meats, wipe them dry, and slice and fry if to be served immediately.
(Ribs may also be baked.) If for the *olla,* place them on a rack to dry, in a cool
place, for about a week. Be sure that all surfaces are exposed and pieces do not
touch one another. After drying period, remove from rack, slice loin and separate
ribs as desired, and fry lightly in oil. Pack into earthenware or tin containers and
proceed exactly as for *chorizo.*

Dried Mountain Ham (*Jamón serrano*)

1 fresh leg of pork, skin on	1 tbsp red wine vinegar
approx. 1 lb (500 grams) salt	ground black pepper
1 tbsp paprika	

Note weight of ham before beginning. Have ready a wooden box or some sort
of basin in which a hole can be made to permit drainage. Lay the ham on a bed
of salt in the basin, then cover it completely with salt. Coarse-grained salt is
good, but not rock salt. Place the uncovered basin in a cool, airy place (or same
conditions as for *chorizo*) for as many days as the ham weighed in kilograms.
When this period is elapsed, remove the ham from the salt and wash it thoroughly.
Then press the ham for five to twelve days. This may be done in the same box or
basin, cleaned of salt. An appropriate weight would be a case or two of wine
or soft drinks. The pressing-time depends upon the consistency desired – the
ham should neither be soft nor overly tough and dry; the desirable consistency
is similar to that of *prosciutto* or Bayonne ham. If pressed in very dry conditions,
it is probably best to press for a shorter time, as the ham will also hang. When
removed from pressure, coat the outside of the ham lightly with a paste made
of sweet paprika wetted with a very small amount of vinegar. Suspend ham on
a meat-hook so that it hangs free, away from the wall, in the same conditions
described above and for *chorizo.* Fill the hole left by the hook and coat the knuckle
area generously with black pepper. This helps to prevent maggots. (Commercial
preparations are also in use.) Do not cut for six months, or perhaps slightly
sooner if kept near central heating. The outside layer of fat is the choicest
tocino or back fat which is used in stews and is also eaten plain with bread. The
ham itself is cut in thin slices from the leg as it hangs.

Three Country Dishes

Migas (crumbs) are daily fare as well as being prepared especially (and differently) on the day of the *matanza*. Every region has a version of this dish, which
is normally served before the meat course. Note its potential as a poultry
stuffing.

Migas, using *chorizo* and *tocino*

Cut about 1 lb (500 grams) stale bread (crusty French or Spanish type) into small cubes. Sprinkle with water and leave overnight in a covered earthenware dish or in a jar. Next day, fry thin slices of *chorizo* and/or *tocino* (or *torreznos*) in olive oil, which should be the pungent 'green' oil from the first pressing. Remove meats and brown two or three cloves of garlic, chopped, in the same oil. Add ½ tsp of sweet paprika and about ½ wineglass of water or red wine. When this is boiling, add salt to taste and the bread cubes. Stir and fry until brown. To serve, add the *chorizo,* etc., and scatter small, seedless grapes over each plate of *migas.*

Broth (*Caldo*), using *jamón serrano*

Spanish *caldo,* or broth, may be made from chicken alone or from any combination of veal, chicken and beef meat and bones. A common way of dressing up a rich *caldo* is to include in the bottom of each large cup some ham, shredded or in small dice, diced hard-boiled egg, and shredded or diced soup-meat or chicken. In areas where the ham must be cooked, heat it with the broth before serving.

Ribs with Potatoes (*Costillas con patatas*), using ribs from the *olla*

Bring desired quantity of ribs to the boil in water to cover. Skim when water boils, and add potatoes, peeled and sliced, chopped onion, chopped green pepper, a clove or two of chopped garlic, a bay leaf, and salt and black pepper. Ingredients should be added in proportions to taste. The dish may be made predominantly of potatoes, in which case it is properly called *patatas con costillas,* or of ribs, as desired. The same dish may be made with fresh ribs, which will need more seasoning than ribs from the *olla.*

BIBLIOGRAPHIC NOTE

A recent specialized work, possibly unique in Spanish, is Mateo Garrigas' *Manual del chacinero* (Pork Processer's Manual), (3rd ed., Barcelona, 1967). It is devoted wholly to the discussion of the *matanza,* its techniques and its products. The section on hams is most thorough, that on sausages somewhat weaker on details of technique.

In cookery books, pork products and country dishes are perhaps most completely described by Emilia Pardo Bazán in *La cocina española antigua,* published in Madrid around the turn of the century. Teodoro

Bardají Mas' *La cocina de ellas* (2nd ed., Madrid, 1955) includes excellent instructions for classic country dishes of several regions along with more elegant creations, but does not discuss the preparation or pork products. A more recent work by Rosario Cifuentes, *La cocina práctica* (5th ed., León, 1967), *Cocina regional*, published by the Sección Femenina of the Spanish Falange (3rd ed., Madrid, 1966), and *El libro de la cocina española: quastronomía e historia*, by Néstor Luján and Juan Perucho (Barcelona, 1970), include much from classic rural cookery, as do a few other modern books. Descriptions in English of Spanish cuisine begin at least with Richard Ford's *A Handbook for Travellers in Spain* (London, 1845), and a variety of recipe collections is now in print.

NOTES

1   For a discussion of traditional communal meals and a culinary classification of feasts in the Sierra Ministra, see my *Neighbors: the Social Contract in a Castilian Hamlet*, Chicago, 1970.

2   Most breads are incised at the last rising for practical reasons. What is important here is the symbolic content of the form of the incision and the fact that it is made solely on the large, round loaves which are traditionally the only loaves eaten daily in the home.

3   The symbolic value of analogous conversions is, of course, dealt with by Lévi-Strauss in *The Raw and the Cooked*. Food classification and commensal traditions of the Sierra Ministra provide a rich field for symbolic analysis – for example, in the contrasts between festal and non-festal foods for different agegroups – but these are far beyond the scope of this essay.

Susan Plant Dos Santos

Salt and Sugar in Portugal

The rural, and indeed the urban, food of Portugal is still very much governed by the natural fluctuations of the seasons which bring freshness and pleasant variety in the fruitful months and a respite from the underlying ancient cycles of scarcity. The methods used to cheat the seasons and vary the monotony of the winter diet are very old arts, which require skill, time and dedication. Drying, smoking and salting, cheese-making and sugar preserving, the making of wine, brandy and liqueurs, and the pressing of olive oil, all demand a high utilization of labour and natural energy. They may involve all the members of a family at many stages in the process; and in the case of harvesting corn (the *ceifa*), and olive (the most important of various *colheitas*), and the grape (*vindima*), the co-operative group will expand to include what may be the entire population of a small hamlet. Harvesting and pressing are occasions for festivity involving a whole region, the picnics and dances being celebrations of the bread (wheat is called bread, in many parts, hence the 'bread harvest' and the '*Festa do pão*') or the new wine. Specialist skills are also called for at crucial stages, and these may be acquired by apprenticeship or be a fortunate gift – like having hands of exactly the right temperature for beating the curds of ewe's milk in making a fine cheese.

A remarkable example of the traditional dependence on labour-intensive techniques and natural energy was the annual voyage of sailing schooners to the Grand Banks of Newfoundland in search of cod. The *bacalhau*, slit open and salted on board during the return journey and dried in the sun in Portugal, was a staple food for centuries. Cod was fished by line from tiny coracle-like *doris* which held only two men. Until recently, the sailing fleet assembled each year in the Tagus, but despite the replacement of sail by motor the fall in the catch since the war has made *bacalhau* a luxury item. It was, however, a common and popular dish, and there are more than 100 recipes recorded for it.

Fish-salting seems to have been an organized industry from prehistoric times. Ancient salting tanks dated within the first millennium BC have been

45

excavated at various centres, some of which exported the popular condiment *garum*, in the form of a paste or sauce to Rome in the days of the Luso–Romans. These centres supplied the large new ships of the fifteenth and sixteenth centuries for their voyages of discovery, and nearly all continue to flourish today, producing salt and processing fish.

Ursula Bourne's excellent *Portuguese Cookery* (Penguin, 1973) gives several recipes for dried salt cod, including this one.

Bacalhau à Gomes de Sá (Serves 4)

1½ lb (750 grams) dried salt cod	1 lb (500 grams) cooked potatoes,
½ pint (285 ml) olive oil	sliced chopped parsley
2 onions, sliced	2 oz. (57 grams) black olives
1 clove garlic, crushed	4 hard-boiled eggs

Soak the cod in cold water for 24 hours, changing the water several times, then simmer until tender in just enough water to cover (2–3 hours). Remove the skin and bones and flake into large pieces. Heat the oil in a heavy casserole, put in the onions and cook gently until soft. Add the potatoes, cod, olives and garlic and bake in a moderate oven (350°F, gas Mk 4) until browned, about 10 minutes. Garnish with quartered eggs and sprinkle with parsley.

The Arabs first brought sugar-cane to Portugal, the 'Garbe of Andaluz', and so introduced an area of Portuguese cuisine which almost constitutes a parallel and antithetical world to that of salt and salt-preserving. The first plantation was in the Algarve, near Tavira, but although planting was revived after the Reconquest, sugar was still a luxury in the middle ages. Imported 'pink' and Alexandria sugar cost more than fifty times as much as local honey. By the mid-fifteenth century, however, there were plantations on the Atlantic Island of Madeira, and soon afterwards in the Azores and Cape Verde Islands. It was then transferred to Brazil in the early sixteenth century, and by the seventeenth and eighteenth centuries a large variety of home-made sweets was produced in Portugal, stimulated by an apparently endless supply of Brazilian sugar. The convents, notorious centres of gastronomic luxury, manufactured enormous quantities of sweet delicacies from the basic ingredients of egg-yolks and sugar. These were sold, and many became customary foods at religious festivals. Only a limited number of these sweets are still made, but the *docaria* of Portugal represents the most extensive repertoire of home-made sweets in the world. The ingredients are still mainly egg-yolks and sugar combined in an infinity of different ways and varied by the addition of almonds, coconut, walnuts, bean curd and sugared pumpkin, flower essences and liqueurs, vanilla and cinnamon and delicate pastry cases and wrappers. Convent sweets are still to be found, identified by erotic names – 'Nun's bellies', 'Angel's crops', and 'Maiden's dribble', for example.

Golden Sops (*Sopa dourada*)

1 small loaf of day-old white bread
125 grams (4½ oz.) butter
500 grams (1 lb) sugar
10 egg yolks

125 grams (4½ oz.) ground almonds
cinnamon
¼ pint (140 ml) water

Make a strong sugar syrup with sugar and water, boiling until the temperature reaches about 220°F on a sugar thermometer; this is called '*ponto de cabelo*' or '*ponto de fio*' (hair- or thread-point) because a little cooled syrup taken between thumb and forefinger will make fine strands when the fingers are opened. Cut the crusts from the bread and slice the white part into small wafers or tiny cubes. Fry in the butter until golden, drain on kitchen paper, and then add them to the pan containing the sugar syrup. Boil for a minute or two, stirring with a wooden spoon. Cool. Beat the egg-yolks with a fork and sieve, then beat them until they are frothy. Add the egg-yolks little by little to the syrup mixture, stirring in between. Add the ground almonds and heat again until the mixture thickens, stirring well all the time. When the mixture is thick, pour into a china or glass bowl and dust the surface generously with cinnamon. Serve cool.

China Slices (*Fatias da China*)

12 egg yolks and 2 egg whites
butter

250 grams (9 oz.) sugar

Beat the yolks and whites until they are pale, frothy and very thick. Pour the egg mixture in a baking-tin, 10 × 20 cm, which has been well buttered. Spread evenly, and stand the tin in a meat-dish with water, so that the mixture will cook in a low oven or in a *bain-marie* The mixture is properly cooked when a knife-blade can be inserted and drawn out clean. Cool and turn out the pudding and cut very carefully into slices about 1 cm thick and 5 cm long. Lay the slices side by side on a large shallow plate, or form them into a crown. Boil the sugar with water to make a thick syrup and pour it over the slices so that they are saturated. Serve when cold, or chill before serving.

Anthony Jackson

Faroese Fare

Faroese cooking is simple and unsophisticated. There are two basic methods: boiling and frying over the peat fire. Nowadays, roasting is also employed since there are electric ovens. The simplicity of Faroese food reflects the limited variety of food available: sea-birds and their eggs, fish, sheep, the pilot whale, cows and milk products. Only the potato is cultivated besides the rhubarb. At one time barley was grown but corn has always had to be imported. This was used to make unleavened bread (*drylur*) which accompanied most meals before the potato was introduced.

For the most part, fish, flesh and fowl were salted down for the year and later boiled. However, there is in addition another older major method of preparation and that is to wind-dry fish and meat. There are two stages to the drying process: (a) after a few months the fish or meat would be 'strong' (*raest*); (b) after several more months it would be 'dried' (*turrur*). Drying took place in special drying-sheds (*hjallur*) which have gaps between the planks to allow the wind to blow through them.

Both salted and 'strong' meat are boiled before eating. However, dried meat is simply carved in thin slices and eaten with bread and butter. Dried fish is pulled apart and eaten with butter or salted blubber.

Puffins are caught on 2 July, which corresponds to the 'Glorious 12th' and the season continues until the end of August. They are captured in mid flight by a triangular net (*fleyg*) at the end of a 10-foot pole (*fleygastong*). The fowler sits in a traditional site on the cliffs and awaits the returning birds. There may be as many as fifty sites along the bird cliffs which have been in use for centuries. One does not change the sites as this would awaken the suspicion of the birds. The fowler lays his pole alongside the rocks so that it cannot be noticed, but he holds it ready. When a puffin is hurtling towards the site, the fowler sweeps up his pole into an arc which, hopefully, transects the puffin's flight. The bird gets entangled in the net and its neck is wrung. This proves the downfall of the others since the initial catches are set upright

Catching a puffin | *Puffin*

around the site by skewering them with sticks. As the puffin is notoriously inquisitive, it will swoop over these propped-up corpses to see what's going on. The only puffin that's allowed to escape is the 'herring-bearer (*sildberin*) – that is a bird coming back with little fish hanging out of its coloured beak for its young.

In the spring-time, adult puffins are caught sitting in their burrows. A shaft is sunk down a little way from the entrance to the puffin's underground tunnel and a short stick with a bent 6-inch nail at the end of it is inserted in the hole. The puffins are dragged out and their necks broken. The puffin's head is placed under a string around the fowler's waist so when he comes home he wears a colourful feather skirt.

Roast Puffin (*Lundar*)[1]

Pluck and draw the puffins; singe and truss them. Place some fat bacon over the breasts and spread with softened butter. Roast them in a hot oven (400°, gas Mk 6) for 15–20 minutes, depending on size, basting well. Remove the bacon before the cooking is completed to allow the breast to brown. Serve with boiled potatoes, brown gravy and rhubarb jam.

Although fishing is the mainstay of the present economy, this development took place only within the last hundred years. Before then agriculture and sheep-rearing were far more important. Until the last war, fishing was conducted in open boats using a hand-line. Fishing grounds were a closely guarded secret for they were very small – perhaps only 10 square yards or so. One of the trade secrets was the bearings of these grounds taken from significant sites on land.

Like many people who live by the sea, the Faroese have definite aversions to certain animals. This is seen in two ways: they refuse to eat eel and any form of shellfish; they don't use the proper names for some animals when at sea; thus 'cat' becomes 'short-nose', 'cow' becomes 'long-tail' and 'ewe' becomes 'short-tail'. However, it is not simply domesticated animals that receive 'half-names': the seal is 'bitter tasting'; a knife is 'the sharp one' and a minister is called a 'puffin'!

Some of these beliefs are woven into stories that used to be told in the evenings when the family gathered round the peat fire to continue their daily tasks – carding and spinning wool and knitting. One such story concerned a farmer who had a 'grey one' (*huldremand*) as a neighbour. These 'grey ones' were like humans in every respect except they lived underground and had supernatural powers. One day the farmer spotted a strange cow on a small island belonging to him and which he used for grazing. So he rowed over with his man to take the cow home. They were rowing back with the cow in the boat when they heard oars behind them – it was the 'grey ones' in pursuit. The 'grey one' caught up with the farmer and leapt into his boat. They struggled and the farmer got the advantage and called to his man to pass him 'the sharp one'. His servant didn't hear him, so the farmer shouted, 'Give me the knife, you fool!' With those fatal words, he was in the 'grey one's' power because he had uttered that which should not be said afloat. The farmer was taken to the southern isles as a thrall to the 'grey one'. He was seen from time to time by fowlers up on the mountains but he never came home again.

Fish Balls (*Fiskaknettir*) (To serve 6)

3 medium-sized haddocks or 3 lb
  (1·5 kilos) cod fillet
2 to 4 tbsp (sheep) suet (to taste)
2½ tsp salt
2 tbsp potato flour

2 to 4 tbsp milk (depending on the
  consistency of the fish)
1 small onion
pepper to taste

Clean the fish, rinse, split and fillet them. Grind the fish several times in a grinder (or mince finely) together with the onion and suet. Mix in the flour, salt and pepper: adding milk gradually until the mixture is of a dough-like consistency. Form into balls about 10 cm in diameter. Drop into boiling water (or a broth made from the fish's head, bones and skin) and cook for 1 hour. Serve with boiled potatoes, melted butter and sweet mustard.

It's an old saying that 'Faroese wool is Faroese gold' because one of the chief exports of the Faroes was knitted stockings. Indeed some people believe that the very name of the Faroes derives from the word *får* (meaning 'sheep'). (John Buchan wrote a novel called *The Island of Sheep* which was set in the Faroes.) In any event, sheep are a very important source of income and of food. At the autumn round-up of sheep in the hills they are driven down into the infield and some of them are killed for winter food. The slaughtering is done in the cellar of each house. A knife is plunged into the sheep's neck, killing it instantly. The sheep's feet are bound together and it is placed on a table with the head overhanging the edge. The jugular vein is cut and the blood is drained into a bowl on the floor. The head is cut off and thrown to one side. The sheep is laid on the floor and skinned. Then it is disembowelled and the innards are placed in a bucket. The whole process takes a very short time and no blood spills on the floor, since the cutting-up is done on the inside of the sheepskin. The blood is used to make a pudding which is boiled in the stomachs. The intestines make good sausage-skins for the chopped-up lights.

The heart and kidneys can be stewed, the lungs made into soup. The hind legs are hung up to dry for several months while the rest may be salted down (nowadays, frozen). What happens to the head follows.

Boiled Sheep's Head (*Seyðarhøvd*)

Burn the wool off the head with a flame. Saw the head in two longitudinally between the eyes. Put the halves in a saucepan with boiling water, add salt and herbs and peppercorns to taste. Simmer for about 2 hours until the meat slips away from the bone. Allow half a head per person. Serve with boiled potatoes and melted butter. Place the heads on a plate in the centre of the table where everyone can reach and pick or cut off what they want. Everything can be eaten except the bones. Fastidious persons may omit the eyeballs and the gums.

NOTE

1   A few medieval delicacies, among them puffin, were regarded as fish. Roasted puffins were served as part of the fish feast held for the enthronement of the Archbishop of Canterbury in the early sixteenth century – see Anne Wilson, *Food and Drink in Britain*, Constable, 1973.

Eugene Hammel

Bosnian Coffee

A dark roast of coffee, preferably freshly roasted, should be used. The beans are placed in a cylindrical brass coffee mill (*mlin*) and ground to a fine powder. Muscular non-Balkan males will be astounded by the effort required and the aplomb with which Balkan females grind up the required amount. Usually, one ordinary *mlin* filled to capacity will provide enough coffee for one standard coffee-pot and will serve 4–6 persons. When the coffee is ground, or while it is being ground, fill a standard coffee-pot with water. This pot (*džezva*) is made of copper, in the shape of a truncated cone with flaring lip and a long brass handle. The standard one is about 9 cm high, 8 cm in diameter at the base, and holds about 225 ml. Pour off enough water from the *džezva* to fill one small coffee-cup (*fildžan*, about 60 ml capacity). If sugar is to be used, add it to the cold water (to the pot), one teaspoon per *fildžan* (again the small cup); if this much is used, the coffee will be Bosnian coffee; if less, Serbian. Bring the water to a fast boil, preferably over an electric fire (charcoal was used formerly, but has gone out of fashion). When the water boils, remove the pot from the fire and add the contents of the *mlin* to the standard *džezva*. (This works out to about 175 ml, 10 tsp powdered coffee.) Stir. Place the *džezva* back on the fire and allow to come to a boil, removing quickly to prevent the froth from overflowing. Repeat this twice more. The grounds may be settled by pouring in the cup of cold water that has been kept aside, but this must be done so as not to disturb the froth (*kajmak*) on the coffee. When in doubt, do not pour in the cold water but wait for the grounds to settle; do not, however, wait too long or the *kajmak* will disappear. Pour a little *kajmak* in each *fildžan*. Then pour the coffee out into the *fildžani*, floating the *kajmak*. Drink.

One does not ordinarily eat with this coffee. However, it is not uncommon to take a glass of fruit-juíce or a plum brandy (*rakija*) as an accompaniment.

Joseph Rykwert

On Strata in the Kitchen, or the Archaeology of Tasting

The proverbial thirty-two chews recommended by Gladstone are hardly enough to consume the rough and contrasting stuffs – hard-crusted and clay-like wholemeal bread, nuts, shredded vegetables, unhusked rice and so on – served in health-food restaurants and salad bars. Eating-places providing such a diet have multiplied in Anglo-Saxon countries particularly. The fastidious eaters who attend them have not usually rationalized their urge for the coarse food enough to consider why they have reversed a tendency in the preparation of food at least two centuries old. The climax of this tendency was reached about the time of Napoleon's First Empire, and was then maintained on a plateau of invention, without changing course until the middle of this century: this French *haute cuisine*, following the French language, became the staple of courts, of diplomacy and of the cosmopolitan world of hotels and restaurants.

The devising of *haute cuisine* was marked by a number of inventions: the fundamental one was, I think, that of the *velouté* sauce to which Louis de Béchamel, in the time of Louis XIV, gave his name. The second, which must have been devised some years later, is the *mayonnaise* which, as Carême rightly pointed out, is also quite different from other sauces (in which the boiling of liquid for reduction is the essential operation), since it is based on emulsifying a fat and a protein by brisk stirring. Legend attributes its invention or discovery to the unnamed cook of the Maréchal Duc de Richelieu after the capture of Port Mahon, on Minorca, which would date it to 1756. About the same time, King Stanislas Leszczyński popularized another cooking discovery: the *meringue*. All three have one property in common: they are transformations of relatively simple aliments, egg whites or yolks, olive oil, sugar crystals or butter and dripping or flour through a single culinary process into a complex 'masking' substance. Even a cursory reading of eighteenth-century cookery books will show the importance of the operations of *liage* to produce smooth texture, and of masking. As the century advances, and passes over into the nineteenth, so the cookery books emphasize the rationalization of the menu and the greater use of scientific information to render food more appetizing, and more easily digestible. This tendency is summed up by the most illustrious writer on gastronomy, Jean-Antheleme Brillat-Savarin, who was born in 1755, and died in 1826. A year before his death, he published his best-known work, *La Physiologie du goût*.[1] Its agreeable, racy prose has endeared it to many who could not follow the author in his gastronomic tests. Brillat-Savarin was the contemporary of a number of men whose precept and example codified *haute cuisine*. Antoine-Auguste Parmentier, economist and agricultural expert (1737–1817), ennobled the potato; Marie-Augustin Carême (1748–1833) codified the high style in a number of books, of which the most monumental were the five volumes of his *Art de cuisine au dix-neuvième siècle*, which appeared in Paris in 1816. Grimod de la Reynière devised a new style of ephemeral literature: the *Almanach des gourmets* which appeared from 1803 to 1812, as well as the system of classifying food through what he called *légitimisation*, a written approval, which he and a group of friends – a self-styled gastronomic academy, the Société des Mercredis, who claimed to remember the fine food of the Ancien Régime – issued to any *restaurateur* or *traiteur* who submitted dishes for consideration.

In spite of his vaunting of the Ancien Régime, and for all that the development of a cuisine must be gradual, Grimod, like Brillat-Savarin and Carême, belonged to a new dispensation. This began truly with the opening of the first restaurant by a cook called Boulanger, who challenged the guild monopoly of the *traiteurs*, the cook-shops, who worked to specific orders, given well in advance. In 1770 they brought a case against him, but the Paris Parlement decided that the sheep's feet in white sauce, for which Boulanger's establishment became known, were not a *ragoût*. This decision opened the way to the creation of a new kind of commercial eating establishment, more luxurious and better equipped than the older *cabarets* and cook-shops. They proliferated under the terror, when unemployment afflicted the *chefs* and the *maîtres d'hôtel* of the great, exiled families.

The new *restaurants*, as they were called after a poor joke of the original Boulanger (*venite ad me vos qui stomacho laboratis et ego restaurabo vos*), provided meals cooked to order, as well as a fixed menu. With them the habit of elegant eating-out became a regular element of bourgeois life. They, and the hotels with which they were associated, imposed the standards of the French cuisine throughout the world.

The eighteenth-century menu, to which this kitchen was appropriate, was articulated into a series of *services* (usually three), from the most delicate (*potages*, boiled meat or fish in their broth) to the most savoury, up to the *gratins* of game; the wines moved from light 'cooked' ones (madeira, sherry) to sweet white, dry white, clarets, burgundies, to conclude with heavy sweet wines at the dessert. These *services* consisted of symmetrically apparelled dishes, which were served together: so there might be seven or eight different preparations on the table at one time. The enormous demand this layout of the meal made on the carvers and servers, the inevitable cooling and drying of the most laboured sauces, led to the modification of this form of the meal, known as the *service à la française*, into the form of the menu which we now know, and which came to be called at the time *service à la russe*, and which is the basis of modern restaurant and banquet menus, with their succession of *hors d'oeuvres*, soup, fish, meat and game dishes, cheeses and sweets. The rationalization of the kitchens was an inevitable concomitant of rationalized eating: the *batterie de cuisine*, composed mostly of copper pots and dishes, tinned on the inside, belongs to this period, as does the division of labour among a strictly hierarchized group of kitchen staff.

With them, the *genre* of literature (to which Grimod's *Almanach* contributed) inevitably came into being. These were books about informed eating – gastronomy. The word was coined about the time of the Revolution, long before Brillat-Savarin gave it currency, and was the subject of a long poem by Joseph Bérchoux in 1800. The previous literature of eating was concerned, on the whole, either with providing cooking-recipes or suggesting a medically-approved diet. The two types appear early: the recipe-book of a Roman writer, M. Gavus Apicius, is known through its Carolingian copyist-editors; about the same time, the Galenic medical tradition was reformulated in a long poem called the *Regimen Sanitatis*. Both texts were popular throughout the middle ages, and were printed before 1500. There were plenty of cookery – and household management – books written during the middle ages in France, as in Italy. Bartolomeo Sacchi, who is better known as 'il Platina', the author of a very popular collection of the lives of the popes, also wrote one of the earliest of modern cookery books, and the first important one to be printed: *de honesta voluptate*; it appeared in Rome in 1473, and in Italian translation in Venice soon after; but in fact the Italian *cuisine* which was to come nearest to the way Italians eat now, the Italian *cuisine* of international cookery (*La cuisine italienne est le triomphe des pâtes*, as Ali-Bab puts it) was not formulated until the latter part of the sixteenth century. Many of the essential dishes and flavours associated with it came from the new world: the *polenta* of maize and the tomato are the most obvious examples. As we know it, it was codified by Bartolomeo Scappi (secret cook to Pope Pius V), whose *Opera* appeared in Venice in 1570 and by a number of writers on the art of carving and managing banquets, which form another by-way of culinary literature; since they are somewhere between a treatise on manners and house management and a cookery-book. The showiest of the category is the *Trinciante* of Vincenzo Cervio, who had worked mostly for Cardinal Allessandro Farnese (1520–89). It is the almost theatrical aspect of these treatises which is impressive and important. They expend much attention on matters of protocol, but also on the almost choreographic direction to the carver on how to hold the meat he is carving high on his fork before his lord, in feats of graceful, acrobatic display.

The French cooks of the sixteenth century, and of the early seventeenth, were very influenced by Italian example: Charles IX's Italian expedition had a notoriously powerful influence on French culture; as did the two Medici ladies, Catherine and Maria, wives of Henry II and IV respectively. What goes for architecture and literature goes also for cooking. Italian cookery books were translated into French; more important, a number of Italian cooks worked in France. Their influence is notable in the increase of salads, vegetables and fruit dishes, ices, and the generous use of cheese in cooking; Italian cooks also changed the *cuisine* of several other countries: of Britain, to which they imported the use of vegetables, almost unknown before the seventeenth century, as well as to northern Europe, where they merged their art with certain local procedures. In Italy itself the image of the 'traditional' Italian meal has much altered since the seventeenth century. The dominance of French *cuisine* has asserted itself over Italian cooking by a number of importations, of which the 'masking' sauce is the most obvious. But certain essential and perhaps even structural differences remain.

Take the matter of the sauce. While the French sauce is not only a means for transforming the essential ingredients of the dish into a culinary preparation from which it must often be quite unlike in texture and appearance, it almost always – and particularly in the case of hot sauces – involves the use of reduced liquids from the cooking process, so that there is a continuity of flavour between the main ingredients (meat, fish or vegetables) and the sauce or garnish. The typical Italian sauces – such as the *salsa verde* or the *agrodolce* sauce or, for that matter, the Genoese *pesto* and Lombard *mostarda* – are garnishes of quite distinct and alien texture to the main ingredient which they accompany. The thickening is never the *roux* of French cookery, but the herbs themselves, breadcrumbs, nuts or cheese. In any case there is a vast variety of sauces which are used primarily as a condiment for the various forms of *pastasciutta*. This basic Italian dish was already well known in the middle ages: *maccheroni*, *ravioli* (or *ravivoli*), *tagliatelle* appear in fourteenth-century books; and although they were commonly used by the people – being filling and cheap as well as nutritious – they also appear on the menus of elaborate banquets; and sometimes as 'foreign' dishes on French menus. The formal variations of *pastasciutta* are an essential factor in the make-up of Italian *cuisine*, although they bulk somewhat less in Italian meals than foreign observers suppose. The prodigal variation of shape, especially now that *pasta* is dried and produced commercially, and its flavouring with a vast range of sauces, actually depends on the uniformity of the ingredients: flour and water, to which eggs, butter or vegetable colouring are occasionally added: a bland, unrisen dough which is then cut and shaped in dozens of ways. It is the emphasis on shape and texture (sometimes heightened by stuffing) that makes *pasta* so interesting: this emphasis still dominates Italian eating habits. Meat is, as often as not, served without vegetables, which may be a separate course; the succession of dishes is as much a sequence of textures as of tastes: raw vegetables are as important for their textural as for their gustatory value, even cheese is eaten with a knife and fork, like meat.

By contrast, French *cuisine* is based on the shading of colour and flavour. The use of reducing cooking liquids, of thick masking sauces and aspices to change the shape of ingredients, the high favour of *quenelles* as garnish, are outward symptoms of a more important characteristic: the systematic rationalization of the division of labour in the kitchen which corresponds to the equally formidable and detailed organization of the *batterie de cuisine*, all aiming at the quality for which Brillat-Savarin coined the word *esculance*; and all this belongs firmly to the end of the eighteenth century.

To re-state it all in stylistic terms, you might almost say that French cooking is as much neo-classic as Italian cooking is baroque, and for that matter, British cooking is Victorian neo-Tudor. All this leaves many questions begging: French domination of cooking, established after 1800, led to the adaptation of masking sauces (*mayonnaise* in *vitello tonnato*, *béchamel* in *pasticcio di lasagne*) to Italian dishes, and to a relative impoverishment and provincializing of autochthonous Italian cooking. French domination is the last eating hegemony to be established; indeed French is, apart from the Chinese, the only surviving *haute cuisine* still practised, and with an impact on eating habits all over the world. Go to any supermarket outside Italy, and you will be hard put to it to find more than three or four varieties of *pasta*, while in Italy, and in shops catering for expatriate Italians, you will find up to thirty or even forty varieties. But almost anywhere there are (and in abundance) the industrial surrogates of the *cuisine classique*: plastic sachets of *mayonnaise*, of smoked salmon, packed and tinned sauces including *béchamel* and *velouté*, *potages*, stock cubes: even surrogate truffles and caviare – the whole gamut of a *kitsch* high life reduced to terms of eating. Even Grimod de la Reynière's system of *légitimisation* has been extended, and democratized through a whole literature of good food guides. At their apex, the Michelin guide dispenses its stars with all the solemnity of Grimod's 'academy'.

Against this provision of a surrogate but popular *haute cuisine*, the merchants of roughage set their 'genuine' wares: the wholemeal breads, the bran cakes, the coarse-cut salads in wooden bowls. The texture of the 'real thing', however, is not the large-scale formal variation of the Italian cooks, but the rough graining of cereal and root vegetables. As far as Europe is concerned, it is also a preference for home-grown, as against imported, foods. This requirement does not correspond to any major movement observable either in literature or in the visual arts; in any case, we are too near to the phenomenon to make any simple equation.

The desire for the rough, uneven texture of the hand-made thing is a major cultural shift, which appears at its lowest level in such phenomena as the mechanically serrated edges of greetings cards or even photographs; at a higher level in the ostentatiously knobbly surface of most modern artists' prints or the hand-beaten, unfinished look of much modern jewellery. It is almost a mirror image of the equivalent desire for the smooth and regular, the finish which only machine production can really guarantee, which eighteenth-century printers sought to satisfy by the use of hot-pressed papers, engravers by the perfecting of the use of the graded bloom of mezzotint, and cooks by the development of *liage*.

It had a precedent in the 1930s, when the heirs of the arts-and-crafts movement still prospered, and 'limited edition' presses churned out large numbers of books on the thickest and roughest paper possible, which are in high demand among collectors and therefore booksellers; and in fact facsimiles of such books are already being produced, much in the way producers of industrially made foods are already producing surrogate 'wholefoods'; and paradoxically, the phenomenon is affecting the outer reaches of the consumer economy, with cosmetics not only – as in the past – nominally based on fruit and flowers, but even on cereals: the sociology of the 'real thing' would be a most interesting investigation!

The home-produced, rough-textured ethos corresponds closely to the mood of social revisionism its detractors call doom-watching. It is all too easy to underestimate at the current rate of increasing mobility and commercially enforced cosmopolitanism. It must remain incomprehensible unless the whole of the man-made world, the world of culture, is considered as a continuum – in which food preparation is given its right, its dominant position among other cultural phenomena. It must, of course, also be considered in the context of the social *mores* in which eating is done; and related to what is generally thought of as its 'goodness' in the medical and in the gastronomic sense.

Health food, then, is a minority fad which publicity dissipates through over-imitation, but which in turn affects attitudes throughout industrial society. *Kitsch haute cuisine* is already a major industrial phenomenon. They meet in a binary opposition which signifies a radical division in what might be called the north-western world (the Anglo-Saxon countries and western Europe), which can be understood only through a discursive examination of the historical horizons or strata in which the complexes were first formulated.

NOTE

1   *The Philosopher in the Kitchen*, Penguin, 1970.

SECTION 2

The Middle East

Woman reaping wheat

Marianne and Jerry Leach

Meydiha's *Kısır*: a Wheat Dish from Southern Turkey[1]

This is our favourite cereal dish and foremost culinary discovery in twelve years of travel. It comes from the Adana province of Turkey, especially the floodplain called the Çukurova which borders the Mediterranean. We learned it from a Turkish villager named Meydiha who lived outside the city of Adana in 1965.

The dish is essentially a steaming heap of spicy cracked wheat eaten in lettuce leaves. It is like a cross between the Turkish national dish *bulgur pilavı* (cracked-wheat pilaf) and southern Turkish *kısır* or Lebanese–Syrian *tabbouleh* (spicy cracked-wheat salad). The offspring we find superior to the parent dishes.

Cracked wheat is made by boiling or soaking whole wheat kernels and then cracking them by grinding or pounding.[2] The cracked particles are then dried and stored until time for cooking.

Bulgur pilavı is made by boiling the cracked wheat, causing the particles to swell to several times their original size. Salt is added, and butter (if available) is melted over the dish just prior to eating. Chopped onions and tomatoes are sometimes included in the preparation. Among farmers, the dish is often served as a main course on communal trays or in individual bowls and is eaten by hand or spoon. Among urban middle-class Turks, the dish is an intermediate course, often substituting for rice pilaf.[3]

Southern Turkish *kısır* and Lebanese–Syrian *tabbouleh* (spicy cracked-wheat salad) are closely allied dishes. *Tabbouleh* is a cold hors d'oeuvre or side-dish made by mixing soaked cracked wheat with onions, mint, pepper, parsley, olive oil, and lemon juice. The preparation is eaten with romaine lettuce or cabbage-leaves used as spoons.[4]

Turkish *kısır* is similarly a cold appetizer made from soaked wheat with onions, parsley, pepper, olive oil and possibly tomatoes. In southern Turkey, the liquid additive is sour pomegranate juice (*nar eksisi*) or liquefied tomato paste mixed with chilli pepper pulp (*biber suyu*). Outside the south, lemon juice is more common. The dish is sometimes eaten in lettuce leaves or sometimes moulded into a ball by hand. It is a popular accompaniment to the aperitif arrack[5] (Turkish *rakı*). Though southern in origin, *kısır* has become fashionable in Turkish cities over the last fifteen years.

Meydiha's *kısır* is not this currently fashionable dish but one rather like it. It is eaten in the villages of the Çukurova area and not, to our knowledge, in restaurants or middle-class homes.[6]

Grinding wheat with a hand-mill

Meydiha's *Kısır* (To serve 6)

1 lb (450 grams) cracked wheat, usually obtainable at health or foreign food
    shops under the labels 'Bulghur' or '*Labsi*'
12 spring onions with tops (or substitute a mixture of white and spring onions)
2 cloves garlic
⅓ cup (100 ml) mild olive oil (or substitute a mixture of strong olive oil with
    vegetable oil)
2 or 3 chicken bouillon cubes. Note that this is is our suggested addition to the
    recipe and not a part of the dish we were originally taught.
2 pts (1·2 litres) boiling water
2 tsp tomato purée (or substitute tomato sauce or ketchup)

¼ tsp cayenne, if you like pungent tastes, or red pepper, if you don't. Note that
the tomato purée and cayenne are a substitute for the liquefied tomato
paste and chilli pepper pulp found in southern Turkey. The substitution
maintains some authenticity because red pepper and cayenne come from
the same species as Turkish chilli peppers.

black pepper, to taste

salt, to taste

4 to 8 oz. (100–200 grams) parsley, finely chopped. The flat French or Continental-
type parsley is preferable if available

⅔ cup (200 ml) lemon juice

3 heads of romaine lettuce (or substitute cos or ordinary lettuce)

3 or 4 lemons, sliced for squeezing over final preparation

Chop the onions using all the green of the tops. Chop the garlic finely. Heat the
olive oil slowly in a large pot and sauté the onions and garlic until soft. Boil
2 pints of water in a separate pot. Dissolve the bouillon cubes in a small amount
of water in another container.

Pour the cracked wheat into the large pot with the onions and garlic. Mix the
wheat until it has taken up all the oil. Pour in the bouillon and the 2 pints of
boiling water, completely covering the wheat. Drop in the tomato purée and stir
well. Bring the wheat to the boil, cover, and reduce the heat to low.

Cook the wheat until it is soft and fluffy. Be careful not to overcook, as the
wheat can become too soft and mushy.

Season the mixture to taste with salt, pepper, and cayenne or red pepper.
Pour in the lemon juice to taste. Add the parsley and mix well. Cover and let
stand until ready to serve. The flavour deepens the longer it stands.

Prepare a small bowl of romaine (canoe-shaped) lettuce leaves for each person.
Chilling the leaves well adds flourish to the occasion and contrasts pleasantly
with the steaming wheat. Chilling, however, is our addition to the dish and
therefore departs from Turkish authenticity.

Inside of a hand-mill

Serving

Serve the wheat hot or warm in a large bowl or platter in the centre of the table. Place two or three bowls of sliced lemons, preferably chilled, around the table. Place the bowls of lettuce at each place. People should spoon the wheat from the platter with the lettuce, adding a dash of lemon juice before eating.

Meydiha's *kısır* can be served as a main course in a meatless dinner or as an accompaniment to many meat dishes, especially kebabs. It also substitutes nicely for rice. Cold water goes best with the dish, though light red wine is also good. Note that letting the dish stand for 24 hours and then reheating it in a little added water brings the preparation to its fullest flavour.

Farmers of the Çukurova plain would normally eat this dish in segregated groups, men before women, though this rule is not so rigidly observed any longer. The men would be served several dishes in bowls on a large flat tray. The tray is placed on a stand in the middle of the room. Those eating gather round the tray sitting cross-legged or, more politely, with their right knee up and left leg flat on the floor. Right shirt-sleeves would normally be raised above the elbow. The host or elder begins the meal with *'Bismillah!'* ('In the name of God!').

On varying occasions, especially when lettuce is not in season, spoons or fingers may be used for eating the wheat. Fingers work well if the wheat is a little sticky. Small wads are made between the thumb and forefinger. For Turks, the right hand is the culturally 'clean' hand and appropriate for all eating. Water would normally be drunk after eating is finished. Fingers are not licked after eating but washed with poured water. Belching and lip smacking are not acceptable.

A guest at such a meal will find the dish served with the ritual phrase *'Afiyet olsun!'* ('May it do you good!') to which the reply is *'Elinize saǧlik!'* ('Health to your hands!'). This exchange is often repeated after eating as well.

Wheat Taboos

Though lacking prominence in the Koran, wheat nevertheless has great significance in Turkish religious beliefs. Wheat is considered a blessing from God and offences against it are open to divine retribution. The common warning to children about violating wheat and other prohibitions is *'Allah çarpar!'* ('God will strike you!').

It is forbidden to urinate or defecate, or have intercourse in a wheat-field or to urinate or defecate with wheat, especially bread, on one's person. Wheat should be eaten after hands and face are recently washed. While eating, one should keep wheat always above the waistline, thus dissociating it from the lower 'profane' half of the body. This is why servings of wheat should never be placed on the floor but put on elevated stands. Bread should never be allowed to touch the floor or ground and, if it has, it is doubly heinous for one to step on it. Turkish children are taught to kiss fallen bread and touch it to their forehead as an apology to God. Above all other foods, bread should not be left uneaten at a meal and, if it is, it should not be thrown away as waste. Wheat taboos help protect the power of fertility and are important in maintaining the proper relationship between people and God.

The Origin of the Name

The dish we learned was called *kısır* by the maker. However, we have converted this to 'Meydiha's *kısır*' to avoid confusion with the more widely known cognate dish called *kısır* (spicy cracked-wheat salad).

The label *kısır* for either dish presents an interesting problem. *Kısır* means 'barren, infertile, unproductive, insufficient, incomplete'. The term is commonly applied to barren women or animals, infertile soil, fruitless work or insufficient talent or quantity. The Turkish equivalent of the English idiom 'vicious circle' is '*kısır döngü*' ('barren or unproductive turning'). Why should either of the dishes labelled *kısır* have any association with this range of meanings?

Turks and Arabs have given us six explanations. (1) The dish's name is 'just a name' and does not relate to the range of meanings of *kısır*. (2) It is a borrowing from Arabic. (3) It denotes the 'defertilized' state of the cracked wheat. (4) It stands for the 'insufficiency of quantity' that one feels when eating a delicious dish. (5) It denotes the meatlessness of the dish. (6) It comes from the cultural disjunction between wheat and spiciness making a staple food culturally 'dangerous' to women because of certain pregnancy taboos.

We have found the 'just-a-name' explanation unacceptable because the majority of our informants think the name of the dish and range of *kısır* meanings are related. Furthermore, both *kısır* dishes are recognized to be recent innovations and, since *kısır* is not known as a personal or place name, the name must have come from some pre-existing stock of semantic items. New names are seldom whole-cloth fabrications but usually are extensions of old meanings into new areas or borrowings from other languages. Finally, it is not exceptional that some people see a label for an innovation as 'just a name'. Most of us receive new labels without an explanation of how they came to be associated with the thing they identify, though sometimes the link is obvious. When the link is not obvious, we are left uncertain, i.e. with 'just a name'. We hold that the word-dish association with *kısır* is not obvious because the key information necessary to understand the association is, to some degree, sex-linked. Sex-linked, in this case, means held mainly by women.

The Arabic-borrowing explanation stems from the fact that *kısır* is thought of as a southern dish, especially associated with areas adjacent to

Lebanon and Syria. In these provinces, Arabic is a strong minority language. Arabic contains a verb, *kasara*, which means 'to break' or 'to break into pieces'. Various forms of *kasara*, because of Semitic-language vowel changes, sound like *kısır*. The argument is that *kısır* could be of Arabic origin, cloaked in Turkish phonology and spelling, and making a straightforward reference to the wheat being 'broken into pieces'. The problem with the argument is that *kısır* is not used by Arabs to refer to the dish but *tabbouleh* is. Furthermore, Arabs see the dish as an import from Turkey because of the prominence of *bulgur* wheat in it. If this 'import' suggestion is true, then, short of an unusual linguistic counter-migration of a second Arabic name which is not used in Lebanon or Syria, *kasara* becomes an unlikely progenitor for the name *kısır*.

The third explanation, that using cracked wheat is using 'defertilized' wheat, meets three serious objections. Most informants see it as far-fetched. No cultural evidence can be uncovered which equates cracking wheat with removing its symbolic fertility. Lastly, many other Turkish dishes employ cracked wheat as an ingredient without any reference to 'infertility' or 'barrenness, unproductiveness, incompleteness, or insufficiency' in their names.

The fourth explanation, that *kısır* means 'insufficient' and is a poetic way of describing attitudes to a delicious dish, is imaginative but weak. It probably stems by analogy from the name of a famous Turkish aubergine dish *Imam Bayıldı* (The Priest Fainted) which carries the connotation of a dish so delicious that it causes even those resistant to the pleasures of food to succumb.[7] Nevertheless, most informants are unresponsive to this kind of explanation for *kısır*. Among other things, 'insufficiency' is one of the weaker translations of *kısır*. Its most frequent reference seems to be to barrenness. Lastly, Turks hedge their bets on whether or not *kısır* (spicy cracked-wheat salad) is so delicious (Turkish *nefis*, *hos*, or *tatlı*) that it would attract a name based upon deliciousness as its distinctive feature.

The fifth explanation, that *kısır* stands for the meatlessness of the dish, has some strong exponents among our informants. The reasoning is that southern Turks are known as meat eaters, mainly because they are thought of as rich due to their agriculture. Hence, wheat dishes are said to contain meat in the south and *bulgur pilavı* to be eaten with meat in it. An example of the wheat-meat association is another southern Turkish dish *çiğ köfte* (raw lamb rissole with cracked wheat and red pepper), now also becoming popular throughout the country. The 'meatlessness' suggestion contains plausibility but does not for us rest on a strong explanatory foundation. It overstresses the closeness of the wheat-meat association in the south. This we maintain from our own observations and from the existence of the very dishes the name of which we are trying to explain in this section. Also there is the problem of *kısır* as 'meatlessness' resting on 'insufficiency' and 'incompleteness', the weaker translations of the main term.

The sixth explanation is placed last because we hold it to be the strongest contender for the key to understanding why the dishes *kısır* should have any relationship to the 'barren, infertile, unproductive, incomplete, insufficient' range of meanings. The reasoning starts with seeing 'barrenness-infertility' as the core meaning of the term *kısır*. This we believe is established by what informants say they think of first when explaining what *kısır* means, by how informants remember the way they use the term, and by the high social significance of fertility and infertility. Of all forms of barrenness-infertility, human non-regeneration is of greatest concern.

Two kinds of causes culturally explain human barrenness: causes not under human control and those under human control. The first kind of cause basically means barrenness inflicted by God. It can affect males or females but is, more often than not, viewed as a 'woman's problem'. Some informants argue that *kısır* applies only to female barrenness. The second kind of cause involves human action in bringing barrenness about. For men this means castration (*hadım*). There are no other cultural practices, to our knowledge, that can make a man barren. For women barrenness is risked by violating certain prohibitions. Bathing, especially in sea water, during menstruation may, it is believed, produce infertility. During pregnancy, women who eat spicy (*acı*) food, drink alcohol, eat raw coffee-beans, drink unsugared coffee, or walk barefooted on cold floors are said to risk damage or death to the foetus. Indeed, eating raw coffee-beans in large quantities is a prominent abortifacient. Women, not men, have cures for barrenness which involve bathing in mineral springs (*kaplıca*), especially in the city of Bursa, or going to other women who have curative magic.

Given these beliefs as a cultural setting, the association between Turkish *kısır* (spicy cracked-wheat salad, usually drunk with arrack) and barrenness is no longer surprising. Wheat as a staple of the Turkish diet does not appear often, if at all, with the exception of *kısır*, in spicy concoctions. Hence a common food becomes in this dish 'dangerous' to fertility, especially the fertility of women. This, we hold, is the distinctive feature which explains why the dish is named as it is. Reinforcing this explanation is the fact that wheat is a pervasive cultural symbol for fertility and regeneration. For example, ears of wheat are sometimes hung over the doorways of homes, especially in rural areas, to foster the fertility, health, and general good fortune of the household. An ear of wheat is the emblem of the New Turkey Party, a secularist and reformist political party of the left. Given wheat as such a symbol, and the fact that wheat (*buğday*) is a female name, we hold that the swelling up of cracked wheat in cooking is seen as a cultural analogue to the natural process of swelling up in pregnancy. Hence, spiciness (with alcohol) relates to swollen wheat as barrenness relates to pregnancy. In other words, one condition is the cultural negative of the other in each relationship. This is a more complex way of stating the simpler argument given previously but has the virtue of allowing other facts about wheat to fall into conceptual place. The other explanations of the name *kısır* as standing for 'meatlessness' or the 'insufficiency of a delicious quantity' or the 'defertilization of cracking wheat' now seem like interesting extensions allowed by the semantic pathways inherent in the original range of *kısır* meanings.[8]

NOTES

1   The best simple pronunciation guide to 'Meydiha's *Kısır*' is to pronounce it with approximately equal stress on all syllables. The undotted 'ı' stands for a Turkish phoneme which is mid-way between the vowels in the English words 'hit' and 'hut'. The closest sound cluster in English to *kıs* is the 'ks' sound in 'hooks'. The final '*r*' is a front palatalized flap '*r*'.

2   For a picture of the cracking process, see Harry G. Nickles, *Middle-Eastern Cooking*, Time-Life Books, 1969, p. 77.

3   For a 'citified' recipe for *bulgur pilavı* see Venice Lamb, *The Home Book of Turkish Cookery*, Faber & Faber, 1969, p. 126.
To get something of the importance of wheat socially in rural life, see the first book about a Turkish village written by a villager, Mahmut Makal, *A Village in Anatolia*, Vallentine, Mitchell, 1954, esp. pp. 4, 15, 28, 30–1, 39, 50, 88, 96, 108, 127, 147, 158, 190.

4   For an excellent recipe for *tabbouleh*, see Claudia Roden, *A Book of Middle Eastern Food*, Penguin, 1968, p. 86. There is a picture of *tabbouleh* in Nickles, op. cit., p. 115.

5   For arrack, see Nickles, op. cit., p. 22.

6   For Turkey's most acclaimed novel, which is, incidentally, about the Çukurova, see Yashar Kemal, *Memed, My Hawk*, Collins and Harvill, 1961.

7   For the *Imam Bayıldı* recipe, see Roden, op. cit., p. 316.

8   We gratefully acknowledge the help of Sinan and Arin Bayraktaroglu, Saime Timms and Martin Hinds in preparing this article, and we thank Meydiha who taught us the dish.

Elaine Baldwin

Israeli Food

The reaction of most Israelis when asked to define 'Israeli food' would be to say that there is no such thing, or perhaps as an afterthought to mention olives, hummous and tehina (made from chick peas and sesame seeds respectively), which they would then admit were really Mediterranean and Middle Eastern foods. When pressed for an explanation for the absence of 'Israeli' food, the hypothetical Israeli would point to the peculiar history and social composition of Israel's Jewish population: a mixture of Jews who have come from all parts of the world, bringing with them their own food habits and traditions. There is much to this point of view and certainly even after twenty-eight years of statehood it is still possible to predict with a high degree of accuracy the kind of food that will be cooked by members of certain ethnic groups.

The major and simplest division that is made in Israeli Jewish society is between 'Orientals' and 'Ashkenazis'; the former category being those Jews who themselves, or whose families, came from the Middle East or North Africa; the latter being those who came or whose families originated from eastern Europe. It is along these lines that food stereotypes have developed: Orientals eat hot, spicy food, while Ashkenazis eat a blander food and usually such things as gefilte fish, chicken soup with noodles, and borscht. To some extent these patterns have been changed by marriage across ethnic groups (though this is still statistically less frequent than could be expected), but nevertheless the preparation and method of cooking food seems surprisingly consistent with ethnic group boundaries. This is particularly evident on such occasions as Jewish festivals and domestic celebrations such as weddings and circumcision ceremonies.

However, the relationship between the preparation and cooking of food and ethnic origin is not a simple, uncomplicated one, and there are many factors that cut across ethnic groupings and unite them. One of the most significant is the adherence to Jewish religious beliefs and practices about the consumption and preparation of food, and observant Jews of whatever ethnic group share the same broad and basic attitudes and follow the same practices according to Jewish dietary laws. A second important factor, and an obvious one, is the state of the domestic food market. Israel has a thriving and efficient system of agriculture which for both practical and ideological reasons was based on the principle of self-sufficiency in food production. One result of this is that there are plentiful and relatively cheap supplies of chicken and turkey meat, milk, eggs, cheese and fresh vegetables, and it is these foods that tend to form the main diet of the whole population.

It is probably safe to speak of the 'Israeli breakfast' and the 'Israeli supper', meals which are almost identical, both being composed of eggs, cheese and salad. And most Israelis eat their main meal of the day at lunchtime, the exception to this being on occasions of national and Jewish festivals and on Friday evening, when the Sabbath meal is eaten; so, again, Judaism imposes a pattern of eating habits on the whole population.

Government and semi-government agencies such as baby and child care clinics have had an enormous influence on the feeding patterns of young children, and here again the tendency is to a uniformity in the population. Israel's position as a food exporter to western European markets has also had an influence on the type of food that is eaten at home, many products which have been grown with the overseas markets in mind having found their way to Israeli tables; so foods such as celery, lettuce, avocado and strawberries are fairly common in the Israeli diet. As a result of all these factors and more, there does seem to be a tendency to similarity in the kinds of food that Israelis eat, but the main difference between ethnic groups still seems to lie in the preparation of food and method of cooking.

Not surprisingly, foods are linked with status in Israel no less than anywhere else. I was told by an anthropological colleague that while he was doing fieldwork in a predominantly Moroccan community, the Moroccan shopkeeper (believing him to be unemployed!) offered him credit at the shop so that he could buy white bread for his family instead of black bread. The shopkeeper did not think that it was becoming to the status of an educated man to eat black bread. Similarly, drinks are linked to status, and the offer of whisky, brandy or vodka is a significant statement about the social and economic standing of the household, even though to western European eyes the occasions on which they are offered seem to be very strange – I was rather nonplussed to be given a glass of brandy as an accompaniment to a supper dish of fried eggs and salad.

Aubergines are a very popular vegetable in Israel and are served in a variety of ways – as a spicy salad or stuffed with minced meat, or cheese. Usually they are served as a first course as an introduction to the main meal. This recipe can be served either hot or cold, as a first course, and occasionally it was served to me with spaghetti or macaroni as a light luncheon dish. Typically, this aubergine dish when served as a first course is followed by grilled or roast chicken served with potatoes, rice or macaroni.

Aubergines in Tomato Sauce

2 or 3 aubergines, depending on size	salt
1 or 2 beaten eggs	1 tsp sugar
1 small tin tomato purée	margarine
(2½ oz./65 grams)	oil

Peel aubergines (if they are young and fresh, the skin may be left on) and cut into slices 1 inch thick; lay, sprinkled with salt, on a chopping-board and leave for 1–1½ hours (the aubergines will 'sweat' and this removes the bitter taste).

Wipe dry. Dip the slices in beaten egg and fry lightly in deep oil until soft. Remove from oil and drain. Prepare tomato sauce by adding three times the amount of water to the purée (using the tin as a measure), add a teaspoonful of sugar, pinch of salt and a knob of margarine. Mix together until well blended – this can be done over a low heat if desired. Place layers of aubergines in a wide, shallow, flameproof cooking dish (two layers are preferable) and pour over the tomato sauce. Cook over a low heat until almost all the tomato sauce has been absorbed by the aubergines, usually 20–30 minutes. Can be served hot or cold.

Spiced Aubergines

Spiced aubergines is a very attractive dish which is served cold as an accompaniment to cold meats and salad. It needs time and care in preparation and presentation, and as such it was usually served only on special occasions in the village where I worked, since the women were too busy with farm- and housework to prepare this dish for every day. I am assured that it is eaten at cocktail parties in Tel-Aviv, Jerusalem and Haifa, but I have eaten it only at New Year dinners or at weddings and other festivities, when it was accompanied by large glasses of vodka or whisky – this makes a very fiery combination and it is advisable to have cold drinking water available for guests who are not accustomed to such 'hot' food.

2 or 3 aubergines	salt
2 red peppers ⎫ capsicum variety	vine leaves (if available)
2 green peppers ⎭	wine or cider vinegar
2 pickled cucumbers	water
ground black pepper	oil, approx. ½ cup (142 ml)

Wash and slice aubergines 1 inch thick, sprinkle with salt, lay out on chopping-board and leave for 1–1½ hours. Wipe dry.

Fry aubergines in deep oil, until soft, remove from oil and drain. Dice green and red peppers and pickled cucumber and fry lightly in the oil until soft. Remove and drain.

Prepare vinegar sauce by diluting 2 cups vinegar with a little water according to taste, add black pepper and vine leaves and bring to boil. Simmer 5–7 minutes.

Place a layer of aubergines in a deep dish, and on top of each aubergine spoon the diced pepper-and-cucumber mixture, continuing doing this until all aubergines and pepper mixture have been used. The dish looks most attractive when there are at least four layers of aubergine and peppers. Pour vinegar over aubergines, making sure that those on the bottom layer are also covered. Place in fridge for a couple of days, to allow aubergines and peppers to absorb vinegar.

A light cake of eastern European origin based on a sweet dough mixture is called a *babke*.

In the farming village where I did fieldwork, it was usually baked on Friday morning in preparation for the Sabbath. Friday and Saturday evenings are the usual times for social gatherings in the village, when neighbours get together to gossip and to discuss the happenings of the past week. Such gatherings would begin about 8.30–9.00 o'clock in the evening when spruce and well-groomed villagers, looking very different from their workaday selves, would arrive, after having eaten their Sabbath eve meal at home. In the house where I stayed, guests gathered around a large table in the kitchen; the table was covered with a white cloth for the Sabbath and on it the Sabbath candles burned in their silver candlesticks. When all the expected guests were assembled, the candles were removed and in their place was put the *babke*. The lady of the house cut a slice for each guest, and very often the *babke* was served with a home-made strawberry preserve, which was eaten with a spoon (not spread on the cake), and guests would take alternate tastes of cake and strawberry. Tea was usually served and this was drunk in Russian style, from a glass, without milk or sugar but with a cube of sugar held in the mouth, through which the tea was strained. It took me quite a while before I became adept at manoeuvring the cube of sugar into the right place in the mouth and then holding it there until I drank the tea. If anything remained of the *babke* after the evening's gathering, it was eaten the following morning as an early breakfast, this time usually spread with butter and jam, to be followed some two hours later by a full breakfast of eggs and salad after the early morning work on the farm had been done.

Babke

1 oz. (30 grams) yeast or 2 tsp
   dried yeast
4 tbsp sugar (2 oz./60 grams)
few drops vanilla essence
4 cups sieved flour (1 lb/450 grams)

3 or 4 eggs (separated – yolk and white)
2 oz. (60 grams) chopped nuts ⎫
2 oz. (60 grams) raisins or   ⎬ optional
   sultanas   ⎭
1 cup (approx.) warm water

Sprinkle yeast in ⅓ cup of warm water (40°), to which a teaspoon of sugar has been added. Allow to stand in a warm place for 10–20 minutes. Place flour in a large bowl, make a small hollow in the middle and add the yeast mixture. Gradually work flour into the liquid. Add egg yolks, a few drops of vanilla essence, the remaining sugar and warm water. Knead well until the dough no longer sticks to the hands. Mix in raisins and nuts if desired.

Place the dough into a well-oiled, warmed bowl and cover with a damp cloth. Allow to stand in a warm place until the dough has doubled in bulk (about 1½–2 hours). Punch down and then place it in an oiled cooking tin and allow to rise again (approx. 20 minutes). Brush the top with some beaten egg-white to which a little sugar has been added.

Bake in a medium oven (350°, gas Mk 4) for 35–40 minutes, or until cake is brown on top.

SECTION 3

Africa

The Bechuanas put their milk into sacks made of untanned hide, with the hair taken off. Hung in the sun, it soon coagulates; the whey is then drawn off by a plug at the bottom, and fresh milk added, until the whole sack is full of a thick sour curd, which, when one becomes used to it, is delicious. The rich mix this in the porridge into which they convert their meal, and, as it is thus rendered nutritious and strength-giving, an expression of scorn is sometimes heard respecting the poor or weak to the effect that 'they are mere water-porridge men'. It occupies the place of our roast beef. (*Livingstone's Missionary Travels in South Africa*, London, John Murray, 1857)

William and Dorothy Shack

Cooking in the Garden of Ensete

Culinary specialists often engage in preparing foods to resemble what they are not, an art that could be called *faux cuisine*. French cookery abounds with *faux spécialités*. For example, *langues de chat* are, in fact, 'cooky cups', *Reine de Saba*, a 'fruit-filled sponge cake', has no historical relation to the legendary Ethiopian Queen of Sheba, and the Christmas cake called *Bûche de Noël* is, of course, eaten, not burnt as the festive Yule log. Culinary art also presents us with the Anglo-American 'Mock Turtle Soup', the basic ingredients of which are veal bones and calf brains; Afro-American 'Soul Food' is not a sacrificial offering to appease spirits of the dead, but serves to whet the appetite of the living.

One twist to such culinary sleight-of-hand is the food prepared from the staple crop that dominates the small, densely cultivated gardens of the Western Gurage, in south-west Ethiopia. Their staple is *la fausse banane* (*Ensete ventricosum*). Ensete belongs to the family of *Musacae* that produces *la vraie banane*. However, because the former genus does not bear an edible fruit, never will it be found among the produce stocked by the local green-grocer. For that reason, Ensete has earned the appellation coined by other Ethiopians and Westerners: the 'false banana plant'. This botanical curiosity that resembles in its vegetative form and shape the true banana (*Musa*), or the plantain (*Plantaginaceae*), begs the obvious questions for venturesome culinary artists bent upon experiments with 'exotic' cookery. Namely: if the fruit of Ensete is false, and inedible, what parts of the plant do the Gurage eat? what methods of preparation, or culinary sleight-of-hand, do Gurage employ to make what is 'false' to be 'true', and edible? what suitable substitutes for Ensete and other Gurage foodstuffs are available in markets outside Gurageland, and Ethiopia generally? Before turning to the culinary aspects of Ensete, let us briefly put the false banana in its true cultural setting.

The Western Gurage, who speak a Semitic language and number approximately 300,000, are only one of several ethnic groups in south-west Ethiopia for whom Ensete is their food staple. One of the few indigenous

African cultigens, Ensete was known to the Egyptians of the early dynastic eras. This easily led to speculations that Ensete must have spread south into Ethiopia from the Nile valley. Indeed, Sir James Bruce, while travelling in northern Ethiopia during the eighteenth century in search for the origin of the Nile, recorded his observations of wild growths of Ensete around villages in the region of Lake Tana; the lake proved to be the source of the Blue Nile. It is now fairly firmly established that the centres of origin of Ensete are the lowland areas located between Uganda and Tanganyika, around the Ruwenzori, Mt Meru, Mt Kivu, and in the Kordofan mountains in the Sudan. Voluntary growths of Ensete are still to be found in all these regions, as well as in the grain-producing Ethiopian highlands where the plant is consumed sometimes as an emergency crop under severe conditions of famine. However, on the ethnographic map of the world, let alone of Africa, only in south-west Ethiopia is the genus *Ensete* cultivated as a food staple today.

Unlike *Musa* and Plantain, which produce edible fruits, it is the root of Ensete and the inner layers of the pseudostem that provide substance for food. After harvesting, these parts of the plant are decorticated to extract the edible portion which is then chopped, minced and kneaded into a fibrous pulp, the consistency of which is similar to mashed unripened yams. Small batches of the pulp, measured in quantities sufficient to supply food for three to four days, are wrapped in Ensete fronds and buried in deep earth-pits sunk in the garden of each homestead to allow fermentation. Fermentation in the earth-pits, which continues from two months to several years, produces in the food a sour, unpleasant odour that permeates the garden area, especially when the earth-pits are opened. Gurage themselves are quite sensitive to the smell and frequently comment about it; Ethiopians of other ethnic groups and foreigners unaccustomed to the Gurage diet usually experience difficulty in digesting Ensete. Indeed, Gurage complaints of stomach disorders are not infrequently attributed to having eaten Ensete before it had been properly fermented. However, when removed from storage in the earth-pits, the pulp is again kneaded, shaped into a large, round, flat, but slightly thick pancake-like 'bread' which Gurage call *wusa*. *Wusa* is pan-fried, rather than oven-baked, on an uncovered metal disc that has been greased lightly with oil pressed from *nug*-seeds (*Guizota abyssinica*). On ceremonial occasions, or when important guests are feasted, the finest quality Ensete is used to make *wusa*; it is called *ṭəquräya*.

Food is only one of the many needs Ensete meets for the Gurage. All parts of the plant are consumed in one way or another, thus increasing considerably the importance of Ensete in Gurage culture. A few examples of the varied uses of Ensete shall suffice. In house construction, the outer layers, 'bark', of the pseudostem are used as insulating material; it is also burnt as fuel. Dried Ensete leaves, cut into small 'plates', are used for serving *wusa* and other foods at all festive occasions, secular as well as religious. For wealthy Gurage, it is a status symbol to eat daily from Ensete fronds at the

Preparing ensete
for baking

evening meal. In matter of fact, a man's status is determined principally by
the number of Ensete in his garden, and the height and girth the plants
reach, some exceeding 10·5 metres in height. During harvesting, Ensete
fronds are used to form a lining in the deep earth-pits in which batches of
the pulp are stored. Finally, after the plant has been decorticated to extract the
edible food substance, the remaining long, coarse fibres are dried and marketed
as a minor cash crop for use in the manufacture of ropes and paper sacks. It
is worth noting that Gurage hold to the belief that nearly all forms of illnesses
can be cured from medicines concocted from the roots of certain types or
'clones' of Ensete. Medicinal foods prepared from some clones are claimed
to aid in healing fractured bones, presumably due to the high calcium content
common among certain Ensete types. Ritually afflicted illnesses attributed to
the activities of malevolent spirits invariably involve exorcism rites in which
the patient consumes Ensete especially prepared from the roots of plants
cultivated for this purpose. Customarily, Ensete claimed to have pharmaco-
logical properties is stored secretly in one of the earth-pits, hidden well below
the *wusa* that is consumed in the daily round.

Meat, usually beef, but occasionally lamb, a type of kale (*Brassica
oleracea acephala*), and lentils, are the principal supplementary foods Gurage
eat, and then sparingly. These are prepared in the form of hash, the Gurage
word for which is *kətfwä*. The evening meal usually consists of some type of
kətfwä and *wusa*. Barley-beer (*ṭallä*) flavoured with *gešo* (*Rhamnus prinoides*),
coffee flavoured with salt and rarefied spiced butter (the latter for its believed
curative power), and mead, are the principal beverages. Not infrequently a
distilled potent liquor, *aräge*, is served as an after-dinner drink.

A Gurage meal, therefore, is not a Gurage meal if Ensete is not laid on. The symbolic structure of the meal represents a variation on the placement of Ensete as the centrepiece, the staple, or the trimming, according to the hour of meal-taking, or when eating serves a function other than a strictly nutritional one. Typically, at morning and mid-day meals, Ensete is the centrepiece. Coffee and perhaps roasted barley may be served, but not other food. When *kətfwä* is prepared and served for an evening meal, Ensete becomes the trimming, which Gurage view as the only appropriate supplement. On such festive occasions as weddings, circumcisions, or annual celebrations to one of the major deities, feasting takes place on a grand scale. Then meat from freshly slaughtered bulls is the centrepiece. Most of the flesh is eaten raw, the pieces being dipped in red pepper and washed down with barley-beer. Some of the meat is set aside, and with kale and lentils prepared as *kətfwä* saturated with butter, red pepper and topped with a layer of curd. In the structure of a festive meal, then, *kətfwä* becomes the trimming, whereas the fine quality *ṭəquräya* 'bread' is symbolically the staple.

To prepare a typical Gurage meal consisting of *wusa* and *kətfwä* by substituting food items available in markets in large cities catering to continental tastes poses no serious problem. Plantain, a common staple in the Caribbean and coastal regions of Central America, is an adequate substitute for Ensete; it can be prepared as the Gurage do, that is, excluding the fermentation in earth-pits! Beef or lamb, kale and lentils acquire a different, if not 'exotic', taste when cooked in the style of Gurage *kətfwä*. The following recipes provide a simple guide to a culinary adventure into the cuisine of the garden of Ensete.

Plantain–*Wusa*

Remove the skin from one or more well-ripened plantains. Mash or pulverize the pulp and shape into a flat 'sheet' about 1 inch thick. Pan-fry until the 'bread' acquires a light crust. Serve whole, or slice into 2 inch squares.

Meat–*Kətfwä* (4 servings)

1 lb (450 grams) beef or lamb, finely minced, *not ground*	2 oz. (60 grams) rarefied spiced butter (see below for recipe)
red pepper to taste	4 oz. (110 grams) cottage cheese
½ tsp coriander	salt

Pan-fry the minced meat until medium rare; add spices, varying the mixture until the desired taste of piquancy is obtained. Stir constantly. Add the butter which has been melted in advance. Serve in an open casserole; top the *kətfwä* with a dressing of cottage cheese.

Kale–*Kɘtfwä* (4 servings)

1 lb (450 grams) kale	2 oz. (60 grams) butter
red pepper (cayenne) to taste	4 oz. (110 grams) cottage cheese

Boil the kale leaves until tender. Remove from the pot, mince finely, return to the pot and cook slowly until all the liquid is evaporated. Pour melted butter over the minced kale and add red pepper before placing in a serving dish. Top off with cottage cheese, lightly sprinkled with red pepper.

Lentil–*Kɘtfwä* (4 servings)

1 lb (450 grams) brown lentils	red pepper to taste
2 oz. (60 grams) butter	4 oz. (110 grams) cottage cheese

With a mortar and pestle, crack the lentils, then roast lightly and boil in water until tender. Drain the water from the lentils; add butter and red pepper to the lentils after placing in a serving dish and top off with cottage cheese.

Rarefied Spiced Butter

1 lb (450 grams) unsalted butter	1 piece ginger
½ medium-sized onion	5 cardamon pods (approx. 1 tbsp seeds)
1 tbsp red pepper	

Butter, a basic ingredient in preparing *kɘtfwä*, can be rarefied and spiced to achieve a taste that closely approximates the Gurage flavour. Simmer for 15 minutes the butter mixed with the sliced onion, red pepper, fresh, finely minced ginger, and crushed cardamon. Strain and cool. Butter should be prepared several days in advance and stored in the fridge.

Thick curd cottage cheese, drained of the 'milk', is almost indistinguishable from Gurage curd, especially when mixed with melted, rarefied, spiced butter and red pepper. For beverages, unchilled Guinness stout is an ideal substitute for Gurage barley-beer; the Greek liquor, ouzo, is a reasonable stand-in for *aräqe*; mead is mead, if made from pure honey.

In the culture of *la fausse banane*, as in almost all cultures, there is the formality of extending polite expressions of thanks for hospitality rendered, a custom we as anthropologists readily adopted in the garden of Ensete. For whatever the symbolic position of Ensete at mealtimes, the staple, centrepiece, or trimming, Gurage habitually express satisfaction of the food served, uttering with a sigh, several times, '*ṭäfwahum*', literally, 'I am satisfied.' And they do so, as people often do in other cultures, even though the cook might well, as it were, have spoiled the brew.

Ṭäfwahum?

William Bascom[1]

Some Yoruba Ways with Yams

Except for describing stews and yams as the customary diet of all economic classes and for the subsequent introduction of tea, coffee, and the baking of bread, Bowen's brief description still holds good today for most Yoruba after over 100 years:

> Their manner of cooking is quite different from ours. They bake nothing, but all their food is boiled or fried in earthen pots. Various kinds of bread of corn and peas are fried in palm oil or tree-butter. Sometimes they cook Indian corn in whole grains, like our 'big hominy' but the usual preparation of corn is the *ekkaw* .·. . Meat is always cut fine to be cooked. Sometimes it is stewed, but it is usually made into palave sauce which the Yorubus call *obbeh*, by stewing up a small quantity of flesh or fish with a large proportion of vegetables, highly seasoned with onions and red pepper. Obbeh, with ekkaw or boiled yam, pounded or unpounded, is the customary diet of all classes, from the king to the slave. They take three meals a day, breakfast a little after sunrise, dinner about twelve, and supper after dark. No people are so much in the habit of eating in the streets, where women are always engaged in preparing all sorts of dishes for sale to passers by. Their usual drink is water. Tea and coffee are unknown, but hot ekkaw, diluted to the consistence of gruel is much used as a morning beverage. The women make beautiful malt, and passably good beer, of Indian corn and millet. In many parts of the interior, palm-wine is very scarce and highly prized. (T. J. Bowen, *Central Africa*, Charleston, Southern Baptist Publication Society, 1857, p. 300.)

The staple food of the Yoruba is the yam, but there is regional variation, and in some areas yams are less important than other crops. Yams are the most desirable of the vegetables, but because of the prestige associated with

82

serving them, they may be reserved for social occasions while in private the family relies on cassava, taro, or maize. This point is implied in the Yoruba proverb, '*Igba dodo li agbado igbani*' ('Corn is the support of a people'). The staple food and the relative importance of yams in the diet varies also with economic means; in Ife the poor can rarely, if ever, afford to eat yams. A large number of varieties are recognized, most of which are also classed as 'white yams', 'yellow yams' or 'water yams'. Although new yams have been introduced from other parts of the world since first contact with the Portuguese in the fifteenth and sixteenth centuries, 'white yams', of which there are the greatest number of varieties, are native to Africa. Yams are boiled, mashed in two forms, steamed in three forms, fried and made into fritters, flour, porridge and a loaf and mixed with other loaves or masked with other vegetables.

Most people have a few favourite dishes which they eat meal after meal and day after day with little variation. They are discriminatingly critical of the way in which these are prepared. Not only with regard to the ingredients, the method of preparation and the amount of seasoning, but also as to the stiffness or consistency of gruel, porridges, mashed vegetables, and vegetable loaves. These are matters of individual taste and preference, which are recognized by the Yoruba and catered for in cooking. It is the duty of the Yoruba wife to learn the favourite dishes of her husband and to prepare them exactly as he wishes; and in a polygynous family the favourite wife (*ayo*) may prepare her husband's food regularly because she can do it best to his liking.

The food of an unmarried man is prepared for him by his mother or sister. Lacking these, a single man will ask some woman in his compound to buy cooked food for him in the market. Yoruba men do not cook for themselves for fear of gossip and ridicule; it would be assumed that they were either so bad that their wives and their close female relatives refused to cook for them, or that they were so miserly that they were trying to save a little that their wives might waste. The apparently innocent question, 'Why are you cooking?', asked of a man cooking his own food, is regarded as an insult.

Beside the questions of nourishment and of individual taste or preference, patterns of food consumption also involve the factor of prestige. In order to maintain a particular social status certain foods must be served to guests, regardless of what may be eaten in private. For entertaining, the most desirable menu consists of a meat stew and yam loaf. In recent times boiled rice has become the next best substitute for yam loaf, followed by yam porridge, or cassava meal porridge, and somewhat below all these, cornstarch porridge. The attitude toward the traditional dishes is expressed in the proverb: 'Yam loaf is real food; yam porridge is just medicine; if we do not see either, we can eat cornstarch porridge; to keep the mouth from being idle is the purpose of toasted corn.'

The rules of hospitality forbid a man to eat at home without offering food to all visitors and, even if he himself does not eat, it is bad form for him not to offer food to his guests. For prestige reasons, furthermore, it is necessary for a man of any social pretensions to keep a pot of stew in the house at all times in case visitors drop in. It would be shameful for him to send out to the market to buy food for his guests. They would eat market food without comment, but he would know well enough they would be thinking, 'What does he mean? A man of his position without stew in his house!'

Yam Loaf (*Iyan iyan isu iyan orufo, dombai*)

Yams are sliced, boiled (*se*) on a fire, and peeled either before or after boiling. They are then pounded in a large wooden mortar. As they are pounded they become stiffer or tougher. As the Yoruba proverb says, '*Igun iyan ko jo ti elubo; mimu ni iyan, kiku li elubo iku*' ('Pounding yam loaf is not like pounding dried yam slices; yam loaf becomes more adhesive; dried yam slices separate into powder'). When they have been pounded to the desired degree of stiffness, they are moulded into a large doughy loaf somewhat resembling an unbaked loaf of bread. Yam loaf is always eaten with stew, and anyone who eats a vegetable loaf alone or with any food other than stew may be ridiculed, saying, 'He is eating yam without sauce, *onsan iyan*'.

Yam Fritters (*Ojojo*)

Yams are peeled, washed, grated, mixed with pepper, salt, and, if desired, onion, and moulded into round balls about the size of a lime. These are deep fried (*din*) in a large pot of palm oil until crisp.

Steamed Yams (*Amuyale*)

Fresh yams are peeled, grated, mixed with pepper and salt, and moulded into small lumps which are rubbed with the palm of the hand, adding water until they become soft but not liquid. They are then wrapped in leaves and steamed (*se*) in a large covered pot. This dish is usually eaten alone, but may be served with palm oil as a sauce.

Stew Sauce (*Ata, ata soro, obe ata*)

All stews are prepared from a sauce or seasoning made from gourd-seeds, locust beans, or, further north, benni-seed. These are boiled and then soaked for about four days until they are soft, during which time they ferment. The seeds prepared in this way are known as *ogiri*. They are then ground on a grinding stone with pepper, set out on leaves in the sun to dry (*sagbe*), and dried further by placing them beside the fire to toast (*yan*). This mixture is then ground again and mixed with water as needed in making stews. The salt, pepper, onions, palm oil, and other ingredients used with *ogiri* and meat or vegetables in making stew are known as *elo obe* or *nkan obe*.

Meat Stew (*Obe, obe eran*)

Meat is boiled (*se*) and added to stew sauce, with palm oil and salt. The meat (*eran*) of domestic animals, fowl, fish, or wild animals may be used, giving a variety of types of stew, including snake and locust stews. Such distinctions, however, are generally reserved for the kitchen, and it is considered impolite to make specific reference to the kind of meat served in front of guests, unless they are very close friends.

When served with a vegetable loaf the stew is poured into a depression made in the top of the loaf, and mouthfuls of yam are broken off the side and dipped into the stew with the fingers. As a Yoruba proverb says, '*Imogunjuo li afi ifa obe la*' ('With the forefinger one licks up the stew').

NOTE

1   William Bascom did fieldwork in Ife, in the deciduous forest zone, in 1937–8. The paper from which this contribution is extracted may be read in full in *Africa*, vol. 21, 1951.

Robert Brain

Cameroon Koki:
a Bean Pudding from Bangwa

The staple food of the Bangwa – a group of Bamileke-speaking peoples living in the steep mountains dividing the plateau grasslands and forest lands of Cameroon – is *taro* (or cocoyam) eaten as a pounded *fufu* with various meat, vegetable and fish sauces. On special occasions, and there are many of them (funeral feasts, dances, men's and women's meetings), the menu is varied by the addition of extra meat dishes and a variety of boiled or steamed puddings which are usually eaten with yams or plantains or cocoyams. These puddings are boiled in leaves and are made from ground beans, egusi melon seeds, maize or groundnuts. Fresh corn is ground in a mortar and mixed with oil and pepper and wrapped in the green sheath of the corn cob. Melon seeds are also ground and mixed with oil and season delicacies such as flying ants and tadpoles – melon seeds make a pudding as light as a soufflé or an Italian *sformata*.

The most common of these dishes, however, and the most appreciated, is made from haricot-type beans, palm oil, pepper and the delicate inner leaves of the cocoyam plant. It is boiled in the larger outer leaves. Apart from the cocoyam leaves and the palm oil, none of the ingredients is difficult to get and these are satisfactorily replaced by spinach or groundnut oil. Without the palm oil, however, the pudding loses its attractive red-gold colour and a certain pungent flavour; I add onions to counteract this. In Bangwa the making of these dishes requires hours of patient preparation, usually by children, whose job it is to remove the skins of the soaked beans and grind them in the stone mortar. It is possible to make it without removing the skins and the stone pestle and mortar can be replaced by a blender. Mix the ground beans with the oil, onion or garlic, and salt; then add the whole, washed, uncooked spinach leaves. The leaves should be left whole for when the pudding is cooked and sliced the leaves make an attractive marbled effect. The beans are then boiled for 1½–2 hours in an oiled pudding-basin.* It is a very good warm or cold dish. The amount of hot pepper depends on the taste, but it is used very liberally indeed in Cameroon. A good winter accompaniment to a meat stew.

* Alternatively, the mixture may be tied, not too tightly, in a buttered and floured cloth, placed in boiling water with a plate at the bottom of the saucepan, and allowed to simmer for a couple of hours.

Laura Bohannan

An Adaptation of Tiv Sesame Chicken

The Tiv cook this dish especially on such occasions as when a man welcomes his first wife to the homestead and is under the obligation of offering a rich chicken stew to the married men of the homestead. The chickens must be caught by the bridegroom (or his agents, i.e. his mother, his brothers, his age-mates), the sauce ingredients provided by the mother and her co-wives, the wives of her husband's age-mates, bridegroom's sisters, etc., and should be cooked by the married men. In point of fact, on such a night everyone in the homestead seems to be out chasing chickens, catching chickens, searing the feathers off chickens and cooking chickens. The dish should be eaten with the typical African 'porridge', a stiff confection of yams the Tiv call *luam*. It is considered even better when the *luam* is made of African white sweet potatoes. For the Western palate I recommend rice. I have discovered, however, that it is also excellent eaten poured over hot French bread cut lengthwise down the loaf.

Tiv Sesame Chicken

1 large frying chicken
½ cup sesame seed
salt
½ cup peanut (groundnut) oil
2 or 3 hot red peppers

½ tbsp parsley (optional)
2 large ripe tomatoes
1 lb (450 grams) okra or 'spinach'
1 or more large Spanish onions

Notes on ingredients
Use *chile pequeños* or black pepper; cheyenne or white pepper comes out wrong. For a bitter taste, appreciated by Tiv, use mustard greens, beet greens, or spinach well washed. For an oleaginous quality, also much appreciated by Tiv, use lots of okra, broken so that the seeds and 'glue' come out in the cooking.

In a deep, very heavy pot (the best is iron lined with porcelain) heat peanut oil and brown chicken. Remove chicken. Crush $\frac{1}{2}$ cup sesame seeds in mortar; brown gently in oil from which chicken has been removed. Remove as much of sesame seed as possible, add to chicken. Take pot from fire and pour off the oil. Add minimal amount of water, just enough to make browning from chicken and seeds into a suspensible mixture. Add layer of sliced and heavily washed vegetables, sprinkle with seasoning and sesame, add layer of chicken. Repeat till vegetables and chicken are used up. If you are using only the one chicken, cook on top of gas stove over the smallest possible flame (with an electric stove, use an asbestos pad, or cook in oven). If using several chickens (I've done a casserole of this for twenty people), put in slowest possible oven at about noon. Mid-afternoon, remove and turn the topmost layers to the bottom. Serve in the evening.

Warnings. Do not add water. It cooks in its own juices, and in using the leaf vegetables one must be very careful not to come up with a thin soup. Do not use a stewing chicken: it becomes unbearably fat. African chicken is a lean and gamy bird.

Esther Goody

Ghanaian Groundnut Stew

The basic food in Ghana consists of a starch of some kind, served with a rich, highly spiced soup. Just what is served with the soup varies from one part of the country to another and with the time of year. In the savannah, where grain crops thrive, the basis of the daily main meal is porridge, cooked very well until thick. Cassava flour is also used to make porridge, either mixed with maize or other flours, or in lean times by itself. Where the rainfall is sufficient, on the borders of the forests, yams are the staple. They resemble a denser form of potato, and are usually pounded with water until they form a sort of dough which is known throughout Ghana as *fufu*. There is a mysterious boundary between Ghana and her neighbours to the west which the cultivation of rice has until very recently largely failed to cross. So while imported rice is eaten in the towns, and sometimes bought for special occasions by those who can afford it in the rural areas, it has not been a staple in Ghana as it is in the Ivory Coast, Liberia and the countries to the west. There are interesting exceptions. A few isolated peoples like the Avatime of the Volta region have cultivated rice for centuries, and in the most important of the annual politico-religious ceremonies of the Gonja of northern Ghana rice, not grain, must be used for the ceremonial meal. I suggest that groundnut stew should be served with rice, because this is readily available and easy to prepare. But the stews of which this is an example are not ordinarily eaten with rice except by better-off people in the cities, or on special occasions.

During the colonial period, groundnut stew was adapted by expatriates to the model of the Indian curry and served for Sunday dinner, surrounded by a variety of small dishes of condiments. Sunday lunch of groundnut stew became an institution, when one entertained, ate a great deal, washed it down with cold beer and dozed and talked the afternoon away. But the basic groundnut stew is simply a meat or chicken stew, based on fried tomatoes, onions and little hot red peppers, seasoned with a paste made from pounded (or ground) lightly roasted peanuts. The meat is simmered in the broth until it is tender and has absorbed the blended flavours. It is, incidentally, a wonderful

89

way to cook a really tough bird or piece of goat. (In northern Ghana, unless you are living in a town large enough to support a butcher, there is little else by way of meat.) While processed peanut butter is widely available in Europe nowadays, in Ghana we always bought fresh groundnut paste, which, it must be admitted, is tastier. If there was no groundnut paste on the market, Seidu, the cook, simply took a bottle and used it as a rolling-pin to crush groundnuts for the stew. Ghanaian women use the small round grinding-stone and shaped stone trough, at which they spent several hours a day until motor-driven grinding-mills became available.

Estimate quantities of meat or chicken as for any stew. You can use boiling fowl or stewing steak, or more tender cuts according to available time and cash. If the tougher meat is used, first simmer it *slowly* with onion, celery, bayleaf, etc., until partly cooked, and use the broth for the stew.

Ghanaian Groundnut Stew

For medium chicken or 2 lb meat:
2 large onions
5 or 6 tomatoes (according to size) or 1 medium-sized tin peeled tomatoes
garlic (optional)
2 or 3 small red peppers or $\frac{1}{2}$–1 tsp cayenne pepper. Half a teaspoonful will add
    tang, but not be at all hot. If you start with this amount, more can be added
    later according to taste.
1 8-oz. jar (220 grams) peanut butter (I prefer the crunchy sort, but it doesn't
    matter)
about $\frac{1}{2}$ cup oil for frying (groundnut oil for preference)
4 to 6 cups broth, either from soup cubes or pre-cooking of meat

Joint chicken or cut meat into cubes, partly cook first, if tough (see above).
Fry onions and drained tomatoes over high heat. Crush one tomato, garlic and
red peppers, or crush tomato with cayenne powder, and add to frying onions in
pan. Fry all together for a couple of minutes and then add meat pieces, browning
on all sides. Use hot fire and enough oil to fry vegetables and sear meat pieces.
You want to avoid stewing them in their own juices. Turn, don't burn.

While meat is browning, mix peanut butter with chicken broth, first to a smooth
paste, then add more broth to make a rich soup, sufficient to cover pieces of meat
in a casserole. (If you mix peanut butter into broth with your fingers, it's quite easy.)

Take browned meat from frying pan and put into casserole. Add peanut soup
to frying-pan and stir to mix with fragments of onion, meat and tomatoes left
in pan. Simmer gently a few minutes and taste for salt and pepper; add to taste
and pour soup over meat. Cover casserole and cook in slow oven (350°, gas Mk 4)
until meat is tender.

Serve with plain boiled rice and whole (shelled) hard-boiled eggs. Side-dishes
are optional – you can use chopped raw onion, fried onion, chopped bananas,
chopped green pepper, fried shedded coconut, nut meats – *ad lib.*

Gay Cohen

Groundnut Stew
from Sierra Leone

This has been referred to by a nineteenth-century observer as the national dish of Sierra Leone.[1] 'Every country has its national dish and "ground nut soup", a rich white compound of boiled fowl and the almond-like kernel of the groundnut is one of the grand dishes of this part of the world.' This Sierra Leonean version of the dish was given to me by a Freetown housewife. The most important ingredients are groundnuts, which provide the thickening medium. In any market in Freetown you will find tables on which are set out mounds of sand-coloured balls, which are sold for a few pence each. These are groundnut balls. Groundnuts are boiled in their shells; then the shells are removed and the nuts roasted. When the nuts have cooled, their skins are removed and the nuts are ground on a grinding-stone or pounded into an oily paste. The paste is mixed with salt and formed into the small balls which are found on market stalls. However, as the western housewife cannot buy the nuts prepared in this way, she may use peanut butter as an alternative.

Groundnut Stew

2¼ lbs (about 1 kilo) lean meat
1 large onion
1 lb okra or 1 large tin okra
3 chilli peppers or 1½ tsp ground chilli
¾ pt (400 ml) stock

1 small jar (8 oz./ 220 grams) peanut butter
salt
2 tbsp tomato purée
½ cup groundnut oil

Cut up meat and onion and pepper. Fry in oil until the onions are soft. Add salt and stock and cook until the meat is tender (about 1½–2 hours for stewing-steak). Half an hour before the meat is ready, add okra, peanut butter and tomato purée. When it is ready the sauce should be the consistency of a thick soup.

As in Ghana, this dish can be served in the 'colonial' fashion, with side-dishes

91

of bananas, dried fruit, coconut, oranges or apples. Sometimes in Freetown it is served with fried plantain, a West African fruit which resembles a grossly over-grown banana. It is also delicious if cut in slices and fried in groundnut oil.

NOTE

1   M. S. Melville, *A Residence in Freetown*, London, 1849.

Lynn Brydon

Snacks and Stew from Ghana

The recipes here are of two kinds: recipes for snacks, which are sold throughout Ghana, and a recipe for a type of stew, which is traditional throughout southern Ghana in general and among a small group in the Central Volta region in particular.

Two Snacks

Kele Wele

2 very ripe plantains
3 tsp ground ginger (or 2 stems fresh
  ginger root, crushed)

1 small onion
salt and chilli pepper to taste
oil for deep frying

Chop up the onion very finely. Put it into a bowl and add the ginger, salt and pepper, and mix well. Peel the plantains and chop them into roughly 1-cm cubes. Mix the plantain pieces into the onion thoroughly, until each piece has come into contact with the onion. Heat the oil until it is very hot. Add the plantain pieces and fry until they are brown on the outside and well cooked (soft in the middle).

Alternatively, one can peel the plantain, slice it very finely, and fry the wafery slices in hot fat until they are crisp. These plantain chips make excellent nibbles at a party.

Roasted Groundnuts (peanuts)

This is very simple, and the nuts have a much fresher taste than bought ready-roasted nuts. Buy as many unshelled peanuts as are needed. Remove the shells. Take a heavy frying-pan and put it onto a medium-to-hot heat. Add enough nuts to cover the bottom of the pan. The skins of the nuts will begin to split.

Turn the nuts occasionally with a wooden spoon until they are roasted thoroughly on all sides. The nuts can be tested, to see if they are thoroughly done, by picking one up and rolling it between the fingers until the skin comes off – if the skin comes off easily, then the nut is done. Care is needed here, since the nuts are very hot. If the nut is brownish on all sides, then it is done. Pour out these nuts onto a flat dish to cool and start roasting the next batch. When all the nuts have cooled, pick up handfuls and squeeze or roll them in the hands. This removes some of the husks, which can then be blown away. The Ghanaian women winnow the nuts, but this requires some skill: continue de-husking the nuts until all, or as many, husks have been removed as desired. The nuts can be shaken with salt, if preferred.

There are other ways in which groundnuts are eaten in Ghana. The fresh nuts, which are softish and rather watery, may also be roasted or boiled in their shells.

Snacks like this are sold along the sides of the street in all southern Ghanaian towns and in many villages. Groundnuts in all forms are sold throughout the day. Depending on how much one wants to spend, the seller (always a woman or child) will scoop up the required amount onto a square of old *Daily Graphic*, add a 'dash' (an extra amount), and screw up the paper. The usual thing to eat with roasted groundnuts is banana or roasted plantain. The plantain is roasted at the roadside on a makeshift charcoal burner. Plantain and groundnuts make an excellent lunch, as many Ghanaian office workers seem to have discovered.

Kele wele is sold mainly at night, and usually in towns. After dark a different set of traders seems to appear on the streets, each with his own wares, utensils and home-made kerosene lamp. When there is no other street lighting, the flickering of the traders' lamps tracing out their positioning looks very attractive.

The '*kele wele* lady' has her makeshift brazier with an enamel bowl full of palm kernel oil on top of it. Beside her brazier is a small stool with an enamel tray on top of it. The tray is piled up with pieces of the *Graphic*, together with a tin for money and her lamp. She sits on an even smaller stool with her basket of ripe plantains beside her. Ghanaian women are very deft with the enormous kitchen knives-cum-cutlasses that they use. The woman tops and tails the plantain, makes a slit down the side of the skin, and then rips off the whole of the skin – truly a case of 'unzipping'! The ubiquitous *Graphic* comes into its own again: *kele wele* can taste no finer than when it is eaten straight out of a square of oil-sodden newsprint.

Green Leaf Stew (or, in Avatime, *Sigase*) (To serve 4–6)

2 lb (1 kilo) green leaf vegetable (spinach is probably best)
3 tomatoes and/or ½ small (1½ oz./40 grams) tin tomato purée

1 medium onion
palm oil
chilli pepper or ½–2 chillies, depending on personal taste
    (for mild effect, use 1 chilli or 2 tsp pepper)
½–1 lb (220–450 grams) tinned fish (pilchards or sardines) or left-over meat

It is difficult to gauge exact quantities for this dish, as it depends very much on personal taste. However, what is important here is the method of making the stew.

Wash the spinach carefully and cook using very little water. (Use enough for average-sized portions for each person, remembering that spinach reduces in quantity when it is cooked.) Chop the onion and tomatoes *very finely* and fry lightly in a large heavy pan in 3 or 4 tbsp palm oil. Add salt and chilli pepper to taste. Ideally, fresh red or green chillies should be used, but these are not always available. If they are, add two or three to the onions and tomatoes in place of the ground pepper. (Palm oil can be obtained from Asian or West Indian food stores. It is bright orange in colour, opaque when cool, but clearer and brighter when hot. Take care: it stains.)

When the onions are almost soft, remove them from the heat. Strain the cooked spinach. Mix the onion mixture with the spinach and add tomato purée, if used. Blend together in a liquidizer.

Transfer back to the frying-pan and add more oil (for Ghanaians, as much as you like; for four people not used to oil, about 2 tbsp). Cook gently. Meanwhile open the sardines or pilchards. If you can face more oil, pour the oil from the sardines into the spinach mixture. Alternatively, buy the fish in tomato sauce. Chop up the fish roughly and add to the spinach mixture. Stir and cook until the fish is heated. If left-over meat is used, chop it up and add it to the stew. Cook until the meat is thoroughly heated through. Serve with plain boiled rice.

This recipe is a very free interpretation of the Ghanaian original. In Ghana many different types of green leaves are used, from the well-known and widespread *nkontommire* (cocoyam) leaf in Ashanti and elsewhere, to local plants grown especially for this kind of stew. This recipe is a lazy substitute, because a Ghanaian would grind the tomatoes, peppers, onions and salt on a grinding-stone before boiling them together with the green leaves. When the leaves are cooked, everything is removed to a grinding-dish (a locally made earthenware dish with a rough inside surface), and is ground up with a wooden ladle. Much palm oil is then added and the whole can be heated for a little longer. The fish or meat is usually regarded as a luxury extra.

The method of grinding up the vegetables is common to many Ghanaian stews. For example, in 'light soup', a stew eaten with *fufu* (pounded starch

Grinding-bowl and spoon

vegetables), the onion and tomatoes and peppers are boiled whole with fish or meat, removed, ground together, and then returned to the stew base. The same goes for groundnut and palm nut stew. For a quick sauce, onions, peppers, tomatoes and salt are ground together raw, mixed with a tin of mackerel or sardines in oil, and served with other 'slices' (slices of boiled vegetables – yam, plantain, cocoyam, cassava) or with *kenkey* (steamed, fermented maize dough).

Among the Avatime, a small group of people living in the Togo hills, this type of stew is very popular, and at least four different types of green leaf are grown for it. A stranger to the area is described as one who 'doesn't eat green leaves'. In Avatime too, the stew is usually eaten with roasted maize flour porridge, or with 'slices' (*kakupa*).

The dish is also traditionally important among the Avatime. Before a girl attended her nubility ceremony, there was a ceremonial feast during which this stew (without fish and pepper) was prepared with roasted rice-flour porridge and white garden eggs. Some of it was sent to the fetish priests, and the remainder was eaten by post-menopausal women on the morning of the girl's nubility ceremony. (Rice is the traditional staple of the Avatime, and there is much ritual attached to its cultivation.) Bush meat (i.e. 'natural' meat) could be included with the dish of food sent to the fetish priest, but no fish or domestic fowl could be included. The pepper was left out on purpose, since this was thought to act as an irritant, and to have an adverse effect on the relationship between the girl and her future spouse.

Later on in the cycle of the nubility ceremonies, there was a further occasion on which the stew was cooked. This time it was made in the same way as before, and was poured over small balls of rice porridge, arranged on a flat winnowing dish. On the appropriate day, in the evening, the dish of food was taken into the central place in the village where children gathered and rushed to eat the food as soon as it was set down. After it was finished, they all went around the village calling out that on the next day they were going to perform the ceremonies for the girl.

Nowadays, however, the stew and porridge are cooked on the night before the modern version of the nubility ceremony is due to take place. The girl sits quietly on a low stool while a woman, who stands in the relationship of the father's sister to the girl, places porridge and stew on the ground in front of the girl. Eager young children are then called, and they wolf down the food. Water is then brought and poured over the children's hands to fall into the empty food dish. The children are then sent away and the father's sister gives the girl this water three times to drink.

In some of the Avatime villages this food is prepared on the morning of the nubility ceremony and is eaten by old women. Some of the old women say that, if prepared, this is kept secret, since it is not the Christian thing to do, and today most of the population are Christians.

Carol P. MacCormack

A Sauce from Sierra Leone

Strength and health-giving goodness is symbolized in the official Seal of the Republic of Sierra Leone by the oil palm tree. Its strong trunk bridges streams, and its leaves, as roof thatch, give protection from heat and rain. The leaves also provide tough fibre for fishing nets. The heart of the palm contains a large quantity of starchy food, now fed to pigs. However, women know how to cook it, suggesting that it is famine food, and it may have been utilized more extensively as a staple starch before alternative crops were introduced from Asia and America. Palm wine is the quickly-fermented sap, tapped directly from the crown of the living trees. But the oil palm is best

Pulling cassava leaves off stems and putting them in mortar, where they will be pounded to break up the fibres

beloved for the thick red oil extracted from the fleshy pericarp of its date-like fruits. The Sherbros living in the coastal area of southern Sierra Leone where the tree grows abundantly attribute great virtue to the oil, which nourishes as it wards off worms and disease. A clear oil can be extracted from the inner kernel of the palm fruit, but Sherbros export the kernel as a cash crop, its thin, colourless, tasteless oil being suitable food for 'effete' Europeans.

Red palm oil, found in West Indian corner shops in London, and in black neighbourhoods in Washington, DC, and New York, is used in Sierra Leone as the basis for most sauces eaten with rice. The most common sauce is called Palaver Sauce, or *Pla'sas* in the creolized form. Its hot, pungent ingredients mingle in the pot as heated voices mingle in the excitement of a palaver.

In addition to red palm oil, *pla'sas* must have chopped or pounded green leaves. The kind of leaf chosen gives a particular taste and texture to the sauce, so that one speaks of cassava-leaf *pla'sas* or potato-leaf *pla'sas*. Cassava leaves and sweet potato leaves are most popular with Sherbro cooks. Women pick the leaves from living plants in their kitchen gardens, taking care not to impede the growth of the starchy root by plucking too much of the plant's foliage. Cassava leaves are pounded in a free-standing wooden mortar to break down the fibres before cooking. Sweet potato leaves and spinach greens are held in a bundle in the fist, then cut across in very close parallel cuts, giving a shredded appearance to the greens before cooking. Frozen chopped spinach also makes a tasty *pla'sas*.

Palaver Sauce (*Pla'sas*) (To serve 4)

1 cup red palm oil
4 oz. (110 grams) beef, cut in small
  cubes
4 oz. (110 grams) smoke-dried fish
  (kippers will do)

1 onion, chopped
$\frac{1}{2}$–$1\frac{1}{2}$ tsp cayenne pepper or 1 to 3 fresh
  chilli peppers
2 cups chopped green leaves
  (cassava, sweet potato or spinach)

Fry the beef in palm oil. Remove the beef and add chopped onion and cayenne pepper or fresh chilli pepper to the oil. (If a small fresh hot pepper is used, it should be deseeded and pounded in a mortar or chopped very fine before being added to the oil, but powdered cayenne may be used.) The sauce should be hot.

When the onion is soft, add the finely-chopped greens. When the greens are cooked, add the beef, crumble in the fish and boil for 5 minutes. Serve on rice.

The Sherbro story-teller begins his riddle thus: I was going to a far country. I met a man by the way and killed him, drank his blood, ate his flesh, and threw his bones away. What was he?

Answer: Coconut.

The coconut, cracked open (with a shiver of cannibalistic analogy), provides food for a traveller, away from kin who hold him to social responsibility, and a wife who cooks for him.

Socially immature boys, always hungry and without wives to cook for them, often pick coconuts on the sly from trees to which they do not yet have rights. These boys favour coconuts whose flesh is immature, which have the consistency of jelly. Mature coconuts, with firm flesh, are picked by men who own the trees. Their wives grate, boil and squeeze the flesh to extract its oil. Women store the oil, cook with it, and portion the food out to the adult (mature) men first, and lastly to the young (immature) children.

On feasting occasions rice is sometimes flavoured with coconut as described below and served with chicken dishes.

Coconut Rice (To serve 4)

Open a mature coconut, discard the water and remove the flesh. Grate the flesh, add 4 cups boiling water, mix and allow to stand for 10 minutes; then pour through a strainer, saving the liquid. Squeeze the grated coconut in your hands, extracting the remaining juice. Discard the fibres, and cook 2 cups rice in the strained, coconut-flavoured water.

Ivan and Patricia Karp

Social Aspects of Iteso Cookery

The Iteso of Kenya are an Eastern Nilotic-speaking people who live in the northern part of Busia district of the Western Province of Kenya. In 1969 there were about 250,000 Iteso in Kenya. There are also well over 500,000 Iteso living in Uganda, most of whom live in the Teso district. They are separated in space and by the accident of colonial history from the Kenya Iteso. As a result considerable differences in dialect and custom have developed between these two groups.

Our fieldwork was conducted for a period of two years, from 1969 to 1971, among the Iteso of Kenya. During this period, we lived as members of an Iteso family in the Amukura area of Busia district.

In this family Ivan Karp was treated as the younger brother of the household head and Patricia Karp assumed the role of a young Iteso woman learning to be a wife. As such she was taken under the wing of the household head's mother, Fulgaria Toto, and treated as a somewhat dull but eager young woman. From Toto we gained some of the most important insights into Iteso culture and society.

Certainly one of the first and most continuous aspects of Iteso society that impressed us during the two years of our fieldwork was the importance (for the Iteso) of the sharing of food and drink. This is stressed in the etiquette of everyday greetings. It is proper to greet people and then to ask for any news. After an exchange of news, the persons involved enquire after each other's health. The Iteso are a forthright people and treat these enquiries as serious requests. After all these issues have been settled, two questions are asked. The first, '*An'ajon?*', asks at whose home beer is to be had that day. The second, '*Inyena inyam'ijo ore kon lolo?*', can be translated as 'What kind of food is there in your home today?' We, as white 'Europeans', were always asked this kind of question because the Iteso assumed that our eating habits would be very different from theirs. When we answered that we were eating *atap*, the Iteso form of maize or cassava and millet bread, people would go into gales of laughter. When asked why, they replied that *atap* was 'African food' and not for Europeans.

101

From the Iteso point of view, one of the sad features of the colour-bar that accompanied colonialism in Kenya was the refusal of Europeans to share an African's food or his food with an African. Hence, Iteso often tried to make us welcome in their homes by giving us foodstuffs to take home instead of sharing a meal in the more usual fashion. They were surprised and pleased by our willingness to share food and drink. If there was hospitality to be offered, we asked to be fed like kinsmen or neighbours, instead of being given food to consume in the privacy of our hut like selfish strangers. Once we were taken at our word and served the meal of the day. It consisted of cassava bread, without the usual millet added. The relish was composed of a vegetable gathered in the bush, boiled in sour milk and flavoured with salt made from the ashes of the leaves of certain grasses. This was the only meal we had while among the Iteso that we found unpalatable; under the circumstances of our declaration, there was no choice but to eat stoically.

Virtually all rituals are accompanied by the sharing of a meal and beer made from finger millet, the traditional Iteso food. This quality of willingness to share is also part and parcel of the judgments that Iteso make about each other. One of the worst terms that one Iteso can call another is *epog*, which most English-speaking Iteso translate as meaning 'selfish'. The term is a little different from the conventional meaning that we assign to the word. The Iteso also mean by *epog* something we might translate as 'self-sufficient'. A person who is *epog* is someone who believes that he can get on without anybody else's help. As a result, he does not feel an obligation to share the food in his home with his kin and neighbours. The Iteso describe someone who is *epog* as the type of person who eats in secret. Their image is of a greedy and foolish person hiding in the darkness of his hut consuming his year's supply of food. Anyone who is like this is foolish because, as Iteso will point out, technology is limited and the environment is uncertain. As a result, people need to share with each other in order to build up a set of reciprocal obligations which will provide a hedge in difficult years. Hence Iteso neighbourhoods and kin-groups fulfil the function of distributing subsistence products under conditions of scarcity. We might say that, for some purposes, an Iteso neighbourhood has a common economy reinforced by the values of mutual commensality.

The Iteso eat their meals in a variety of places, and the place in which it is eaten is significant for the meaning which the meal has for them, as well as the type of cooking that is involved. Most meals are taken inside the sleeping house of the wife that has done the cooking. If a few guests are involved, the meal is served in the husband's guest house. Each wife in an Iteso polygamous family is a separate domestic unit and feeds herself and her children. A husband is supposed to alternate his attendance at each of his wives' homes so that he does not show favouritism to any wife. Few husbands do this and their failure to behave equitably is a constant cause of marital strife. In any case, meals are often served to a larger variety of persons than a wife and children. Children especially eat wherever they happen to be when food is served, and the sight of a woman eating with a variety of neighbourhood children is common. Men often arrive late in the afternoon at the home of a friend or an important person in order to share a meal. A local notable will have several men drop in at his home after the cattle have been returned from pasture and commonly a meal will be dispensed with his advice and counsel. These informal meals are eaten outside the guest house of the person who is host. This is a sign that anyone who drops by is welcome. The opposition between meals eaten inside or outside is important in understanding Iteso notions of hospitality and sharing. Special guests on special occasions are served inside the house.

The typical Iteso meal is based on an opposition of starch and a relish. The starch is a 'bread' made by pouring a flour of cassava and finger millet or sorghum into boiling water. Sometimes the bread is made of cornmeal or plantains. The relish may be made from boiled vegetables or meat served in a sauce consisting of the broth in which they were cooked. Curry powder is used by most households as a flavouring. Once we were visited by some Austrian friends and taken to an Iteso household for a meal. The household head asked our friends what was the main food of their country – was it maize or cassava or plantains or millet?

The starch: meat-or-relish opposition is very important in Iteso conceptions of cookery. No meal can be eaten without a starch. When something is eaten without a starch, it is not a meal. What is interesting about this is the manner in which cooking is tied up with behaviour associated with the two sexes. Only women can cook a starch, and it must be cooked inside the cooking-house on the women's fireplace constructed with three stones. Men, on the other hand, can cook meat, but only outside and only by roasting. The primary occasions when roasted, as opposed to boiled, meat is eaten are during funeral sacrifices and, during precolonial times, when oxen were sacrificed for the age-set ceremonies of the men. These age-set ceremonies were held in the bush during the dry season and only men who had been initiated or were about to be initiated were allowed to attend. If any women happened to pass by, they were tortured. The opposition of roasting, associated with men, and boiling, associated with women, is very important. It fits together with the opposition between inside and outside and a further opposition between nature and culture. As the Iteso system of categories encodes it, women are associated with boiling, the home, and domesticity, while men are associated with nature, the outside world, and political life. The meaning of this can be understood by relating this set of categories to Iteso concerns. In a society that is subsistence-based, the survival of households is a primary concern. Given the uncertainty that Iteso face about rain and productivity of land, most households follow a strategy of producing both for the survival of their members and in order to maintain relationships of exchange with other households that will insure the sharing of subsistence products under conditions of scarcity. This strategy induces a tension between the satisfaction of domestic wants and the satisfaction of requirement for production for the needs of neighbours and kinsmen. This tension is reflected in the different context of cooking associated with men and women. On the one hand we have cooking and eating associated with the inside and women. In this context, it is primarily the requirements of a family unit composed of a mother and her children (sometimes a husband) that are satisfied. On the other hand, we have cooking and eating on the outside associated with men. What are satisfied in these contexts are the requirements of a household as a social group associated with other households which will help each other in times of want.

In what follows we describe Iteso patterns of cooking and eating. *Atap* (called *posho* or *ugali* in Swahili) is the basic starch food. We provide two recipes. The first, for *akapulu*, is for a vegetable relish that we often enjoyed in Iteso homes. The second, for *alaboro*, is a special dish, probably adopted from the Baganda, that is served on special occasions.

The Iteso begin their day with a small meal. Most people eat a very thin porridge made of cassava flour or millet flour and water. A few people, those with some income, sometimes purchase a loaf of white bread and a tin of butter at the local store, and this serves as breakfast. A very small number of people eat eggs for breakfast, a custom probably learned from the Europeans. A common breakfast food is a piece of boiled cassava. The common item at all breakfasts is the beverage – a strong, smoky-flavoured tea, made by boiling tea and water together with large amounts of milk and sugar.

Even the simplest meal involves a great deal of work for the women, whose responsibility it is to grow or purchase whatever food is necessary, collect water and firewood, and prepare the meal. A woman and her children collect as much firewood and water, the latter in tin containers holding 4 gallons (about 18 litres) each, as they can carry on their heads. They usually have to make more than one trip to the bush and stream in any one day.

The fire for cooking is started on the floor of the cooking hut on a fireplace built on a foundation of three stones. On these stones rests an enormous pot of water which must boil for the porridge, tea, or *atap*, the main food of the Iteso. When the water boils (and it seemed to take forever when we were hungry) the cassava or millet, or combination of the two, is added in the form of ground flour, and this is cooked until the right consistency is reached. Each person has a small bowl of porridge and as much tea as he or she wants.

This Iteso meal was sometimes supplemented by cutting or buying a piece of sugar cane. Children, especially, cut large pieces of cane and peel it with sharp knives or *pangas*. They pull it through their teeth, extracting the sweet juice and fibrous strings of sugar cane. It is a very filling snack.

It is recognized that children need more food than adults. Some foods are referred to as a 'children's food'. We grew raspberries to which children would help themselves. Children also collected other fruits and berries, including wild gooseberries from the bush, and ate them as they walked along or played. We often ate such things with the children and the Iteso were mildly amused by our taste for 'children's food'.

The second and last meal of the day is the late afternoon or evening one. This calls for more extensive preparation than breakfast. This meal consists of *atap* ('sold food') and an accompaniment, referred to as a 'relish' or 'vegetable' by the Iteso. Again, the woman of the home builds a fire in the cooking hut. First she prepares the relish. This can be either a vegetable or meat. The meat is always beef or, for special occasions, chicken, and the vegetable is usually something that grows wild and is collected by the women during the day. A favourite is *ekwala*, which is similar in taste to spinach. The meat will be boiled for hours in a little water and curry powder. The vegetable may also be cooked for a very long time, usually with spices or with sour milk. The relish may be flavoured with mushrooms. They are usually gathered by women, but it is not uncommon for a man to find mushrooms as he is walking through the bush and bring them home to his wife to dry and cook.

While the relish is simmering, the *atap* must be prepared. The large pot of water is put up to boil, then the cassava or millet flour is added.* It is cooked until it forms a thick, solid mass. By now the relish is ready and the *atap* is turned out onto a large plate and covered until everyone is ready to eat.

Some people have tables and chairs made by local carpenters. Most, however, sit on the floor of their huts. *Atap* is taken from a communal plate, but each person has his own small bowl of relish. No Iteso use silverware, but may have some on hand to be used by distinguished visitors. A small amount of *atap* is taken, always with the fingers of the right hand, and formed into a ball. Then a depression is made in the centre of the ball with the thumb. It is then dipped into the relish and eaten. Pieces of beef and chicken are also eaten with the fingers.

Other food is collected from the bush by children. After a rain, the air becomes filled with flying white ants. The children run into the bush at dusk and pick hundreds of these ants out of the air and stuff them into tin cans. While they are doing this, they eat as many as they put into tins. All the termites collected in the tins are brought to the children's mothers. The ants are then light fried in *ghee* (clarified butter) and eaten by the men and children of the home. They are quite tasty prepared in this way.

* See Anne Sharman's recipe for *kwon*.

Bush Vegetable (*Akapulu*) (To serve 2–4)

1 lb (450 grams) fresh spinach or
  1 8-oz. (220 grams) pack frozen
  spinach, defrosted
1 medium onion, coarsely chopped
1 tomato, chopped

3 tbsp *ghee* or butter
2 tsp curry powder
1 tsp salt
2 cloves garlic, finely chopped
  (optional)

Wash spinach and remove stems. Cook in the water that clings to the leaves, until tender (about 5 minutes). Drain and set aside. Cook the onion and garlic in ghee until lightly browned, stirring occasionally. Add salt, curry powder and tomato. Cook about 1 minute. Add the onion mixture to the spinach and heat through. Serve as an accompaniment to *atap*.

Alaboro and Groundnut Sauce (To serve 2–4)

6 green plantains (*alaboro*)
1 large onion, coarsely chopped
5 tomatoes
2 tsp curry powder

1 tsp salt
3 or 4 tsp groundnuts, chopped or
  ground
1½ cups water

Peel and wash the plantains. Boil until about half-cooked. Add onion, nuts, salt, tomatoes and curry powder, stir well and cover. Cook over low heat, stirring occasionally until the plantains are soft. May be eaten as an accompaniment to *atap*.

Anne Sharman

Food and Recipes
in Padhola

Situated in south-eastern Uganda, Padhola is filled with a variety of foodstuffs – grains, rootcrops, plantains, diverse legumes and green vegetables,
mushrooms, nuts, fruits, termites, fish, wild and domestic birds and animals.
But variety does not always mean abundance. Old people remember the
devastating famines of the past, the young are often malnourished, harvests
and stores of grain are a constant concern, and government officials struggle
to ensure the planting of cassava and sweet potatoes as famine reserves. For
the local people, the Adhola, food is finally what keeps a person alive. All
other edibles, however delightful, are a tasty embellishment. This distinction
is reflected in their language. The word *chiemo*, translated into English as
'food', is used only for staples, for that which is both filling at a meal and
sustaining afterwards. Food is for everyone, when there is enough. When
there is not, men take precedence. Relishes of all sorts are called *fufa* and some
of them are prohibited to certain categories of people and thus form a source
of distinction and discrimination at all times.

The long history of certain foodstuffs sustaining and giving pleasure to
the Adhola can be seen in the way their cultivation and use is intertwined
with all aspects of social life. But as new lifestyles spread and as new crops
gain in importance, and bought foods become a source of prestige, so the
significance of these relationships fades. 'Why are elaborate rituals associated
with the cultivation of cow peas being curtailed and abandoned?', one asks.
'Because today we have insecticides,' is the answer.

The Adhola recipes I have chosen to present here are for the preparation
of one staple, a basic component of any meal, and two relishes, the first
representing the use of a traditional crop, the second the use of a new one.

Staples

For a staunch Adhola person finger millet surpasses all others as a staple, as
well as being used to brew the best beer. It is the traditional food of Padhola,

of strong and wise men and women. Of other staples widely grown, cassava and sweet potatoes are regarded as inferior – hardy and easy to grow, quick to prepare, adding a little variety to life, but barely satisfying and no fare for a guest. Plantains are variously described as suitable for foreigners, those of high status, the educated and people with weak stomachs. Light and watery, the illusion of fullness they give so readily soon passes, leaving hunger in its place. Only *kwon* made from finger millet provides the bulk and solidity essential to a good food. The term *kwon* is translated as 'millet bread', although its density, consistency and taste have little in common with any English bread. It is often prepared in large quantities and consumed in large amounts, a number of people helping themselves from a single big lump. It is eaten with the fingers and pieces can be swiftly used as utensils for consuming *fufa*.

Millet is also important in people's lives apart from meals. It is essential on certain ritual occasions, both in the form of beer and of food, and fear of poor harvests reinforces acknowledgment of authority in the society. Members of a kin-group can sow their millet only when they have helped the most senior member with the same task, the penalty for ignoring this stipulation being crop failure.

In Padhola great skill goes into preparing the ingredients for *kwon*, so that the final result will suit the particular tastes of those for whom it is being prepared. No recipe based on bought ingredients can do justice to this food as prepared by the Adhola, though it may take some time for a foreigner to develop a real taste for it. In preparing the flour one has to select a suitable variety of finger millet. Some varieties produce a slightly sour bread or give a coarse texture, however finely the flour is ground. Once selected, the grain is roasted. Traditionally the grain was then ground by itself, but today pounded cassava is often added at this stage. Cassava makes the *kwon* lighter and smoother, and is added in varying amounts according to taste. The tough old men reject it. The millet, and cassava if added, must be ground to a very fine flour, in contrast to flour for beer.

Kwon is occasionally made in Padhola with packaged maize flour bought in the local shops, so that this can be used where millet flour is not available.

Millet Bread (*Kwon*)
The quantities specified are for about 6 helpings. Precise quantities are seldom measured.

approx. 3 cups millet or maize (American cornmeal) flour
approx. 6 cups water

Boil the water. Very slowly pour in the flour, stirring continuously. Continue to add flour until the mixture has a stiff consistency, so stiff that it takes all your strength to stir it. Serve while still hot. For a foreigner it is best to serve it with a moist relish such as *magira* or *kifuligo* (see below) rather than dry relishes such as roasted termites.

Relishes

The most coveted relishes are those prepared from certain animals, animal products, birds and fish. They are luxuries, signs of wealth and prestige, and often forbidden to women and children. An important exception is milk, but other considerations restrict the situations in which it can be consumed, since it is thought to look like semen and may also turn a pregnant woman's baby white. A characteristic prohibition in Equatorial Africa is against women and children eating chicken and eggs. These relishes are said to give them anaemia, but the part such prohibitions play in maintaining their subordinate position is more blatantly stated by the Adhola than in some other societies. The forbidden food, it is often said, will turn them into greedy thieves and they will steal or demand that which rightfully belongs to their husbands, fathers and brothers. Today a popular song bewails the changing world and the waning of female compliance, and women say that men thought up the prohibitions to keep the tastiest edibles for themselves.

In Padhola there are, however, other delicious and socially important relishes which are not so directly linked with subjugation and unequal distribution. They are also generally the cheaper ones. The cow pea plant provides dishes of various sorts. The leaves are picked and eaten at different stages during the growth of the plant. Early leaves may be dried and are the only greens which are stored. The peas themselves are eaten in many forms, my favourite being *magira*. *Magira* is primarily a relish, but it is so sustaining that it may also be eaten by itself as *chiemo*. One occasion on which *magira* must be eaten is after the birth of a woman's first boy and after the birth of her first girl. The growth of cow peas is linked with the wellbeing and fertility of all living things. With the first flowering comes the time for spring-cleaning, the cleansing of homes by throwing ashes from the hearths into the bush. There follow fertility rituals filled with merriment and lewd songs and gestures, which provide sex education for young girls while berating men. These are female rituals and unwary men who wander into the women's cavorting path are abused and chased.

Magira (To serve about 6)

3 cups fresh cow peas*	salt to taste†
approx. 6 cups water	milk or clarified butter (*ghee*) to taste

Shell the peas, remove the germ and grind lightly. Add enough water to cover the peas and add salt. Bring to the boil and leave to boil gently for some time.

Remove scum from the surface as it accumulates. Stir occasionally and add more water and salt as necessary. Do not add too much water, as *magira* should finally be firm. When the peas are cooked, stir them vigorously until they are soft (preferably with a three-pronged wooden stick). Remove from the heat and stir for a little longer. Before serving one may add milk or clarified butter.

Although groundnuts are seldom used for making *magira*, they are a common ingredient in making other relishes, especially *kifuligo* (soup). The extensive use of groundnuts is a relatively new development, promoted by the ease of preparing them and their cultivation as a valuable cash crop. As a relish they have replaced sesame, but it is only for such modern purposes as the quest for money that they are important outside the context of meals. Tradition persists in ritual where small sesame seed cakes are given in food-offerings to the spirits. But as ritual time comes round each year the price of sesame in the market rises.

The quantities and variety of ingredients used in *kifuligo* vary greatly depending on the availability of foodstuffs. A very thin soup can be prepared if resources are short.

Kifuligo Mayido (To serve 4–6)

1 cup groundnuts	other vegetables as available
2 onions	4 cups water
3 tomatoes	salt and pepper

Roast the groundnuts gently. Peel off the skins and pound finely, or liquidize with a small amount of water. Add boiling water. Cut up other vegetables and add, together with salt. Simmer for about 20–30 minutes.

* These are not lentils. Their botanical name is *Vigna unquiculata*; the best substitute for them would be black-eyed peas (*Vigna sinensis*). It should be possible to use dried peas, if they are soaked for a sufficiently long time. In Padhola very occasionally groundnuts are used for making *magira*.
† In Padhola, *kadho thndho* is used in preference to salt. This is made by burning banana leaves or other suitable plants, which are placed in the top of a special receptacle. Water is then poured over the ashes and drains into the bottom of the receptacle. The resulting liquid is *kadho thndho*.

Bakoly Domenichini Ramiaramanana

Malagasy Cooking

Most Malagasy cultures distinguish between cooking done in the fields and village cooking: that is, between cooking outside, characterized by such ingredients as insects and tubers grilled in the fire, and more refined cooking, characterized by rice and milk sprinkled with honey.

Cooking in the bush, while crossing the vast uninhabited areas so common in Madagascar, or during seasonal work away from any village, requires no water or fat, and may even dispense with any containers. It is not quite the same as the method of the few true nomads still to be found in Madagascar, although it derives from it. Rather it is a technique for preparing snacks for long journeys on foot or by canoe – a common enough occurrence in a country with little public transport. Ideally, men eat only at home, or at least in conditions where nothing is left to chance. However, if one has to feed oneself for a day or two away from home, and with no acquaintances or inns to hand, one will equip oneself with meats, tubers, salt and pimento and take snatched meals of meat barbecued over a wood fire, or placed directly on the charcoal (*saly*, *tono*), or perhaps grilled on skewers (*tsatsika*), and of various tubers (manioc, yams or sweet potatoes) baked in the ashes. In season, ears of maize, still in their leaves, may be grilled. On such occasions one may also carry a little smoked or dried fish or meat (*kitoza*, *hahy*), preserved with the techniques used by herdsmen, hunters and fishermen.

However, for longer journeys, or for those who attach importance to varying their menus or (even more) to not declining into savagery, pots are necessary. A number of provisions, in any case, need to be cooked in water. More important, these people, who have codified to the last detail conduct relating to food, regard the pot as a mark of civilization. True meals begin with the pot, and sticking to pots whatever the difficulties is a way of affirming self-respect. Although the use of pots in cooking is not as highly valued as in the (not far distant) days of earthen pots, which were so delicate to carry about, pot-cooking is tending more and more to supplant direct cooking, even on brief trips, for as the proverb says:

111

Courage makes for pot-cooking,
Laziness makes for direct cooking.

Anyone doing bush-style cooking in a village, or even using tubers, would incur disapproval and ultimately shame. The exception to this rule is taro, which is never cooked directly in the ashes, and which is honoured with the title, 'rice's elder brother'. The terms which describe this form of cooking and its ingredients are revealing. It may be called *hani-mainty*, the food of the blacks, or *hani-kotrana*, the food of troubled times. The well-to-do would eat this sort of thing only for breakfast, an unimportant meal, or serve it as snacks to children or to servants preparing meals. Roasting tubers is one of those shameful acts which should be hidden, and thus we have the phrase, 'When a crowd of visitors arrives one pretends not to notice the sweet potato cooking in the ashes'; or, in a similar vein, one may say, 'If the children are in the habit of poking about in the ashes it is because the parents are in the habit of putting something there', as a way of saying, 'Like father, like son.'

By contrast, what distinguishes village cooking is the use of containers which can hold liquid. Here too, however, there is a hierarchy, depending on which liquid is used. In order of importance we have water, fats, coconut milk and, most precious of all, milk. This hierarchy is again marked by many proverbs. For example, one may say, 'Anybody may have a pot for meat, but a pot for milk is something to boast about.'

The basis of village cuisine is rice, even in those regions which had other staples in the recent past, but it gains variety from the great richness of other products available in the country. A meal in a good Malagasy home is rarely monotonous, even if it does not reach the perfection of the *hanom-pito-loha*, the 'meal of the seven relishes'. The number seven should be understood as symbolizing abundance, perfection and distinction, since the possible ingredients for such a meal include not only the famous rice with milk sprinkled with honey, but partridge, guineafowl, eel, crayfish, sucking-pig, capon, veal, crab, deer, fish, mushroom, brains, ox tongue, pigeon and rabbit (both luxury foods, especially rabbit, which was the object of extensive financial speculation in the nineteenth century).

The Malagasy entertain rarely (guests in transit normally receive raw food, fuel, and the help of a servant), but on great occasions they throw real banquets, inviting all their friends and relatives. The most famous such meal in the gastronomic annals of the Malagasy was given by a Prime Minister, Rainilaiarivony, on 22 August 1880 to celebrate the wedding of one of his sons. Queen Ranavalona II was present, and an English missionary, Clark, recorded that there were thousands of guests of various nationalities. In the magnificent setting of the Amboditsiry estate, described by Clark as 'fairyland', more than forty dishes of especial rarity were served.

At the level of, for example, a good village inn, a typical meal will consist of what is called *vary sy laoka*, that is a large plate of rice (*vary*), and two or three relishes (*laoka*) including *ro*, meat or vegetables boiled in water, and *lasary*, a mixture of freshly chopped tomatoes, onions and pimentos. Fruit may be eaten as dessert, but many people prefer to eat fruit as a snack between meals. The meal will often end with a drink made with grilled rice (*ranonampango*) which is also poetically called *ranovola*, 'golden water', and which may be drunk hot or cold. Rice and relishes are eaten together and on the same plate, but the rice is served first, the *ro* being placed in front and to the right of the plate at the same time as the *lasary*. One takes a little *ro* in the spoon used for the rice, and eats the two together.

Here are one or two recipes involved in such a meal: first for the rice, then for *loaka*, and finally for *lasary*.

Rice

Rice is served as *ampangoro* at midday, and as *sosoa* in the morning. In the evening either may be used, according to taste and wealth, since *ampangoro* needs more rice. In the form of flour (*koba*), rice is used in various dishes.

Ampangoro

Any variety of rice may be used, though preference is given to *vary lava,* which has long grains and which separates easily after boiling. If the meal is without bread, use 100 grams (about 3½ oz.) per person. Wash the rice and place in a saucepan with one and a half to twice its volume of water, depending on the consistency desired. Cover and place over a strong flame. When it boils, lower the flame and skim if necessary. When the water has been fully absorbed, you smell the characteristic scent of golden rice and need not wait until the grains turn yellow. Prepared in this way, the rice keeps its flavour and smells delicious. Its success is the *sine qua non* of a good meal.

Ranovola

In taking the *ampangoro* out of the saucepan, be careful not to scrape out the grains sticking to the side. You don't have to allow the *ampangoro* to cool, since it can be taken out as a block, like a cake. Replace the saucepan on a strong fire and wait until the grains are well browned; but they must not be burnt. Pour water into the hot saucepan, and the golden drink is ready.

Sosoa

Some varieties of rice, particularly white and long-grained varieties, make an insipid *sosoa*. *Vary mena,* 'red rice', is best, with a medium grain, but you can use round rice. Use 30 to 50 grams per person.

Boil in three to four times its volume of water, placing the washed rice in the pan when the water is hot. Cover until boiling, then leave for 15 to 20 minutes. In a good *sosoa* the rice is slightly more cooked than in *ampangoro*, and the water should be left until it becomes oily and a little milky. Add sugar or salt and finally pepper or pimento. It may be taken with milk or used to accompany meat or grilled chicken.

Vary Amin-Dronono

Use any type of rice. Rice in milk is an *ampangoro* in which water is wholly or partly replaced by milk. Since one does not mix water and milk, the rice is first cooked in its volume of water, and then its volume of milk is added, but only when all the water has been absorbed. Serve cold. Rice with milk is often flavoured with cinnamon or vanilla (of which Madagascar is the leading producer of the best varieties), sprinkled with honey, and eaten today either as a main dish or as a dessert. The same procedure using coconut milk is used to make *vary amin-boanio*.

Ro

The term *ro*, literally 'juice', is used for all the dishes without cereals which, after preparation, still contain water: ranging from the true *ro mazava*, which is a soup. To the *ro mahery*, an extract of zebu meat, and including the (*ro*) *ketsaketsa*, which are dishes with a sauce.

Ro

Ordinary *ro*, normally salted, is made by boiling for a long time, after seasoning, zebu meat cut into pieces (with salt, garlic and tomatoes), chicken, also cut in pieces and seasoned with ginger, or dried goat kid or fish (with salt and tomatoes).

Lasary

Lasary Tongolo sy Voatabia

Any *tongolo* (*Allium*) will do, except for garlic. One can use chives, chibol (Welsh onion), shallot, and onion or green onion. One can add grilled, crushed groundnuts. Chop the *tongolo* very finely without putting in too many greens; then peel the tomatoes and chop them finely too. Add salt and pimento. Some people add a little oil. Mix well.

Lasary Manga

Use green mangoes. Cut into strips and put them into a highly seasoned vinegar sauce (salt, pimento, ginger, red pepper, white onion, etc.). Stir from time to time, waiting at least three days before serving.

The same method may be used for vegetables (carrots, cabbage and green beans) or green papaya. Some add saffron, and pimento is often replaced by pepper.

Alan R. Meyers and Anne R. Meyers

Two Recipes from Southern Morocco

> O believers, eat of the good things
> wherewith We have provided you, and give thanks
> to God, if it be Him that you serve.
> (Koran, II: 169)

Food is more than sustenance to the people of Morocco. Good food is a sensual pleasure and people speak fondly of favourite recipes and lavishly praise their own and other peoples' culinary skills. Food-sharing is an important way of establishing and reaffirming social relationships, and it would be unthinkable for a visitor to leave his or her host's home without sharing a meal or, at least, several glasses of mint tea. But above all, food is a gift from God. Each meal or snack is a reminder of God's providence, and no right-minded Moroccan would begin a meal without consecrating the food to God, nor end it without praising God for the food which had just been enjoyed.

Food also plays an important role in religious events. Some ritual meals and special recipes are associated with such life crises as marriage and boys' circumcisions, while others are associated with the periodic cycles of holy days. The two recipes which we would like to recommend are both associated with periodic religious holidays, one of which is celebrated by Moroccan Muslims and the other by Moroccan Jews. We recorded both of these recipes during fieldwork in Taroudannt, Morocco, between January and December 1972.

Ramaḍān and Ḥarīra

The first of the recipes is for a thick soup called *ḥarīra*, which is especially popular during the Islamic holy month of Ramaḍān.

During Ramaḍān, adult Muslims are obliged to fast between sun-up and sun-down. Fasting entails total abstinence from food, beverages, tobacco

116

Serving out lentil soup to break Ramadan fast

and sex. In Taroudannt, the beginning and end of the daily fasts are marked by a cannon blast and the sounding of drums and bugles in the different quarters of town; in larger cities, sirens are used.

People generally curtail their daytime activities during Ramaḍān, especially when it comes during one of the summer months.[1] Many shops and offices close and those which stay open have few customers. People tend to nap during the days and postpone all but non-essential activities until after dark. But late in the afternoon, the town begins to come alive as people shop and begin to prepare their homes for sun-down, when they can break their fasts.

At the sound of the evening cannon, people eat a light 'breakfast', which normally consists of dried dates, mint-flavoured *café-au-lait*, and *ḥarīra*. Later, around midnight, they have a larger meal of *tajin* (stew) or *cous-cous* or both. Just before dawn, they have another light meal of bread and jam or porridge and mint tea, to prepare themselves for the next day's fast. Between meals, people eat a variety of sweets and pastries, most of which are more or less characteristic of the fast. But *ḥarīra*, the thick soup with which people break their daily fasts, is Ramaḍān food *par excellence*. People eat *ḥarīra* throughout the year, but during Ramaḍān it is served in homes and restaurants everywhere in Morocco, and the prices of the ingredients always rise dramatically in the weeks before and during the fast.

It is not possible to speak of a 'typical' recipe for *ḥarīra*, because the cost of the ingredients is high, and the quality and quantity of the ingredients of a family's *ḥarīra* will depend, at least in part, upon their ability to pay. Moreover, families pride themselves upon special recipes which distinguish their *ḥarīra* from anyone else's. The one cited here is a composite, based upon several separate recipes. It is considered perfectly good etiquette for each person to season his or her *ḥarīra* to taste.

Ḥarīra (a recipe which can be expanded easily to serve a large crowd, but, for amounts provided below, approximately 6 servings)

½ cup lentils ⎧ split peas or other
½ cup chick peas ⎨ dried beans may be
½ cup barley ⎩ substituted or added
1 lb (450 grams) canned or fresh
   tomatoes, drained and sieved or
   liquidized in a blender
1 large bunch parsley
1 bunch fresh coriander (Chinese
   parsley), if available
1–1½ lb (450–680 grams) meat for soup,
   cut into pieces

2 or 3 stalks celery, diced
beef bones
1 onion, diced
½ cup oil
2 tsp turmeric
water or beef stock
rice or thin spaghetti, if desired
salt and pepper to taste
2 tbsp flour
juice of 1 lemon

Soak lentils, chick peas and barley overnight. Drain and set aside. Add chopped parsley, coriander and diced celery to the sieved tomatoes and let the mixture stand.

    Heat oil in a large pot. Add meat, bones and diced onion, and cook until browned. Sprinkle with turmeric and add water or beef stock to cover. Bring to a boil, add lentils, chick peas, and barley, and simmer for 2 hours or so until meat is cooked. Add tomato mixture, salt and pepper and cook 15 minutes more. If desired, add rice or thin spaghetti and cook until done.

    Fifteen minutes before serving, put 2 tbsp flour in a small bowl. Add some hot soup and mix, returning flour mixture to the soup-pot, and cook, stirring, about 15 minutes. Add the juice of 1 lemon and serve hot.

    We find that the *ḥarīra* has more flavour if it is kept for a day before it is eaten.

Sabt and *Dafīna*

Unlike Ramaḍān, which is an annual holiday, the Jewish Sabbath – or *al Sabt*, in Moroccan Arabic – is celebrated every week. In Morocco, as elsewhere, the Sabbath is a day of rest and celebration for Jews, but since 'rest' includes an interdiction against elaborate food preparation and kindling of fires, people must prepare their Sabbath feasts before sun-down on Friday, when the Sabbath officially begins. Fridays are days of frantic activity in Moroccan Jewish households, as women and children cook and clean in preparation for their Sabbath rests. All Sabbath food must be prepared and all fires kindled before sun-down on Friday, but the main focus of attention is the *dafina*, which is served as Saturday's dinner, at midday, after men have returned from the synagogue.

The *dafina*, which means 'burial' in Moroccan Arabic, is similar to the *cholent* which is prepared by Jews of Eastern European origin:[2] the ingredients are put in a single pot on Friday and left to cook on the *mijmar* (brazier) until Saturday afternoon. There are other characteristic Sabbath foods which also figure in this midday meal: for example, the *halla* (Sabbath loaf) and the *giffan* (sacramental wine). There are also fresh and cooked salads, special sweets, local brandy (*ma haya*: lit., aquavit), and mint tea. But without a *dafina*, the Sabbath would be incomplete.

As in the case of *harira*, each family has its own recipe for *dafina*, and these recipes differ according to each family's tastes and means. So, once again, the recipe listed here is a composite and can be varied according to taste.

Dafina

All quantities in this recipe can be adjusted depending upon how many people you are serving and how much you like each of the ingredients. Therefore I am listing only the main ingredients, and suggesting quantities for seasonings only. although these too can be varied according to taste.

All ingredients are put in the pot in layers and cooked slowly, the longer the better.

piece of beef (about 3–4 lb/1·5–2 kilos) for stewing, preferably brisket
2 onions, cut into chunks
¼ cup oil
1½–2 tsp turmeric
½–1 lb (220–450 grams) chick peas, soaked overnight
½ lb (220 grams) rice
1 or 2 cloves garlic, minced
2 tbsp fresh or 1 tsp dried parsley

about 6 whole eggs with shells and uncooked, optional
about 6 white potatoes, peeled and washed, optional
about 6 sweet potatoes, peeled and washed, optional
1 tsp cinnamon
water
salt and pepper

Heat oil in the bottom of a large heavy pot. Add meat, cubed or left whole, onions, 1 tsp turmeric and some pepper. Cook until browned. Drain chick peas and place in a layer over the meat.

Wash the rice, add water to cover, and warm for a minute or two on the stove to soften it. Drain rice and add a pinch of turmeric, ½ tsp salt, I tsp parsley, 1 clove minced garlic, and a spoonful of oil. Mix it well. Wrap the rice mixture in a piece of cheesecloth or a handkerchief, and place the bundle in the pot.

Wash the shells of some raw eggs and place the whole eggs in the pot.
Place a layer of peeled white and sweet potatoes on top of the eggs and rice.
Sprinkle the top with about 2 tbsp salt, ½ tsp turmeric and 1 tsp cinnamon. Add water to cover and cook slowly, the longer the better.

To serve, remove ingredients from the pot and place in one large serving dish or several smaller dishes. Unwrap rice and place it in a dish. Shell the eggs (the whites will be brownish) and cut up or serve whole.

We have given only two sample recipes for two kinds of Moroccan food. We would like to stress that there are many variants of these two recipes and many other exquisite Moroccan dishes which we have not described: stews, roasted meats, varieties of *cous-cous*, and desserts. Unfortunately, there is no English-language Moroccan cookbook which we can recommend, but we have had many successful meals from Mme Bennani Smires's French-language cookbook, which can be ordered from any French bookstore.[3]

We hope that you will enjoy these and other Moroccan recipes, as we have. *Bi-sahtikum* – to your health!

NOTES

1 The Muslim calendar, like the Jewish, is a lunar calendar, but unlike the Jewish calendar it has no intercalary month. So, while Jewish holidays fall on different dates each solar year, they always fall within a certain time-range. Muslim holidays, on the other hand, may fall on any date of the solar year.

2 See M. Zborowski and E. Herzog, *Life is with People*, New York, Schocken, p. 57.

3 L. Bennani Smires, *La Cuisine marocaine*, Paris, Taillandier.

Sheila Patterson

Tasty Little Dishes
of the Cape

This is the title and refrain of a rollicking song popularized about a decade ago by the Cape Coloured singer, Maxine Day:

The first of January
I went to Salt Rivier
To wish Tant' Sarie
A Happy New Year.

When I got there, the party had begun
She'd invited everyone.
There was plenty to drink and there was
    plenty to eat,
Everything tasting just fine.
There was music and dancing and singing too,
Believe me, we had a good time.

There were three pots of soup,
A whole sheep's head,
A chicken's eggs soaked in brine,
Salted meat, the hock of a pig,
And a whole barrel brandywine.

And then Tant" Sarie
Cooked sausage and tamatie
But there was more to come,
Tender pig's feet thinly spread
And a bottle of Van der Hum.

This splendidly robust spread includes a number of the basics of Cape country cooking, among whites and coloured people ·alike. The menu does not, however, mention fish or table wine, and it is low on the fruit and vegetables whose variety and abundance, fresh or cooked, every visitor to Cape Town, or the old-fashioned country hotels of the Province, will remember with relish. The only fruits involved are the grapes that went into the Cape brandy, and the *naartjies* or tangerines which are the basis of the Van der Hum liqueur. The sausages (probably the meaty spicy *boerewors*) are also cooked with tangy-tasting tomatoes so that, as the singer says later, 'you won't want [need] to clean your teeth'. Altogether, this is a Boer-type meal, similar to those meals with which travellers like George Thompson were received in all but the poorest Boer farms throughout the Cape of the eighteenth and early nineteenth centuries.

The old or traditional Cape cooking, basically centred on Cape Town and the Peninsula, is something much more complex, refined and cosmopolitan. It reflects not only the cuisine derived from Holland and the Low Countries but the Malay, Indonesian, Indian and even Chinese influences exerted on the Dutch way of life in the Dutch East Indian territories. This Dutch–Malay or Batavian cookery is the backbone of traditional Cape cookery, rooted in Cape Town by Batavian officials, well-to-do Dutch settlers, Indonesian exiles and Malay and Indian domestic slaves, and later by Cape Coloured cooks, vendors and café-owners. Coloured people and whites have lived in proximity for centuries and there is no separate Cape Coloured cookery. The only differences are dictated by pocket and style of living, except in the case of Cape Town's large residential Malay or Muslim community, whose cuisine is more specifically eastern and follows Muslim dietary observances regarding meat and alcohol.

There are a few traces of Hottentot influence in old Cape cookery, but not as many as one would expect of the French Huguenots, who joined the original Dutch East India Company settlers in 1688–9. They introduced vines and wine-making, whose products still complement the dishes of the Cape and, in conjunction with the temperate Mediterranean climate, produce a somewhat different gastronomic picture from that of the East or West Indies and most other former slave societies. One of the Huguenots' contributions is said to be the rolled wafers now called *oblietjies*, made with cinnamon and white wine or brandy.

The English began to arrive in numbers in the 1820s, after the Cape had passed from Dutch to British hands in 1806. Their influence on Cape cookery was not marked, since both the heavy Dutch and the spicy East Indian components were closely attuned to existing British colonial culinary tastes. Moreover, the majority of cooks in private houses and public establishments continued to be coloured slaves or freedmen, later Cape Coloured, cooking and serving the dishes which they also enjoyed eating. Until recent years, when most Cape Coloureds have left domestic service for factories, shops and offices, this has been one of the strengths of Cape cookery, by contrast with culinary performances in some other African colonial societies.

The chief English contribution to traditional Cape cookery took the form of Miss Hildagonda Duckitt, grand-daughter of one William Duckitt of Esher, who was sent to the Cape in 1800 by King George III to establish model farms and improve the methods of agriculture. One of his sons married a Miss Hildagonda Versfeld and brought up his family on a farm in the Darling district. This farm was virtually a self-contained world, producing its own food – grain, wine, sheep, oxen; butter and cream; pears, quinces, peaches, lemons, almonds; beet, tomatoes, onions, cabbage and kale; garlic and many herbs and spices. From the neighbourhood came game and tortoise, from the near-by sea fresh *snoek*, the erroneously named crayfish (seawater crawfish or rock lobster) and *perlemoen*. Taught to cook by her mother and a cook called Abraham, a former slave from East Africa, Miss Duckitt also made her own cooking-fat, soap and candles from sheep's tallow, and did her own baking and preserving of meats and fish, jams, pickles, condiments and chutneys, Dutch, English and Malay. She was also versed in home remedies, including tortoise soup for invalids, *dagga* (marijuana) tea for jaundice, and Hottentot fig gargle for sore throats. Miss Duckitt later went to live in the Peninsula, at Waterloo Green, Wynberg, where late in life she published the two classic books which were to become best-sellers and make her the Mrs Beeton of South Africa. These were *Hilda's 'Where is it?'* in 1890 and *Hilda's 'Diary of a Cape Housekeeper'* in 1902, three years before her death.

For a decade or so, many of Cape Town's old hotels and taverns continued to serve traditional *bredies* (meat and vegetable stews), *sasaties* (kebabs) and curries, and the cafés and sweetshops served such delicacies as *tameletjies* (tangerine sweets), *koeksisters* (doughnuts) and *melktert* (milk tart). Thereafter traditional Cape cookery went into a slow decline, until interest in good cooking was revived, partly by immigrants from Europe, after the second World War. In 1951, reflecting this revived interest, Miss Duckitt's grand-niece, Mary Kuttel, published a highly-usable collection of 650 cookery recipes from the two original books.[1] One year before that, Hilda Gerber, a regular cookery contributor to the Cape press and South African media in general, had produced an even more wide-ranging collection of over 900 recipes called *Cape Cookery – Old and New*.[2] This encompassed modern means of food conservation and transportation, and added to the traditional Dutch–Malay cuisine a number of European recipes brought in by more recent immigrants (Austrian, Polish, Italian and French) and adapted to the wide range of ingredients available at the Cape.

When I was living in Cape Town a few years later, there were several small restaurants providing a cosmopolitan cuisine, but the traditional Cape cooking, including the *bredies, sasaties, bobotie* (curried mince), *smoervis* (fried spiced fish), curries and rice dishes recorded by Miss Duckitt, was hardly to be found except in some private houses. Two exceptions were the Netherlands Club, with its splendid *rijstafel*, and the dining-room of the Houses of Parliament.

The revival of interest in Cape cookery was also marked in London by a Wine and Food Society Luncheon with the following menu:[3]

Ertjie Sop (farmhouse pea soup)
Kreef Room (crawfish mould with cream sauce)
Bobotie
Hoender Pastei (chicken pie)
Green Mealies
Granadilla Ice
Soet Koekies

At the more popular end of the scale, however, Cape-style cooking has not declined so markedly. Again, it often displays eastern influences, original or more recent. George Manuel, in his splendid record of Cape Town's District Six before its recent classification as 'White' and despoliation by White property-dealers,[4] describes the many curry shops, cafés and restaurants: some of these, like the Crescent Café in Hanover Street, were popular with Europeans meeting their Coloured friends 'in the good old days before "Group Areas"'. Curry is eaten with *chapatis* or rice and *samoosas* (little triangular pastries filled with curried vegetables or meat). It was and is also often bought as a cheap and filling take-home dish for the family, like English fish-and-chips. Also on sale are cookies and snacks like *slangetjies* ('little snakes') and *koeksisters*.

I was living in the Peninsula and doing a field-study of the Cape Coloured people about the time of this partial revival of traditional Cape cookery. I was luckier than most residents, for I had a Coloured cook-general called Sophie. She was a lively, brown-skinned young woman from a 'good' Cape Town artisan family who had married Agmat, a Cape Malay, and she was known as 'Leggie' to her Malay in-laws. Though charming, Agmat was not a very good Muslim: he worked only irregularly as a cabinet-maker and drank and smoked *dagga* on occasion. He once turned up in the kitchen under the influence of both, brandishing a knife and threatening to kill his wife for going along the coast *to dance* in Simonstown, then a British naval base in whose cafés and dance-halls apartheid was unknown. Together we managed to disarm him, but the 'Bushman girl' (despised for her peppercorn hair and Bushman features) who worked in the flat below had called the police at Fish Hoek, and we had a terrible job getting him bailed and then given a suspended sentence.

Agmat's family did not approve of his marrying out. His mother, however, unbent sufficiently to polish Sophie's knowledge of Malay cuisine, which Sophie, not being a Muslim, did not scruple to apply to pork and other non-Muslim ingredients. In consequence of this tuition, she was a remarkable cook, versed in all aspects of traditional Malay–Dutch cooking, and also English cookery, acquired from working for a naval officer's family in

Simonstown. To this, being genuinely apt and enterprising, she later added a wide repertoire of French and American dishes from my cookery books. Her crayfish Thermidor, sole bonne femme, and turkey à la king, followed by baked Alaska, crêpes Suzette or mint sorbet, were much envied by my friends.

On one occasion, we also prepared a traditional Polish *Wilja* or Christmas Eve meal for a group of Polish friends who had settled in the Peninsula after the 1939–45 war. This included *consommé* of dried *cèpes* (the *cèpes* picked locally by a former Polish officer then working as a farm manager near Somerset West). The traditional main dish was to be stewed carp with a 'grey' sauce (sweet-sour with caramel, almonds and sultanas). The main problem was first to get a carp and then to clean it. A large fish was finally procured from a farmer near Princess Vlei, an oval lagoon on the Cape Flats which is also famous for its *water-uintjes* (*Aponogeton*), a wild lily whose flowers and bulbs have for generations been used to make one of the best *bredies* or mutton stews. Once brought home, there was the chore of cleaning and dressing the large, slithery, muddy, bony fish. This was fortunately undertaken by Gardener, an aged and endearing outdoor odd-job man, entirely Hottentot in appearance, whose long and chequered life had included a spell as a fisherman out of Saldanha Bay. Unlike some of his fellow Cape Coloured workers, he did not sell any of his legal daily allowance of three bottles of sherry wine – sweet strong Muscadel, then retailing at a shilling or so per bottle – to the African workers who were then prohibited from buying anything but 'Kaffir beer' in official beer-halls. Instead, he drank it all.

Gardener (no one knew his real name) demanded a bottle of cheap brandy for cleaning the fish, and he did a good job in the outside sink at the top of the stairs. By the end, however, he had finished the bottle, cut himself, and fallen down two flights of stairs. I returned to find him unconscious, with our doctor neighbour putting in emergency stitches, and the stairs running with water, mud and blood, human and carp intermingled. Gardener, however, survived to maintain his intake of wine for several more years.

Sophie herself is still alive and lively, though she 'suffers with her back', and she and her new husband (Agmat beat her up once too often) have been forced by 'Group Areas' to move to one of the new and characterless 'Coloured townships' far out on the Cape Flats. I hope to eat one of her splendid dishes again.

I have chosen three recipes from Sophie's repertoire, *sasaties* (kebabs), *bobotie* (minced curry) and Sophie's own chicken curry, which I have not found written down anywhere but which, with its adjuncts, is very similar to dishes described in a recent book on south-east Asian food.[5] Some of the ingredients used in Malay–Indonesian cookery were not easily available to the old Cape settlers – notably fresh coconuts, with their flesh, milk and oil, and some herbs, fruit or vegetables. These have become more easily available for anyone experimenting with Cape or indeed east Asian dishes in the Peninsula or Britain, but the alternatives always available (e.g. lard or butter for frying, sweet or sour cream for enriching sauces) have remained in use. Most of the side-dishes (*atjar*, *blatjang*, *sambals*) can be made at home or procured at specialist Indian or Asian shops in Cape Town, London or other large cities.

Sasaties (Kebabs) (To serve about 6)
(A Malay or Indian dish, after Miss Duckitt's own recipe)

Marinade 1 fat leg of mutton or lamb, cut in 1-inch cubes

For the marinade:
1 onion, minced and fried golden
2 oz. (60 grams) good curry powder (freshly prepared)
1 oz. (30 grams) tamarind, drawn on a cup of water (or ½ cup wine vinegar or
    the juice of 2 lemons)
1 tbsp madeira or sherry (optional)
1 tbsp brown sugar
12 lemon or orange leaves (or bay leaves with a little grated lemon rind)
½ cup milk or coconut milk
1 tsp coriander seed (if available)
6 peppercorns
2 crushed cloves garlic (optional)

Mix all the marinade ingredients with the cut-up meat in a deep pan or basin; leave it for a night or longer and, when wanted, place the meat (interspersed with fat here and there) on skewers. Place the gridiron on charcoal to get very hot, or otherwise prepare a hot grill, then grill the *sasaties* a nice brown. Serve hot with rice, salad (tomato, cucumber, coleslaw) and *blatjang* and *sambals* on the side (sharp Malay condiments usually made on a vegetable or fruit base with garlic, chillies, vinegar, etc., added).

Bobotie (Malay or Indian curried mince) (To serve 6–8)
(After Miss Duckitt's mother's recipe)

3 lb (1·5 kilo) meat (beef or lamb)	2 tsp sugar
2 onions	juice of a lemon or 2 tbsp vinegar
large slice white bread	6 to 8 almonds
1 cup milk	1 tbsp butter or dripping
3 or 4 eggs	bay leaves or lemon leaves
2 tbsp curry powder	

Mince the meat, soak the bread in milk and squeeze out dry, then mix all the meat and soaked bread. Fry the onions gently in the butter until soft. Mix the dry ingredients and vinegar with the fried onion. Add a lightly beaten egg, and add the mixture to the meat.

To prepare custard:
Whisk 2 or 3 eggs with ½–¾ cup milk and pour over the meat which has been placed in a buttered pie-dish or into little cups (the old Indian way), with a lemon or bay leaf stuck into each little cup. Put in the oven to bake (350°, gas Mk 4, 40–60 minutes) and send to table in the cups or pie-dish. Serve with rice. (This dish is equally good made of cold mutton.)

N.B. Miss Duckitt adds that the juice from 1 oz. tamarinds soaked in half a pint (280 ml) of boiling water, then strained, when used for *bobotie*, *sasaties* and curries instead of vinegar, gives a very pleasant acid flavour.

Chicken curry was one of Sophie's buffet party dishes at Muizenberg, and has remained one of mine, with minor adaptations and additions, in Montreal, Kingston (Jamaica) and Brighton (Sussex). Its Malay antecedents were validated recently when my husband went to buy rice and other ingredients at a specialist food store in Brighton. The manager, confronted with a request for coconut cream, tamarind and coriander, said: 'So it's a Malay curry your wife is making?'

Chicken Curry (Sophie's own Cape Malay)*

1 3-lb (1·5 kilo) boiling or roasting
   chicken
3 aubergines, sliced and previously
   salted and dried to rid them of their
   bitter flavour

1 onion, sliced
2 onions, chopped
white wine (medium to dry)
salt, pepper and bay leaf
½ tsp coriander

For the sauce:
1 scant tsp curry powder (containing
   turmeric) to taste.
1 or 2 tsp ground coriander
tamarind, lemon or lime juice
   (equivalent to juice of 1 lemon)
garlic to taste

1 pinch saffron (optional)
½ cup (about ¼ pt/142 ml) creamed
   coconut or double sweet or sour
   cream, to taste
½ cup olive oil or butter-oil mixture
   (as preferred)

Boil the chicken slowly in water and wine with salt, pepper, sliced onion, coriander and bay leaf until cooked but firm (about 45 minutes for a roaster, 2½ hours for

* This curry should be mild, with the hot taste imparted by some of the side-dishes.

a boiler). Cut up and put aside. Keep the chicken broth for the sauce.

Lightly brown the chopped onions and sliced aubergines and put aside.

Make a white roux (blending gently over low heat 3 tbsp butter, 3 tbsp flour and 1 cup milk) and add hot chicken stock ($\frac{3}{4}$ cup) and some white wine ($\frac{1}{4}$ cup). Then add the curry powder, fruit juice, squeeze in the garlic, and cook gently for a few minutes, taking care not to allow the liquid to boil. Put in the cooked chicken pieces, aubergine slices and chopped onion, and warm slowly.

Just before serving, stir in the creamed coconut or cream. Colour and flavour with saffron if desired.

Serve with polished rice and an assortment of the following side-dishes: chopped hard-boiled eggs; chopped salted peanuts; sliced bananas; pawpaw balls; crushed pineapple; grated coconut; chopped green and red sweet peppers; sliced pineapple; sliced tomato with chopped onion or chives; pappadums; sliced lemons; any available *atjars, blatjangs, sambals,* chutneys, ranging from mild to hot.

NOTES

1   Hildagonda J. Duckitt, *650 Cookery Recipes*, Maskew Miller, Cape Town, 1951.

2   Hilda Gerber, *Cape Cookery – Old and New*, Howard B. Timmins (Cape Town), for Hodder & Stoughton, London, 1950.

3   Lawrence Green, who records this in *Tavern of the Seas* (Howard B. Timmins, Cape Town, 1947, p. 68), does not record the exact year of this luncheon.

4   George Manuel, *District Six*, illustr. Bruce Franck, ed. Dennis Hatfield, Longmans S.A., 1967.

5   Rosemary Brissenden, *South East Asian Food*, Penguin, 1969.

The Americas
and the
West Indies

One of these Newfoundland Dogs, after he had been constantly worked in the woods during the winter, then slain, is not bad eating. The hams, salted and smoked with juniper Berrys and branches of Rasberrys and their [Indian] tea, in point of flavor, is superior to the celebrated Hams of Bayonne in Gascony. Dog hams are a new article in the Epicure's catalogue. (*The New-foundland Journal of Aaron Thomas*, 1794)

Eva Hunt

A Mexican Fish for Easter

New World cultures have contributed more than a fair share to the cuisine of the world. In fact, it would be hard to imagine how many Europeans would eat without, for example, potatoes. Mexico alone has added the basis of many of the national dishes of European nations. Could Italians cook without tomatoes? Or without polenta corn meal? Would Holland or Switzerland be famous for their chocolates without Mexican cacao beans?

We all know, in the back of our mind, that Mexicans gave us many of the staples of our diet. Many of us have heard that contemporary Mexican cuisine is very hot, with a surfeit of chilli peppers of all sorts. What few people know is that Mexico has one of the most complex, varied and symbolically charged cuisines of the world.

Every town and village in Mexico has hundreds of local recipes, proud specialities, each with a proper time of the year to be eaten. The four seasons are punctuated by holy days, and each one has a different roster of foods which are typical of the day. In one village alone I collected, just for the fun of it, over one hundred different ways of preparing a mild drink made out of corn starch (*atole*), which was invented in prehispanic times. Each variety of the drink was appropriate for different health conditions, but also for different holidays in the round of the annual solar calendar.

Throughout Mexico every day of the ritual year is characterized by a distinct meal, which is made up of components with highly charged symbolic meanings. Some of the meanings are of prehispanic origin, having to do with symbols of deities and spirits which have survived five hundred years of the colonial debacle. Other meanings are pseudo-Christian, and attached to apparently Christian symbols. Most cooked foods are a symbolic hybrid, carrying both prehispanic and Old World meanings simultaneously. Like modern Mexicans, who are socially, racially and culturally a combination of two different historical streams, so is Mexican food. Together with the New World staples such as beans, corn and squash, Mexicans eat pork, veal or lamb imported by their European ancestors. Many foods drifted into the

131

New Spain during the period of the French Empire of Maximilian and in middle-class urban homes, one often finds French recipes, adapted to the Mexican taste.

In the rural areas, less influenced by the European traditions, the most varied food symbolisms exist. In one of the villages in which I worked, in the state of Oaxaca, people are supposed to eat twelve different foods during the Easter week. Each one of the twelve represents one of the Apostles present at the Last Supper. The foods, however, are native 'cold-water foods' in their classification, and are said to be controlled by the rain god, Lord Lightning Thunderbolt. What makes them 'cold-water foods' is that they are white, or transparent in colour, or have a large water content, or all at the same time, such as cucumbers!

But another reason why water foods are to be eaten during Easter is that this religious holiday marks the beginning of the rainy season, during which ceremonies are conducted to ask the gods for rain prior to the planting of the major corn crop. Water foods eaten by man, in sympathetic cosmic digestion, bring water food for the newly planted seed in the ground. The foods, indirectly and through man, bring a message of rain, in a transformed culinary-agricultural code.

In the cities of Mexico, busy urban people know little of corn-planting or of Lord Lightning Thunderbolt. During Easter Week people eat lots of dry shrimp, eggs and fish dishes, because of the Roman Catholic injunction against eating meat during Lent. Fish dishes are liked because a fish is considered an old symbol for Christian identification. By eating fish during this ritual period one symbolizes one's closeness to Christ.

One of my favourite Easter fish recipes is reproduced below. I found it originally in a book published in 1831, *The Very New Art of the Kitchen or an Excellent Collection of the Best Recipes at Low Costs Dedicated to Young Mexican Maidens*. Since then I have checked the proportions with several Mexican friends, and found them furiously divided into the pro-capers and contra-capers factions. The choice is the cook's.

The best fish for this recipe is red snapper, but sole, pike or sea bass (and, in extreme cases of need, fresh cod) can be used.

A Good Stew for the Vigil of Lent or Easter Week (To serve 4–6)

6 fillets (about 2 lb/1 kilo) white meat fish
2 medium onions, cut in rings
1 large green pepper, cut in strips
3 tomatoes, peeled and seeded, cut in circles

Spice mixture:

¼ tsp powdered cinnamon

¼ tsp thyme

¼ tsp powdered oregano

¼ tsp powdered cumin seeds

salt and pepper

¼ tsp powdered rosemary

¼ tsp dry powdered chilli peppers, the
  hot red variety called in Mexico
  chile piquin (if desired)

½ cup olive oil

½ cup dry white wine

juice of ½ lemon

Garnish:

chopped, pickled chilli peppers, chopped capers and green olives

Arrange fish fillets or slices in an oiled oven dish. Cover them with the slices of onion, green peppers and tomatoes. Mix the spice mixture with the olive oil, lemon juice and wine. Pour the spice mixture with the liquids over the whole top. Bake at 350° (gas Mk 4) for 1 hour or until done. Before serving, sprinkle with the garnish of chilli peppers, and, if liked, chopped capers and green olives.

This dish is wonderful served with white rice and a cold glass of dark Mexican beer such as *Dos Equis*. If you cannot get Mexican beer, a Danish dark Tuborg will come close to the taste of a Mexican one.

Stephen and Roxane Gudeman

Rice and Old Clothes

As in many cultures, food is a frequent topic of conversation among rural Panamanians. The peasants, or countrymen as they are known, discuss all their food-producing techniques and worries from the first seeding to whether one strain of rice lasts better than another in the pot. Indeed, all the comestibles, particularly the central food – rice – are considered important, not only for their immediate food value but also for symbolic reasons. Like sex, food is the focus of beliefs, prohibitions and stories: no adult should be seen eating by a hungry child lest the youngster grow envious and die from a 'falling stomach'. Likewise, even in the cramped family sleeping-quarters, parents are modest and surreptitious in their sexual relations. The foods of a meal must be properly selected and combined to meet the strictures of the hot and cold system, a means for classifying foods which ultimately derives from Greek beliefs. And, just as a man hot from work in the fields should avoid cold foods, so also a 'cold' man should avoid a 'hot' woman lest he be drained of his vital energies. But food is not a mere metaphor for sex; a network of subtle threads links both with genetics and nationality. When I revisited Panama after seven years, I carried with me pictures of our two children, the elder of whom was born within a year of our leaving the village. The alert villagers began by identifying which was the elder, questioned me about date of birth, recalled that I had left the field a few weeks in advance of my wife, and then concluded that the child was bound to look Panamanian anyway, since we had been eating 'typical' food for some time. Such a genetic theory is intriguing if not positively appealing in the context of our scientific culture; at least it implies a folk recommendation of their own foods!

But adults are linked to the food quest in a more ordinary, less exotic fashion. A man, to be a man, must be able to provide his family with yearly sustenance. He should be seen going to the fields every day with his machete. Even on days of rest men will often go just to check, but in fact to admire, their growing crops; and a field, cleaned of weeds with young green rice-stalks rippling in the breeze is a pretty sight. Once harvested, the rice is hauled to the house where it is stored in a loft above the kitchen fire. Here, it becomes part of the woman's domain, and her tasks are no easier than the male's, for she must remove the rice from the stalk, pound it with a heavy pestle and mortar to remove the husks, sort it and cook it. Each variety of rice calls for a slight variation in preparation, and just as a man prides himself on having a loft full of rice, so a woman partially defines and realizes herself through food preparation.

When writing for his professional colleagues, the anthropologist always faces the problem of translation and balance. To render a distant culture exactly, he ought to write in the people's own language; but this would tend to restrict his readership. Yet, the more he uses his own native tongue, or even the anthropological lexicon, the more he may misrender the delicate cultural fabric of the people, which he had hoped to understand and convey to others. The 'recipe problem' is somewhat similar. Foods, like wines, do not always travel well; those which satisfy in the hot, humid midday of Panama taste rather different in a cold, dark Minnesota winter. And the ordinary cooking skills of the American or British reader may not include masticating and spitting maize in order to make a delicious, but illegal, Panamanian beverage known as *chicha*. Besides technique, ingredients are a major problem; when availability forces substitution to be made, at what point

Cooking a meal out of doors during the dry season

does the exotic become the ordinary? When gas takes the place of wood, fine-grain white rice is used in place of a broken, coarse variety, and tempered steel cookware is substituted for blackened iron pots, is the similarity only in the mind and not on the tongue? Perhaps it is all a creation of the anthropologist.

At any rate, we present the following three recipes which we have enjoyed out of the field. Preparation is not complex and the ingredients are all reasonably easy to obtain. However mistranslated and re-rendered they may be, each recipe represents something different but important about Panamanian culture. For us, the pleasure has been both in the mind and on the tongue, but we recommend that others re-translate the quantities – as would any cook – and perhaps the ingredients. The Panamanians would understand that. Though their range of fare is limited, there is no standardized version of a dish. And that, perhaps, is a cultural universal!

Beet and potato salad is sold on holidays. Very popular among the peasants, who are the principal consumers, it is made by other peasants. Yet none of the ingredients is locally grown; all must be purchased on the national market and the salad is rarely served in a home.

Beet and Potato Salad (*Ensalada de remolacha con papa*)

2 lb (1 kilo) (non-starchy salad) potatoes, cooked and diced	1 tsp vinegar
	1 tsp cooking oil
2 medium onions, sliced	mayonnaise to mix
4 boiled beets, diced	salt and pepper to taste

Mix the ingredients gently in a large bowl. Use sufficient mayonnaise to blend. The oil and vinegar are optional; to use oil reduces the amount of expensive mayonnaise needed. The beets give the potatoes a bright pink colour. To enhance the colour and flavour, the salad should be mixed while the potatoes and beets are still warm.

Ropa Vieja

Ropa vieja is of special interest in that its ingredients 'say' something about Panama as an international transit zone; the recipe comes from the city, but is known, though infrequently served, in the countryside. We obtained the recipe by purchasing all the ingredients and having a friend come to our house and prepare it. No one else made the dish while we were in the village, but in the past, when times were better, our friend's mother, who was known as a good cook, would be asked to prepare foods such as this for weddings or house-building work parties.

Old Clothes *(Ropa vieja)*

1 lb (450 grams) chuck or stewing steak	pepper to taste
salt to taste	¼ cup water
1 clove garlic, if desired	¼ cup vinegar
2½ tsp soy sauce *(Salsa China)*	1 tbsp Worcestershire sauce
1 medium onion, finely chopped	*(Salsa Inglesa)*

Sprinkle the raw meat lightly with salt and pepper, then place in a flat shallow dish with vinegar and soak for 2–3 hours. Place the soaked meat in a pot with an inch or so of water and simmer for 15–30 minutes. Remove and chop it into small, thin strips, and place in a frying-pan with the onion, salt and pepper and optional garlic. Mix together the water, soy sauce and Worcestershire sauce and add to the meat. Simmer slowly until almost all the moisture evaporates. The result is a tasty meat coated with a thin sauce. As a variation, a little tomato paste may be added to the sauce.

Quick-cooking, corrupted, variation:
If a more tender cut of meat is used, such as round steak, one may brown the meat and onions quickly in 2 tbsp cooking oil, then add the sauce and boil until the moisture almost evaporates. To prepare the sauce, mix 2 tsp vinegar, 2 tsp soy sauce, 1 tbsp Worcestershire sauce and 2 tbsp tomato sauce.

As the day's work in the fields draws to a close, men will begin to speak of how they are looking forward to a good *quacho* upon returning home. Although not eaten every day, the dish is very popular. In our terms a soup, for the peasants it is not, since it always contains rice, though substitution may be made in the other prime ingredients. Nearly all the constituents can be found in the countryside. But this recipe is the most difficult to 'translate'. Our version calls for measured amounts only of the main essential ingredients – beans and rice. The other essential ingredients, the spices and flavourings, termed as a unit *'quiso'*, are common to many dishes prepared in Panama, but our recipe does not specify the proportionate amounts. We have experimented with various combinations, but the result, though pleasing to our taste, may be different from the Panamanian version. The final problem is that the ingredients are truly local. None of the beans in our local international food market is at all similar to the Panamanian ones, while the tubers are virtually unobtainable.

Guacho

½ lb (220 grams) vine or bush beans
(we found 'pigeon beans' to be the
closest)
generous pinch *achiote* (annatto)
4 oz. (110 grams) rice
2 tbsp cooking oil
¼ tsp ground black pepper
1 tsp salt
2 medium onions, chopped

2 cloves garlic, chopped
tinned sweetcorn (optional)
yucca (sweet manioc) (optional)
½ lb cubed beef (optional)
tomatoes (optional)
yam (optional)
generous pinch cayenne pepper or
small amount seeded and chopped
small hot green pepper

Bring water to boil, remove from heat, and let beans, if dried, soak for 1½–2 hours.
Sauté the onion, cayenne (chilli) pepper, garlic, black pepper, *achiote* and salt
in the cooking oil until onion is translucent. If meat is used, brown it at the
same time. Add water, bring to boil, then cook the beans until they are soft.
Add the rice and cook until it is soft. If other ingredients are used, add all with
the rice, except the corn – which should be added 10 minutes before the rice is
done. The dish should be like a stew when finished, drier than soup but with
liquid. (The quantity of water used depends on the number of ingredients.)
Guacho – drained or cooked to be drier – is a nice accompaniment to 'Old
Clothes'.

Eugene Hammel

Peruvian *Cebiche*

Beachcomber's Version

Remove the shoes, stockings, shirt and any other garments, as the situation permits. Lay hold of the *atarraya* (throw-net), stride without hesitation into the surf, and keenly observe. Cast the net over the first suitable fish and draw in. Kill the fish by sharp pressure of the right thumbnail (thumbnails must be kept in condition for this) on the skull. Slit, clean, skin and fillet the fish. Returning to shore, lay the fillets on a driftwood log, as free of sand as possible, but with sufficient splinters to hold the fillets firmly. Chop the fillets into pieces about 1·5 cm ($\frac{1}{2}$–$\frac{3}{4}$ inch) wide. Cut several limes and squeeze these out over the pieces of fish. (The purpose of the lime juice is to 'cook' the fish.) Eat before this has a chance to occur. The most suitable beverage is *chicha* (maize beer), partly fermented. This recipe is from the village of Matacaballo on the shore of the Sechura desert.

More Elaborate Version

Obtain fillets of a reasonably tough-fibred fish, such as red snapper. Slice these into pieces about 2×1 cm and lay in a broad, shallow glass or glazed pottery vessel. (Do not use a vessel with lead glaze.) Slice onions in sufficient quantity to make a layer covering the fish. Slice green or red chillies (chilli peppers) and lay these on top of the onions; the quantity of chillies depends strictly on their strength and one's taste for highly spiced food. If the seeds are left in the chillies, their effect is raised to the power of the number of seeds included. Do *not* touch the eyes or genitals after handling the chillies unless the hands are thoroughly washed. The reverse precaution is unnecessary. The typical Peruvian recipe covers the onions with a solid layer of chillies, seeds included. Pour over all this the juice of limes or lemons sufficient to submerge the topmost ingredients. Cover the vessel with an inverted one of identical size or with an impermeable wrapping material such as waxed paper. (Do not use aluminium foil as it might touch the lemon juice.) Let the dish stand 3–5 hours. (One should take care not to leave the cooking fish uncovered as the fumes are said to cause blindness.) The fish is done when it has been transformed by the lemon juice from its raw to its cooked state (purists may object that this is all more in the category of a salad). The excess lemon juice may be drained before serving, and the pieces of fish tastefully arranged on a platter, perhaps with the onion slices but not with the chillies. A side dish of boiled maize, on the cob, in slices about 3 cm (1¼ inches) thick, or cold sliced boiled potatoes, is appropriate.

Barbara Klamon Kopytoff

Maroon Jerk Pork and other Jamaican Cooking

The Maroons of Jamaica are descendants of slaves who escaped from British plantations in the late seventeenth and early eighteenth centuries and established their own societies in the mountainous interior of the island. There they mixed with a few ex-slaves dating from the earlier Spanish occupation of the island, and possibly with a few surviving native Arawak Indians. After a guerrilla war that exhausted both sides, the British despaired of ever defeating the Maroons and in 1739 signed peace treaties with the two major groups of them. The treaties recognized the freedom of the Maroons, allowed them self-government and established reservations on which they were to live, in return for the Maroons' recognizing the sovereignty of the Crown and agreeing to return any new runaways that tried to join them thereafter. Elsewhere in the New World similar communities of Maroons sprang up during the days of slavery, and treaties were signed between Maroons and colonial powers in a number of places; but it is only in Jamaica and the Guianas that the descendants of Maroons survive as separate and distinct groups. The Jamaican Maroons still live on the reservations granted them shortly after the treaties, ever conscious of their history as guerrilla fighters whom the British could not defeat.

In the days before the treaties, when their presence made the interior of Jamaica too dangerous for white settlers, the Maroons had the free run of the mountains. There, a favourite occupation of the men was to hunt wild hogs. Whites pursuing them sometimes found 'springes' the Maroons had set to catch hogs as the only sign of their enemy.[1] Maroons were so well known for hog-hunting that an eighteenth-century Jamaican historian, Edward Long, guessed that their name derived from the Spanish *marráno*, a young pig.[2] (The more widely accepted derivation is from the term the Spanish used for escaped slaves, *cimarrón*.) The prepared hog meat, a Maroon delicacy, was called 'jerked' hog. The early Maroons were often in want of salt, an essential ingredient for jerked hog, but they made do with[3]

141

> . . . a strong lixivium of Wood Ashes, which they accidently
> discover'd to be Salt; and by dipping their Hog . . . in the pickle
> which They made of them, and afterwards Smoaking them They were
> able to preserve their Hog . . . a considerable time.

After the treaties of 1739, Maroons had free access to the island markets and obtaining salt was never a problem, but their free-ranging hunting area was progressively limited as was the natural habitat of the wild hogs, by settlers who crowded in to occupy the formerly dangerous territory near the Maroon settlements. Nevertheless, Maroons continued to hunt hogs in the less inhabited regions of the mountains, and sold jerked hog in the island markets. Henry Gosse, writing in 1851, recalls the fine figure cut by the Maroon huntsman vending his wares:[4]

> He was generally seen in the towns armed with a fowling piece and
> cutlass, and belts that suspended on one side a large plaited bag,
> known as a *cuttacoo*, and on the other a calabash, guarded with a
> netted covering, in which he carried his supply of water. On his
> back braced round his shoulders, and suspended by a bandage over
> the forehead, was generally seen the wicker cradle, that held inclosed
> a side of jerked hog, which he sold passing along, in measured
> slice to ready customers, as an especial delicacy for the breakfast
> table.

By this time, the Maroon style of cooking wild hogs had diffused to the lowland plantations, and was used for preparing domestic pork. Matthew ('Monk') Lewis, the writer of gothic novels, described the process in his diary of a trip to Jamaica in 1815:[5]

> We had at dinner a land tortoise and a barbecued pig, two of the
> best and richest dishes that I ever tasted; – the latter, in particular,
> which was dressed in the true maroon fashion, being placed on a
> barbecue (a frame of wicker work, through whose interstices the
> steam can ascend), filled with peppers and spices of the highest
> flavour, and wrapt in plantain leaves, and then buried in a hole filled
> with hot stones, by whose vapor it is then baked, no particle of the
> juice being thus suffered to evaporate.

Since emancipation in Jamaica in 1834, the Maroon men, who had previously earned wages scouring the interior as a special police force, have had to turn more of their efforts to agriculture. They have had less time to chase wild hogs, and there have been fewer wild hogs to chase. But Maroons have adapted their recipes for wild hog to domestic pigs, which they began to keep after 1739.

The present-day method of preparing 'jerk pork' in the old style is very like that described by Lewis. Maroons will ready a suckling pig for cooking, season it inside and out with salt, pepper and pimento (allspice); stuff the cavity with cooked rice, seasoned with ginger and chopped onion; and wrap the entire pig in pimento leaves for flavour and green banana leaves for protection. Meanwhile the cooking pit is prepared; a hole is dug about two feet deep, lined with rocks, and wood fire is built in it. When the fire has burned down to coals, the unburnt wood is removed and the leaf-wrapped pig is placed in the hole, and surrounded on all sides (including the top) by live coals and hot rocks. The hole is then covered with a piece of corrugated metal, and earth put on top of that. When the pig is cooked, in three or four hours, it is unwrapped and browned over hot coals or in the oven.

When Maroons don't want to go to that much trouble for 'jerk pork', or don't have a suckling pig handy, they cook a simpler version of it in their own kitchens, which are separate structures adjoining their houses. There, they generally cook over wood fires, which lend their distinctive aroma to the food. A Maroon woman can season any piece of pork with salt, pepper, pimento, thyme, ginger, chopped onions and scallions, and when the meat has had a chance to absorb the flavours, she will hang it over the kitchen fire for a few days to let it smoke. The spicy smoked pork is then cut down as needed, bit by bit, cooked, and added as a special treat to the family's meal.

Below is a recipe for stove-top 'jerk pork', adapted for an American kitchen. It was provided, along with all the other recipes, by Shirley and Ditty Cawley, daughters of the late Colonel T. J. Cawley of the Accompong Town Maroons. While 'jerk pork' is distinctively Maroon, the other dishes are part of a wider Jamaican heritage.

Jerk Pork (stove top)

2 lb (1 kilo) or more pork, with skin
½ tsp salt
freshly ground black pepper
½ tsp pimento or allspice

½ tsp ginger
2 sprigs fresh thyme (or ½ tsp dried)
scallions, chopped
onions, chopped

Rub the meat well with half the seasonings. Let it sit a while to absorb the flavours. In a heavy casserole, brown the meat and let it cook over low heat until very tender, using 2 or 3 cups of water. When the water is down to about ¾ cup, add the remaining seasonings. Let it simmer another 15–20 minutes and serve.

This recipe may also be made with smoked pork.

Dip and Fall Back* (To serve 6)

1 dried coconut	oil for browning meat
2 cups hot water	½ tsp curry powder
1 lb (450 grams) lean pork (salted overnight)	2 sprigs thyme
	1 onion
1 lb (450 grams) salt cod	dash chilli pepper
¼ cup flour	dash black pepper

Grate the coconut very fine and pour the 2 cups of hot water over it. Allow to stand for a while and then squeeze through a strainer to express the juice. Let the juice boil in a heavy pot until it is reduced by half. Meanwhile, prepare the salt fish by boiling it in a quart of water to remove the excess salt. (It can also be de-salted by soaking overnight in cold water.) Remove the bones and skin from the cooked fish. Cut the pork in bite-sized pieces, brown it, and drain the grease. Add to the coconut juice the flour mixed to a paste with a little water, and the thyme, curry powder, sliced onion and pepper. Let it cook for another 10 minutes until thickened, then add to it the salt fish and pork. Let simmer for 15 minutes and serve over rice, potatoes, yams, breadfruit (available locally in tins), or any other starch.

Peas and Pork Soup

1 lb (450 grams) lean pork	2 stalks scallion
1 lb (450 grams) 'peas'† (dried lima, kidney or pigeon peas or beans)	dash of thyme
	dash of red pepper
2 medium-sized white potatoes	1 small onion
2 medium-sized sweet potatoes	salt to taste

Cover the 'peas' with cold water and leave overnight. Drain, and then boil the peas and pork together in 2 quarts of water until both are tender. (This should take about 2½ hours.) Add the white and sweet potatoes, diced onion and all the other ingredients at the same time. Let cook over low heat until potatoes are done.

* Also known as 'dip shake off dip come back': 'descriptive of the action of one dipping food into a sauce, which [runs] back along one's hand, or falls back into the bowl, or of which one shakes off the surplus' (*Dictionary of Jamaican English*, F. G. Cassidy and R. B. le Page (eds), Cambridge, 1963).
† In Jamaica, 'pea' refers to a red or kidney bean.

Stapee a Pass* ('Stop it halfway')

1 whole dry coconut
2 cups hot water
1 lb (450 grams) salt codfish or salt
  mackerel
1 medium onion

1 stalk scallion
dash of thyme
dash of black pepper
dash of paprika or annato

Cook the salt fish in 1 quart of water to remove the excess salt. Express the coconut milk as described in 'Dip and Fall Back'. Heat the coconut milk over low heat until the cream forms on top. Skim off the cream and place it in a Dutch oven or heavy casserole and boil over high heat. Remove the skin and bones from the cooked fish. When the coconut cream starts forming oil, remove from the fire. Add the cooked fish, broken in pieces, and the seasonings. Return to low heat and let cook another 10–15 minutes. Do not boil, as the oil will separate and the cream will then 'pass' into oil. Serve over rice, potatoes, etc.

Rabbit Jamaican Style

1 whole rabbit (minus head)
1½–2 lb (750 grams–1 kilo) herb stuffing
  (or any stuffing suitable for poultry)
3 hard-boiled eggs
1 large onion, or 2 medium-sized
1 clove garlic, finely chopped

1 tbsp vinegar
3 tbsp rum
dash allspice or ginger
2 stalks scallion
dash thyme
salt and pepper to taste

Combine all spices and seasonings (except the onion), rum and vinegar, and marinate the whole rabbit in this mixture overnight, or longer.
    Combine stuffing and hard-boiled eggs, finely chopped. Fill the cavity of the rabbit with the herb stuffing, and chopped onions.
Oven cooking: Pour any remaining marinade over the rabbit and cover, and place in the oven for 1½–2 hours at 350° (gas Mk 4).
Stove–top cooking: In a very large skillet or cast-iron casserole brown the rabbit. Remove excess fat from the pot, pour over the remaining marinade and add 3 cups boiling water. Let simmer until tender and use the stock for gravy.

* 'Stop-(-it-)-A-Pass: a sauce made with coconut, saltfish, pepper and other ingredients, but not boiled all the way down; it is stopped from "passing" – i.e. the coconut oil is prevented from separating' (*Dictionary of Jamaican English*).

Jamaican Meat Patties

3 cups (12 oz.) self-raising flour	1 tsp red pepper
1 tsp salt	1 medium onion, chopped
½ lb (220 grams) butter or margarine	dash of leaf thyme
1–1½ cups cold water	dash of black pepper
1 tsp paprika	1 cup hot water
2 lb (1 kilo) ground beef	salt to taste
2 cups soft breadcrumbs	

For the crust:
In a mixing-bowl combine the flour, ½ tsp paprika, margarine, and 1 tsp salt, knead to a medium soft dough using ½ cup of cold water.

For the filling:
Cook ground beef in a skillet on low heat, using a fork to separate it. Add salt, black pepper and thyme and stir until beef changes colour. Remove from the heat and drain off excess grease. Return to low heat and add 1 cup hot water, chopped onion, red pepper, breadcrumbs, ½ tsp paprika, stirring constantly. (Add more water for a juicier filling.)

Roll out dough to a thin crust (⅛ inch or 3 mm), a small round at a time. Place some of the filling on one half and fold over the other half over to make a semi-circular patty. Seal the edges by pressing them with a fork. Patties can be made in any size.* They are also sometimes coloured with annatto which, mixed with a little oil, is brushed on top before baking.

Bake in a medium oven (350°, gas Mk 4) until the crust is done, about 25–30 minutes.

NOTES

1   Lieutenant-Governor Molesworth to William Blathwayt, 2 November 1686, *Calendar of State Papers*, Colonial Office, America and the West Indies, vol. 2, p. 272.

2   *The History of Jamaica*, 3 vols, T. Lowndes, London, 1774, vol. 2, p. 338 n.

3   James Knight, 'The Natural, Moral, and Political History of Jamaica . . . to the Year 1742', British Museum Additional Manuscript 12419, p. 95.

4   *A Naturalist's Sojourn in Jamaica*, Longman, Brown, Green, & Longmans, London, 1851, p. 396.

5   *Journal of a West India Proprietor* . . . John Murray, London, 1834, p. 151.

* The dough could also be rolled out all at once, and rounds cut from it.

Frederica de Laguna

Fish Chowder with the Chugach Eskimos

The only Eskimo dish I know is boiled seal meat, but you are not likely to find that in the market. It should be full of blood (never bled as we do our meat), boiled in a mixture of sea and fresh water, half and half. A certain amount of blubber should be in the pot for flavouring. The meat is delicious when cooked fresh after the kill, and the broth is perhaps the best. Cold seal meat is delicious with pickles. But, of course, I've learned to like it. Some complain that it tastes of 'fish' . . . that is, not as fish themselves taste, but with the taste of animals (say ducks) that eat fish. The seal liver lacks this flavour and is as tender and delicate as calves' liver, and I've tried it. I should admit, however, that I have never learned to boil seal meat as well as the Eskimos do – nor, for that matter, as well as the Tlingit Indians do. Our tastes are similar in the matter, but I evidently don't know just how much salt and how much fresh water to use: 'half-and-half' may be just a saying. When some Tlingit Indians cooked some fresh seal on a picnic, the older woman and I agreed that the cooks hadn't added enough blubber. So I know my taste is right, even if my method isn't always perfect.

Woman steaming a crab

147

Obviously seal meat is *not* something you will find in the shops, so that and many other northern delicacies are out. It finally occurred to me that I had learnt how to make fish chowder in a simple, delicious and different way from a Chugach Eskimo woman, in the summer of 1933, when she was living at our camp as interpreter to her father, Chief Makari. This was when Dr Kaj Birket-Smith and I were collaborating on a joint archaeological-ethnological expedition to Prince William Sound, Alaska. Americans (at any rate along the Atlantic seaboard) are divided into two armed camps over the preparation of clam chowder (and my recipe would also fit clams). We changed our tastes through contact with clam-eating Indians. The New Englanders put milk in their chowder, and never tomatoes; while Manhattan chowder never has milk, but does have tomatoes. My fish chowder is best made with haddock (now, alas, scarce; though I've made it with Pacific salmon – in fact that was what 'Ma Tiedeman', the Eskimo woman, used). She always made and drank vast quantities of tea with and after the meal, since 'fishes like to swim'.

Fish Chowder

1 lb (450 grams) fish (haddock, cod) cut up and filleted	1 onion, finely sliced
about 4 or 5 strips fat bacon, cut in small pieces	2 oz. (60 grams) macaroni
	salt to taste

Start bacon and onion in bottom of heavy kettle, stirring and cooking until onion gets soft and yellow. Don't burn. Then add pieces of fish, and no more than ¼ cup of macaroni (about 60 grams, or 2 oz.): elbow-style is easiest – otherwise break it up. Ma just liked to throw in 'macaronis, spaghettis, and rice' – but I think that's too much. Don't add potatoes, for they soak up the flavour. Add salt to taste. Cook slowly until macaroni has swelled. You will probably have to keep adding water. Eat with hard tack. (What's left over is always better the next day, because, as Huck Finn said, 'The juices get swopped round.')

Although the recipe for chowder was given me by a Chugach Eskimo woman, chowder itself is not an Eskimo dish. It is a stew containing vegetables, and, usually, seafood. Since the Eskimos aboriginally had no vegetables (except for those who lived far enough south to get berries), their food was almost exclusively meat and fish. Even though this was boiled, we would not call boiled fish 'chowder'.*

* Chowder was introduced to the US settlers by the French: the word is derived from *chaudière*, the fish-kettle in which the dish was cooked. [See R. Tannahill, *Food in History*, Stein & Day, 1973 (ed.).]

Stephen Hugh-Jones

Amazonian Smoked Fish and Meat— a technique from the Barasana Indians of the Vaupés region of Colombia*

(and frogs and ants and caterpillars and termites and beetle larvae and chilli peppers and whatever-you-like)

The anthropological literature refers to this culinary technique as 'smoking' (see especially Lévi-Strauss, *The Culinary Triangle*), but in fact, as practised in Amazonia, it lies half-way between smoking food as we know it and the more conventional grilling or roasting. What follows is more of a description of a cooking technique than the typical recipe listing ingredients and providing instructions on how to combine them.

In Amazonia the smoking rack is either square or triangular. It is made from lengths of thin, green sapling bound with vine onto a frame of green wood (see illustration). Unless you wish to be very 'ethnic' and use authentic materials, the rack can be made from any piece of wire netting or grid supported on four upright sticks. The sticks should be green, otherwise they will burn. The height of the rack above the fire depends in part upon the size of the fire; that is determined by the amount of fish or meat to be smoked. Large hunks of meat need a big fire with the rack fairly high off the ground; small sprats need a small fire and a low rack. The rack must always be higher than the largest flames produced by the fire. In general, a rack around 3 or 4 feet from the ground will suffice.

Sprat-size fish are usually left ungutted and are smoked whole, often threaded through their eyes in rows on a long stick. (Frogs are threaded in a similar way, but through their jaws.) Larger fish are gutted, although not usually scaled. Meat is cut into pieces no more than 3 to 4 inches thick, for if one attempted larger pieces, the insides might begin to rot before the smoking process was completed. But the legs of young pigs can be smoked whole. (Although the Barasana themselves never flavour the food, it may be worth inserting slivers of garlic, herbs or spices into the meat before smoking it.)

The fish or meat is simply placed on the rack and left to smoke slowly over a low fire. The time it takes to cook depends on the thickness of the

* This cooking technique applies more or less across all of Amazonia.

material concerned. Small fish take about 6 hours, herring-sized fish about a day, larger fish even longer. Large chunks of meat might take up to three or four days (and nights) of continuous smoking. The time taken is also determined by whether one simply wishes to cook the food for immediate eating, or to store it. If the food is to be stored, it is left on the rack till it is dry and brittle.

The Barasana usually allow smoked food to become cold before eating – but it tastes good hot as well. Fresh-smoked food is generally eaten as it is, together with cassava bread and a condiment made from smoked chilli peppers pounded in a mortar with salt. Dry-smoked food that has been stored is usually first soaked in cold water, then boiled in water to which smoked chilli peppers are added. The resulting stew is eaten with cassava bread.

Smoking-rack with fish

There is a problem: the Barasana smoke much of their food inside the house and when they do it outside, wind direction is not a problem. When we tried smoking food in England, it was very hard to get the smoke to go anywhere near the food and this made us aware of how windless Amazonia is. But elsewhere one must either choose very still days or construct a screen of old sacks, etc., around the fire.

The reader need not bother to cut the firewood into neat lengths. Instead, lay the ends of the wood together in a star, light the fire and gradually push the ends of the logs into the fire as they burn away.

Aurore Monod-Becquelin

Three Recipes from the Trumai Indians*

You can eat fishpaste provided that you have not just had a baby or are menstruating and that you are not a new father, a recent murderer, or a youth undergoing his initiation during the 'period of the three rocks'. For this dish you need a number of small freshwater fish, either scaly or smooth. *Xui-xui* (*Acara, Ciclidae* family), *iue* (*Curimata, Eritrinidae* fam.), *kutapolak* (*Peixe Pintado, Pimelodidae* fam.), *titlekte* (*Piranha, Caracidae* fam.) are some of those used by the Trumai.

Fishpaste or Paté (*K'ate toxnol*)

Gut the fish, but do not remove the heads or tails. Place them in a pot, cover them with water and cook over a wood fire. As the flesh begins to come away from the bone, add a small amount of manioc (cassava) flour and *iakyr* (waterlily salt). *Torek*, the flour, is obtained by filtering the liquid in which some pulp of bitter manioc has been washed and leaving the remains to dry in the form of a cake, from which one sifts small pieces to thicken and give a smooth consistency to various dishes. Non-Indians are advised to use a suitable alternative such as maize flour or cornflour because the treating of bitter manioc is a tradition requiring knowledge and extreme care. (Manioc contains a high proportion of composites of cyanide fatal to the consumer.)

Iakyr, the salt (in liquid form), is taken from the ashes of dried and burnt waterlily leaves. Eliminate charcoal and other impurities by rinsing with water, and boil down what remains with some water in a pot until the quantity is reduced. Crush a few red peppers with a pestle, and add them to the mixture.

Torek and *iakyr* are mixed into the fishpaste, which is then reheated for a short time. Use a gourd to help you to place some of this mixture on a manioc pancake (made with manioc flour and fried on a plaque of heated clay). Other types of pancakes can be made with rice or wheat flour.

* A tribe located in the rainforests of Upper Xingù, Brazil.

151

Even though the Trumai regard all neighbouring tribes as 'savages' in culinary arts, they have nevertheless borrowed from them a number of culinary customs, including the preparation of game and intestines, which they normally do not do.

Tripe Cooked in Banana Leaves (a more exotic recipe from the Txukahamae)

First kill a wild pig – *mandašatorek* (*Porco queixado, Dycotiles labiatus* fam.) – carry it back to the village, cut off the head (allowing the blood to run freely) and then dismember the animal and place the pieces on a large meat-smoker under which a quantity of wood has previously burnt. The bristles will char immediately, but the meat will take about half a day to cook. The meat can remain on the smoker for as many days as it takes to cook it, but care should be taken to eat the parts near the belly and ribs first as they rot fastest.

To prepare the innards:
Wash the intestines first with great care. Clean the bowel and turn it inside out; discard the gall-bladder, lungs and head. Divide the tripe into small pieces and wrap them in banana leaves, which should be folded two or three times and placed on the meat-smoker at the same time as the rest of the meat. Turn them after 2 hours and allow the other side to cook. When they are ready, unfold the leaves and eat the tripe with a manioc pancake, with or without red-pepper juice according to taste.

Honey-Cake

Take some manioc flour (*ole paraty*) or cornflour (*otet*) and add enough water to make a soft dough. Add wild honey taken from the forest (the Trumai know over twenty varieties of bees and many different kinds of honey both edible and poisonous). On the earth stove normally used for making manioc pancakes place some banana leaves, overlapping each other, and spread them with the honey mixture until the cake is two fingers high. When the base has cooked, cover the top with banana leaves, and with the help of a wooden spatula turn the cake over. Honey-cake can be eaten either hot or cold.

I shall attempt to characterize the above three recipes in accordance with Trumai thought-processes in general. For while the food of the Indians in Upper Xingù is not sophisticated and does not involve detailed rituals of any sort, nevertheless, the methods of preparation – either by roasting or boiling – and the individual ingredients – manioc, fish, meat, salt, honey and red pepper – are invested with symbolic meaning in the kitchen, and can be directly related to different levels in their thought systems.

It may be helpful to describe an aspect of this logical system with reference to a diagram which summarizes the food prohibitions. For women, as

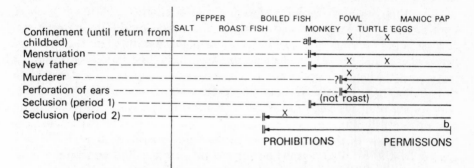

Salt: pepper, roast fish, boiled fish, monkey, fowl, turtle eggs, manioc pap

$a \|$: = tispan, *that is to say 'prohibitive prescription', 'limit of permission'.*

b: *The limit of proscription – from prohibition to permission – regulates equally (and together with other domains of life) sexual consummation and the use of various types of language.*

x: *recommended food.*

can be seen, the blood is the barrier against fish. This is corroborated by the fact that a woman expecting a child, who therefore no longer bleeds, can eat only fishpaste. She cannot eat meat or other hard foods which are considered bad for the unborn child (this is discussed later). For men, the stages of death are the points of reference for proscriptions in both dietary and other forms. The strictest prohibitions are those relating to *ritual death*. The same total immobility and silence are imposed on a child who has just had his ears pierced and on a warrior who has killed *a* man. They lie in both cases in a hammock with their arms and legs straightened out. A greater licence is allowed those in the state of *temporary death*. Here the new father and the adolescent boy in seclusion are confined to a limited space and are able to speak only in whispers. More liberal still are the rules concerning *rebirth*, when the youth in seclusion leaves his shelter progressively finally to enter into adult society. Before this, his parents fish for him and he is allowed to eat boiled fish only; after rebirth, he fishes for himself and can eat whatever he catches. Blood and death – situations in which food prohibitions operate

– also separate what the Trumai call 'savouries' from 'insipid' food; salt and pepper are described roughly in their language as 'having taste', and everything lacking this taste is considered to be unpalatable, difficult to eat – in other words bland food, 'without salt, without pepper, without taste, without everything', as one food-loving Trumai spoke ruefully about the diet observed during couvade.

To this 'savoury/insipid' polarity is added another, 'hard/soft', where both means of cooking and certain parts of the food repertoire are relevant. A roast is hard and as such forbidden to shamans and initiates; the eyes and heads of fish and the bones of meats are also 'hard' and therefore forbidden to pregnant women; thus roasted fish represents a more permissive stage than boiled fish. Finally we note that each kind of food proscribed has its appropriate remedy, *oke*, most often in the form of a root juice to be drunk raw or cooked. Bitter roots, considered strong and highly dangerous, are followed by sweet roots which enable the body to rid itself of the toxins caused by the former, permitting one to break the taboo and return once again to the customs of everyday life.

From what has been said, it is clear that we should place the first and last recipes in the category of everyday food available to all those who are not in a situation socially marked by blood or death; the second recipe probably ought to be put into another category altogether, as it does not form part of Trumai cooking. Only fowl and monkey are traditional foods of the Trumai.

One of the features of Trumai thought is its refined socialization of distance. In many of its manifestations, distance is carefully staked out by the tribal rituals, by rules for preparing ceremonies, by the syntax of possessing – both close possession and far-off relationships – and by various types of language use. We will be content here only with the example of the spoken word, drawing an analogy between this and cooking. Our justification for this parallel is the fact that in both cases there is a distance that separates a danger from its opposite, the absence of danger. In communication, the greatest danger – whether it concerns incest, injuries towards the spirits or the risks of death – is expressed, so to speak, by silence. The rules are rigorous, and the danger of the word can be avoided only by the non-word. On the other hand, the opposite of danger – that is to say, the continuation of inter-tribal solidarity which is indispensable to the survival of the different tribes in this part of the Upper Xingù – is expressed in the form of inverted discourse; by saying exactly the opposite of something, they unveil it ritually. As middle points on this continuum we find *reserved discourse*, which is either modest in content or actually whispered, and which is appropriate to particular roles (initiates, leaders, shamans); and *parodic discourse*, in which mockery has a regulatory value, whether between tribes, when they laugh at one another's customs, or in the 'joking relationships' that are obligatory between cross-cousins who are future brothers-in-law.

Thus we can show that the culinary code follows the same logic as other codes along this axis of danger, marking the continuum from danger to its avoidance by a series of gastronomic stages. Modes of speech and modes of cooking are a measure of one's position in relation to danger. It is necessary to season one's discourse as one seasons a sauce, by means of rules.

Alan R. Holmberg

Cooking and Eating among the Siriono of Bolivia

Preparation of Food

Little care is taken in dressing game, which is done either by men or women. Animals with hair, such as monkeys and peccaries, are first singed whole in the fire, and the burned hair is then scraped off with the fingernails or with a small section of a midrib of a motacú palm leaf. The animal is then gutted with a sharp piece of bamboo, after which the whole carcass is sometimes (but by no means always) perfunctorily washed before it is cooked. Birds are hastily plucked and then singed in the fire and gutted. If an animal is small it is usually cooked whole, but if it is too large for a pot (or too large to roast rapidly) it is quartered or cut up into smaller pieces with a bamboo knife. Armoured animals like the armadillo and tortoise are usually thrown in the fire and left there to roast in their shells. Fish are never gutted before they are cooked, nor are the scales removed.

The division of labour as regards cooking varies a great deal, depending upon the circumstances under which the food is being prepared. Everyone knows how to cook, even young children.

Cooking is an art learned very early in life. When travelling with his mother and father, a child is often given a cob of corn to roast, some motacú fruits to roast or a morsel of viscera to cook for himself. In fact, whenever animals are being cut up, there are always young children (as often boys as girls) around, waiting for some tidbit which they then take to the fire and roast for themselves. Such morsels they share with no one else. [. . .]

No condiments of any kind are used in cooking. Even salt (no deposits of this product are found in the area) is unknown to the Siriono living under aboriginal conditions. [. . .]

I introduced salt to some Indians for the first time, and they expressed a distaste for eating it. By using small quantities in cooking, however, they soon developed a craving for it. In some instances this craving (once the Indians have become accustomed to using salt) has become so great as to become an

156

important factor in establishing and maintaining friendly relations with the whites. [. . .]

Actually little emphasis is placed on the preparation of food. Depending upon the time, place, type and quantity of game, it may be roasted or baked in the ashes of the fire, broiled on a spit or babracot [barbecue] or boiled or steamed in a clay pot. Some vegetable foods, such as maize, are prepared by grinding before they are cooked, and, of course, many nuts and fruits are eaten raw. [. . .]

Eating

It is difficult to establish a schedule of meal hours among the Siriono because of the insecure nature of the food supply and the nomadic character of life. People eat when they have food, and under these conditions they are just as apt to eat during the night as during the day. [. . .]

The principal meal is always taken in the later afternoon or early evening. Other eating is mainly of the between-meal type, and occurs at all hours of the day or night. I was constantly surprised to find, throughout my residence among the Siriono, that food which had been left over from an evening meal was invariably gone by morning. [. . .]

The habit of eating during the night grows not only out of the necessity of hunting and collecting during most of the day but also out of a reluctance to share food with others. When meals are taken during the day, a crowd of non-family members always gathers to beg for morsels, and though little attention is usually paid to them, they do, nevertheless, constitute an annoyance. By eating at odd hours during the night, when nearly everyone else is asleep, an Indian not only gets more food but also avoids the nuisance of having others around to beg it from him.

While I was on the march with the Siriono . . . a few of my loyal Indian companions, who developed a certain interest in my welfare, used frequently to wake me in the middle of the night to share food which they hated to display during the daytime because of the possibility of their having to divide it with someone else. [. . .]

Eating takes place without benefit of etiquette or ceremony. Food is bolted as rapidly as possible, and when a person is eating he never looks up from his food until he has finished . . . The principal goal of eating seems thus to be the swallowing of the greatest quantity of food in the shortest possible time.

Appetites for particular foods are few. There is a preference for meat over all other foods and a preference for fat meat over lean meat, but the cookbook of the Siriono is almost devoid of recipes.

South-East Asia, Ceylon and Japan: 'Rice with Everything'

When the army proceeds on service . . . they carry but little with them . . . They subsist for the most part upon milk . . . Should circumstances render it necessary, in the execution of a duty that requires despatch, they can march for ten days together without dressing victuals, during which time they subsist upon the blood drawn from their horses, each man opening a vein and drinking from his own cattle. They make provision also of milk thickened and dried to the state of a hard paste (or curd) which is prepared in the following manner. They boil the milk, and skimming off the rich or creamy part as it rises to the top, put it into a separate vessel as butter; for so long as that remains in the milk, it will not become hard. The latter is then exposed to the sun until it dries. Upon going on service they carry with them about ten pounds for each man, and of this, half a pound is put, every morning, into a leathern bottle, or small *outre*, with as much water as is thought necessary. By their motion in riding the contents are violently shaken, and a thin porridge is produced, upon which they make their dinner. (*The Travels of Marco Polo*, chapter XLIX, 'Of the Tartar Army')

Jaques Dournes

Time and Menu

. . . with mouths apt to laughter, and to eating, and drinking. And laugh they did, and eat, and drink, often and heartily.
(J. R. R. Tolkien)

So-called primitive people are not necessarily under-nourished. In the Vietnamese Highlands I never saw anyone hungry; there is an abundance of various foods (when it is not destroyed by warriors, and if one excepts the abnormal situation in concentration camps for uprooted indigenous minorities). Those who were once called 'savages', the men of the forest, appear as *bons vivants*, like the lovely Hobbits.

I could describe at length particular recipes or exotic meals, such as fried termites, roasted grubs or red ant soup. Indeed, exquisite culinary pleasures though they may be, many western palates might not be tempted, unless they were brought to try them. Consequently, I shall limit myself to the presentation of several basic recipes and then go on to something more fundamental.

The rice which is generally consumed by the Jörai – as opposed to that of the Lao, for example – is not sticky; after cooking, the grains are not reduced to the thick paste often served on western tables. Glutinous rice is not a consequence of the preparation, but of the botanical variety of paddy (*Oryza sativa*, var. *glutinosa*).

For a family of five or six take a gallon pot, two-thirds full of water, and put it on the fire. Add two or three handfuls of small round aubergines (two smallish aubergines) already cut into halves, as well as a large handful of whole red or green peppers. Let it boil until it overflows, sprinkle lightly with salt, and stir. If you have any snails, you can add them as well (in their shells) after washing. Let boil for ten minutes; when the excess water is evaporated, you can serve. If you prefer you may mash the aubergines, in which case serve the snails separately.

All the meals and their ingredients are locally produced, with the exception of salt. If you have none, there is a process by which it may be replaced: take a gourd, cut off both ends, stop up the neck with a corn cob, and fill it with the ashes of amaranthus and other plants, mixed to taste. You then pour water over the ashes. The liquid which flows from the porous stopper may then be added to the cooking water, thus seasoned.

Another sort of seasoning may suffice to accompany the rice: pick a number of daisy-type flowers, dry and burn them and collect the ashes. Mix them with millet and papaya, and add either sesame seed or amaranthus. Powder and serve.

There is, however, one subtle chapter which should not be neglected in any useful cookbook: how to plan a meal: the organization, the menu. In the present case, I think, recipes (however odd) are less pertinent than the ordering, the nature of the dishes less typical than the structure of the menu. This new kind of speciality may be to the taste of the most delicate reader.

We shall see how the dishes are ordered by the Jörai people (an Austronesian or 'Malayo–Indonesian' ethnic group in central Indochina) and, in this way, learn something of their mental disposition. One might extend this analysis to the majority of the Indochinese minorities; but specialists are jealous people, and so I limit myself to the boundaries of the Jörai territory.

Rice is the basic food – as is very common in South-East Asia. Meat (taken here to include flesh, fish, vegetables, indeed all kinds of food except cooked rice) serves only as an accompaniment. There is one verbal form for 'eat-rice', another for 'consume-meat'; the subject of the latter may be animal or human, while the former activity is proper to mankind when eating rice, the food *par excellence*, never mixed with anything else (neither salt in the cooking-pot nor sauce in individual bowls) because 'she' is noble and sufficient. Pets are fed with rice mixed, in their case, with remnants of the meal, so they 'consume', not 'eat'. Small children are allowed to put some meat upon the rice in their bowls and take it away to eat outside, since they are not yet fully-fledged members of society.

Rice is cooked in a big pot, meat in a smaller one (or two). Then the family takes its meal. They sit together on a mat, and each holds his bowl. The housewife serves the rice from the pot (left near the fire) into the individual bowls. Meat is served in small plates which are put in the centre – for example, a plate of aubergine cooked with snails, one of dried salted fish, another of raw polygonum with chilli. These plates are not handed around; everyone helps himself from the dish he chooses, using three fingers or two bamboo sticks. So it is not the dish which goes to you, but you who go to the dish, while with the rice the opposite happens.

The whole menu is presented at one time, can be seen at a single glance; appreciating the variety of colours, the differences of flavour, you may select what you like, when you like, and savour the rice at your convenience. Jörai meals include neither *entrée* nor dessert; all dishes are presented together, ordered in space, not time. When they are eating, Jörai people do not drink or talk; you may drink before and after but not during a meal, which must not be interrupted but is usually taken quickly – like the sexual act of a married couple; and both acts are concerned rather with the completion of natural functions than with the satisfaction of any hedonistic tendency.

The Jörai people take such a meal twice a day, at home – or sometimes in the ricefield – when the woman who is head of the family (no man is ever head) calls her husband and children to meet.

And between meals? The Jörai do not like gaps. They fill them in with consuming, communicating, drinking, smoking and talking, 'often and heartily'. Going to the forest you may 'consume' (not 'eat') many fruits (90 per cent are edible), the more acid or astringent, the more enjoyable (only very young people prefer sweet things); or you may find some insects, rodents or birds and roast and consume them on the spot, merely from greed, without hunger. Visiting, or receiving friends, fellows, neighbours, you will delight together in relishing a mango or papaya pounded with salt and chilli – very hot delicacies. There is no special time or place for that, and it may be done by day or night, normally outside (in opposition to the regular meal, eaten inside the house by the family); but it is a time for speech and for the pipe, gossiping and smoking tobacco for pleasure, free and informal. Food consumed in this manner is compatible with speech and with smoking, and it is a leisurely activity – like flirtation, which includes, moreover, music and song.

The Jörai meal is continuous (synchronic); the other occasions of consumption act to re-establish a continuum, filling the gaps between the meals. Jörai society approves of discrete people but not discrete events; this is a feature of the culture.

Let me now outline a model of a French dinner, seen from the Jörai point of view; in that way we shall see more clearly some characteristic differences. You are sitting on a rigid chair before a rigid table, between two rigid persons. A dish is served, but you are never able to know what will be served after, you have no choice, you cannot combine tastes. The menu is imposed; worse, the housewife compels you to take your share of each dish, and to take again; sometimes she serves dictatorially onto your plate, and you must eat it all, even if you dislike it. Wine is poured into your glass; if you do not drink during the meal you will appear to be odd, and this will cause comment. At table people talk, talk loudly, talk throughout. The dinner takes such a long time that people smoke cigarettes after each dish. If you are bored you cannot leave; belching is also forbidden.

You eat too much at one time, and after that you have nothing to eat, nothing to do with your mouth. Eating and not-eating are separated, as are the dishes at the dinner. French people like discontinuities, they are fond of discrete things, but they are not too discreet.

Western dishes are considered as entities, for themselves, each one like a *term*, without context, like a performance by itself without reference to the next dish or to the individual being served, whereas Jörai dishes are savoured as *relations* (particularly relations between tastes) and in relation to the context, as musical intervals, rather than notes.

Words in a Jörai phrase act in the same manner; their relative position produces meaning, which is intelligible through context and connotations. But discourse (oral, of course, in languages without writing) is necessarily diachronic, discontinuous, extended through time – in opposition to the continuous meal, so they cannot go together; you eat (in space) *or* you talk (in time). The French dinner being diachronic, eating and talking are compatible.

Sitting at a French table our savage was shocked by an imposed programme and the discrete succession of dishes; he suffered from the gaps and the lack of free choice. The imposition of boundaries ('divide and rule') and authoritative power are both male affairs (even when practised by women). There can be no imperialism without hierarchy or male/female primacy, as is the case among the Jörai, who are not aware of such dichotomies.

It seems – not only to me – that such contrasts in sociocultural features may be superimposed upon other contrasts, such as the spirit of geometry *versus* the spirit of *finesse*, or digital *versus* analog communication.

Note that a set of cultural features is not to be reified as a fixed pattern, determined once and for all. In every living culture change occurs, through its internal potential for adaptation and processes of degradation; and these may be aggravated by external influences. Thus the spread of the imperialist, technical, civilization has already modified the status of women as well as the organization of meals, introducing succession and speech, both expressions of male power, among the more radically colonized groups.

A menu is not a trivial affair; it may be a political matter. We have seen it as an expression in a particular domain (the culinary), a projection on a plan (the table) of an arrangement in the mind.

Alan Davidson

Fish in Laos

The people of Laos include nearly sixty ethnic groups, of which the majority are hill-tribes in the northern parts of the country. The ethnic Lao who inhabit the northern bank of the Mekong and its attendant plains and valleys are by far the largest groups. These are the people who are usually meant when reference is made to 'the Lao', although the term is also used loosely to cover all the inhabitants of the country (for whom the right name is Laotians) and in a general way to denote all the ethnic Lao (of whom the majority live outside Laos, in north-eastern Thailand and the south of China).

The Lao are famed for their amiable characteristics and tolerant, easy-going attitudes. The dominant religion is Buddhism, mixed up with elements of spirit-worship in various forms. The former is immediately visible to the visitor (or has been up to 1975, when the kingdom became the People's Democratic Republic of Laos and a societal revolution was beginning under the auspices of the victorious Pathet Lao). Buddhist monks were to be seen everywhere, filing through the streets in the morning in their saffron robes to receive offerings of food from the willing population, teaching or meditating in the numerous *wats*.* Signs of spirit-worship were less evident, but anyone staying for any length of time in Laos would come to realize how much of the daily life of the Lao, especially but not exclusively in the rural areas, was governed directly or indirectly by this other set of beliefs and customs.

Eating Habits

The easy-going attitudes of the Lao are reflected in their eating habits, which are marked by hospitality and informality and unmarred by any feelings of hurry, anxiety or ostentation. Such, at least, is the impression received by an occidental visitor if he is fortunate enough to be invited into a Lao home. He

* A *wat* is a precinct within which stands a pagoda, together with living and working accommodation for the monks.

will find the food laid out all together on a table, or on a mat on the floor, and that each person helps himself and eats in what appears to be a completely relaxed way.

In fact, however, the relaxed atmosphere invests procedures which are surprisingly formal. These have been described by Dr Amphay Doré in his forthcoming book *De l'Hibiscus à la frangipane*. (Dr Doré belongs to Luang Prabang, the royal capital – until 1975 – of Laos, is of mixed Lao-French parentage and has been able to combine his intimate knowledge of a Lao community from the inside with the expertise in sociology which studies in France conferred upon him. It is fortunate that someone so gifted and so well qualified has been able to record his knowledge of a people about whom very little has so far been published.)

Dr Doré explains that in Lao life the concept of *piep* (which may be loosely translated as 'prestige') is of fundamental importance. Similarly, the concept of *lieng* (feeding, giving nourishment) is a basic one which includes what might be called contractual obligations. Whenever a Lao eats a meal he must do so in a manner which respects the first of these concepts; and whenever he eats outside his own home he must respect them both.

This means, in practice, that at a family meal the father and mother (being the persons of highest rank in the family unit) take the first mouthfuls, followed by the other family members in descending order of age. Once this 'first tasting' has been accomplished, the meal appears to be free for all, but in fact is still subject to rules, for example that no one should help himself at the same time as anyone else or go in front of a person of higher rank, which would cause that person to lose *piep*.

A guest must observe the same rules, and also additional ones. If he begins to eat without first being invited to do so by his host or hostess, he will be deemed to have no *piep* at all. (The logic here is that it is only someone who has nothing who is entitled to appropriate what belongs to others.) He may not continue eating after the others have finished. If he is still hungry, it will be necessary for at least one member of the household to continue eating with him. However, even so, he cannot go on indefinitely, for custom requires that he should leave something on his plate. If he were not to do so, the host's *piep* would suffer, since it would seem that he had not provided enough.

It follows from this last point that the Lao practice is to prepare more food than will be consumed. Moreover, they never know when guests will appear, since relations and (in the towns) people from their own village are apt to appear without notice and must be fed. I recall being told by a member of one of the formerly powerful families in Laos that he had to be ready to feed (and indeed lodge) as many as several scores of people in his house in Vientiane, since he came from a southern town which provided a steady stream of visitors to the capital.

Food

As for the food itself, there are several general points to be noted. Rice is the staple food and the Lao are notoriously fond of sticky rice, which has more 'body' to it than the ordinary kinds. They take it from little panniers and knead it into small balls which can be used like pieces of bread. Another staple is *padek*, a fermented fish product which is akin to the famous *nuoc mam* of Vietnam but which incorporates chunks of fish and which has (although not to Lao nostrils) a more noisome aroma. It is extensively used as a flavouring, but also serves to provide protein. The usual sources of protein – fish, meat, poultry, eggs – are available and are supplemented by unconventional ones such as lizards and snakes (the Lao being more nearly omnivorous, so it seems to me, than any other people of the world). But meat and poultry are relatively expensive and the Lao will often or indeed usually make a meal of sticky rice, vegetables and *padek*.

Fish

Fish, of course, is far more important in the South-East Asian countries than in the western world. About 250 species are indigenous to Laos, land-locked though it is, and some of them abound in such quantity that they never cost much. It is unfortunate that the best of them all (and best by far, in a class by itself) does not abound at all but, on the contrary, seems about to become extinct.

This species is *Pangasianodon gigas*, the giant catfish of the Mekong, called *pa beuk* by the Lao. It is certainly the second largest freshwater fish in the world and may even nowadays, be the largest. Its length can be as much as 3 metres, its weight 250 to 300 kilos. (It is not easy to weigh these fish, as I found when I took possession of the entire head of one in the village of Ban Houei Sai, up by the 'golden triangle' where Laos abuts on Burma and China. I was able eventually to place it on the luggage scale in the tiny office which Royal Air Lao then operated in the village, and it registered 49·5 kilos. The whole fish could not possibly have been weighed there.) In times gone by, this huge fish, which is found only in the Mekong, was fairly plentiful; but in the last few years the number taken annually has dwindled to forty, thirty or twenty, and perhaps in 1976 even fewer. This is sad, as it is a noble fish and a mysterious one, revered by the Lao.

Until recently an elaborate ceremonial accompanied the annual fishing for the *pa beuk* at a deep pool called Ang Ton Nong Chao (the Golden Basin or the Lord's Lake) in front of the village of Ban Ang, upstream from Vientiane. The fullest account of this ceremonial has been given by F. H. Giles, whose paper makes fascinating reading.[1]

Each year at the season of the falling of the waters, the people living in the vicinity of the Golden Basin, the home of the Pla Buk [Giles

uses the Thai name] join together for the purpose of catching these
fish. The observances, rites and ceremonies in connection with this
catching commence on the 8th waxing of the 3rd month and continue
till the 12th waxing. The netting of these fish is carried out from dawn
to midday every day, from the 12th to the 15th waxing of the moon
. . . The ceremonies connected with the taking of these fish are ancient
and have been performed from time immemorial, and carried out
once a year. There are several important Spirit Chiefs who have the
duty of guarding over that portion of the river . . . who must be
propitiated by offerings of food and drink in order to obtain their
help and favour, before the catching of the fish can take place.

After listing the spirit of Siri Mangala, the spirit known as the Golden Swan,
the spirit Chao Dan and the spirit of the Golden Basin, Giles goes on to give
all the details of the propitiatory rites. Thus the Spirit of the Golden Basin
required a procession of boats conveying swords, water gourds, trays of
betel-nuts and leaves, pieces of silver and of beeswax, green coconuts, sweetmeats, candles, incense tapers, sandalwood flowers, a gong and two flutes, all
to be offered to the Spirit with suitable music and incantations.

A similar ceremonial attitude applied to the construction of boats and
nets and to the manner of fishing. One wonders how the fishermen, pre-
occupied by the need to do everything right, could devote the necessary
attention to the actual catching of a fish. They would be further distracted by
the requirement that they should hurl abuse at each other throughout the
fishing: 'O, bald-headed fool; O, ancients in thy dotage. A dog shall lie
with thy mother. I will lie with thy mother. O, Friend, let me lie with thy
wife . . .', and so on. Yet fish were caught. The popular story is that these
ceremonies died out because the appearance of motor boats on the river
disturbed the conditions which had previously encouraged the *pa beuk* to
make the Ang into a sort of headquarters.

Although the rites are no longer observed, popular belief in the magic
nature of the fish persists. It is still sometimes called *pa phi*, meaning spirit
or devil fish. And people at Luang Prabang still relate a story about an
occasion many years ago when the King of Laos caught a *pa beuk* and was
advised to cut it up on the spot so that the local *phi* (spirit) could eat some.
His Majesty preferred to take it first to a near-by village; but the engine of
his boat caught fire on the way. This, it is made clear, was only to be expected.

The above long digression will have served to show that food is used by
the Lao in their ceremonial practices. A whole book could be (and I hope
will be) written on this aspect. But it is time to revert to food as food and to
offer the reader a Lao recipe which is capable of being used elsewhere. There
are not many such recipes; and practically nothing has been written about
Lao cookery. The only substantial and authentic collection of Lao recipes
which exists is contained in two manuscript notebooks which were compiled

by Phia Sing, the late royal chef. These cry out to be turned into a book. Meanwhile I have had the privilege of publishing a number of his admirable recipes in translation.[2] I reproduce below what seem to be the only two for which all the ingredients can be obtained outside Laos. (For the fish sauce, use *nuoc mam* or, if you can't find that, anchovy essence. If you lack banana leaf, use foil – the banana-leaf flavour will be missing, but this is not essential.)

The *Cahiers* of Phia Sing contain two versions of the recipe for steamed fish eggs, numbered 57 and 104. They are almost identical, but the former is slightly clearer, while the latter has a footnote which the other lacks. I present, therefore, recipe 57 with the addition of the footnote to 104.

Steamed Fish Eggs (*Mok khay pa*)*

1 soup-bowlful of fish eggs, which have been stirred in water with a little salt
    so as to separate the eggs (½ pint/285 ml)
1 piece of fish meat, boned and minced, quantity equivalent in size to a duck egg
pork fat, minced, volume equivalent to a hen egg
1 dried red chilli pepper, seeded and
    soaked in water or ½ tsp chilli powder } chopped and pounded together
5 shallots
2 or 3 spring onions, chopped
2 or 3 very small fresh red or green chilli peppers
salt
nam pa (fish sauce)

Take the minced fish and the minced pork fat and mix them together with the ground chilli pepper and shallots. When they are well mixed, combine them with the bowlful of fish eggs. Add salt and fish sauce to taste. Add also the spring onion and the small chillies, and mix well.

Take a piece of banana leaf, roll up the mixture in it and fasten the package with a 'bamboo string' (such as is used for tying packages in the market).

The package is then steamed in a steamer until it is cooked. Then take the package out of the steamer, open it and serve the contents on a plate.

Savoury Steamed Fish (*Mok pa*)

2 lb (1 kilo) (cleaned weight) of catfish, preferably *pa nang* or *pa kot* (a good
    western substitute would be whiting)
3 stalks lemon grass or 3 tsp 'Sereh' powder or citronella
3 shallots
1 head garlic

* This *mok khay pa* usually needs the small chilli peppers and the pork fat; otherwise the fish eggs would set too hard. If you don't like them, take them out, but this is not the way to cook *mok khay pa*.

2 tsps chopped galingale
1 tsp salt
½ tsp monosodium glutamate (MSG)
2 soupspoonsful *nam pa* (fish sauce)
3 cups coconut cream (thick, or a mixture of thick and thin)
6 eggs, beaten
5 or 6 leaves of *mak khi hout* (Kaffir lime) – this is not the same as ordinary lime,
    and can be omitted
1 or 2 tsps chopped dill leaves

Clean the fish and cut the flesh into serving pieces or bite-size pieces, as you prefer.
Finely chop the lemon grass. Chop the shallots. Peel the cloves of garlic (you should
have 6 to 8 from one head) and chop them too. Put these ingredients in a
mortar with the chopped galingale and pound them.

Add the pounded mixture to the pieces of fish and season it all with the salt,
MSG and *nam pa*. Then add the coconut cream and the beaten eggs. Mix all
together.

Now you will need three rectangles of banana leaf. (If they are from a freshly
cut leaf, hold them one at a time and for a few seconds only over a fire so as to
soften them and to eliminate the risk that they will break during the cooking.)
If these are not available, foil can be used. Lay these one on top of the other,
and then deposit the fish mixture in the middle, with fragments of lime leaf and
a little chopped dill sprinkled on top. Fold the banana leaves up and over and
secure them with a piece of split bamboo.

Steam this package for half an hour. Then remove it from the steamer, undo
it and transfer the contents to a serving dish. *Mok pa* is served with plenty of
rice, which may be sticky or non-sticky.

In the south of Laos the beaten eggs would be omitted and the cooked mixture
would therefore be less set and more liquid. However, the amount of coconut
cream used would be much less.

NOTES

1   'An account of the ceremonies and rites performed when catching the
    Pla Buk', *Journal of the Siam Society*, 28, 1935, pp. 91–113.
2   *Fish and Fish Dishes of Laos*, Vientiane, 1975.

Kristina Lindell and Damrong Tayanin

Kammu Dishes

The Kammu live high up on the mountain slopes of northern Laos and Thailand. Although they live in the tropics, temperatures in their villages fall to near freezing-point during the cold season. Their pile houses, constructed mainly from split bamboo, offer little protection against the cold and fires are needed to keep the houses warm. This is reflected in their cooking, for many dishes require several hours of cooking or baking on the fire.

The fireplace – in bigger houses there may be two or three – is made of stamped clay and bordered with wood. Fuel usually consists of three long logs or heavy branches, which are slowly moved towards the centre of the hearth, in a Yule-log-like fashion. Pots may then be placed directly on the

Karen people pouring into baskets rice which has been threshed on woven mats

171

logs or else on a trivet above the fire, while those dishes which are baked in banana leaves are left to cook close to the edge of the hearth. Meat is often laid on sticks and grilled above the fire, and from a shelf above the hearth fish and slices of meat are left hanging to smoke.

Baskets and troughs filled with dried foodstuffs are kept on the shelf. Bunches of herbs and fragrant spice leaves hang from the beams, and small square packets containing crystalline salt wrapped in leaves are laid on the beams. Long thick bamboo tubes which lean against the wall are used as water receptacles, and rice wine is kept in earthen jars. Pounded rice is stored in a basket.

Sticky rice is served at practically every meal, and occasionally taro (wild or cultivated) and yams are also eaten. A great variety of vegetables and fruit is cultivated. Leaves and wild fruits are gathered in the jungle.

Taste varies, of course, as much among the Kammu as among other peoples. Generally, however, most dishes can be described as surprisingly mild – the recipes provided below have by no means been modified, yet they would perfectly suit the European palate. Should one prefer a hot flavour, the rice may be dipped in a pepper sauce, which all people in the area seem to enjoy.

The meal is spread on a low table, and the Kammu seat themselves around it on small round rattan stools. Every person is given a wooden box with a lid or a bamboo basket containing hot rice, and a wooden plate. If soup is to be served, a wooden bowl and bamboo spoon are provided.

The food is eaten together with the sticky rice, which defies any kind of cutlery. A small lump of rice is taken from the box and kneaded into a ball, and a piece of meat or vegetable is added to form a neat mouthful. Usually only plain water is served with the meal, though occasionally the strong rice wine is drunk.

The two main meals of the day are served at noon and at around 6 or 7 in the evening after the day's work is done. People like to take a bath at sunset as a way of ushering in leisure time. Then the meal is cooked, often by the men, who are supposed to be better cooks than women. Members of a family sit around one or several tables to enjoy the meal and a chat after a long working day.

Beef Stew (*Kong ah lampo*)

2 lb (1 kilo) stewing beef cut into ½-inch thick, bite-size pieces
4 tsp salt
2 Spanish peppers
3 or 4 bay leaves
water for boiling

2 or 3 slices of galingale root or ½–1 tsp 'Laos' powder (distributed by Conimex)
1 stalk lemon grass or 1 tsp 'Sereh' powder – i.e. citronella (also distributed by Conimex)

The meat is put in a saucepan and water is added till it covers the meat well. Bring to boiling-point and remove scum carefully. Add salt and spices and de-seeded peppers and simmer over low heat until the meat is cooked (about 2 hours). Serve with rice.

Wildfowl Stew (*Sing tang*)

2 partridges (or pigeons)
1 aubergine (or squash or cucumber)
1 green pepper
½ stalk of lemon grass or ½ tsp 'Sereh'
   powder

1–2 tsp salt
½ tsp monosodium glutamate
water for boiling

Divide the birds into bite-size pieces without removing the bones. Add water till the meat is covered. Bring to boiling point and remove scum carefully.
    Peel the aubergine, cut in halves and remove the seeds. Remove the stem and seeds from the green pepper and mince both fruits. Add minced fruits and other ingredients to the meat and simmer over low heat until meat is tender (about ½ hour).

Fish in 'Banana Leaves' (*Ka koop*)

1 or 2 fillets of fish per person
   (about 6 oz./170 grams)
2 medium-sized tomatoes
1 green pepper
2 limes (or 1 lemon)

2 tsp salt
1 tsp monosodium glutamate
1 stalk lemon grass or 1 tsp 'Sereh'
   powder
aluminium foil for wrapping

Put one or two fillets (depending on size) of fish on a piece of aluminium foil and fold the foil upwards to hold the juice. Press the limes and divide the juice over the different packs. Remove stem and seeds from green pepper, cut in matchstick strips. Slice the tomatoes. Divide tomato, green pepper and spice equally between the packs. Fold the foil tightly around each pack. Bake in oven (375°, gas Mk 5) for 30–40 minutes.

*Kammu food is *mild*, and the peppers used are of the mild paprika variety.

Pepper Sauce (*Pri luh*)

3 or 4 cloves garlic	1 Spanish pepper*
2 limes (or 1 lemon, or ½ cup white wine vinegar)	salt

Peel garlic. Remove stem but not seeds from pepper and cut up in pieces. Pound garlic and pepper till it looks like porridge. Press limes and add salt to juice until it tastes neither sour nor salty. Start with ½ tsp and add more if the fruit is sour. Add garlic and pepper to the juice.

REFERENCES

For further reading on this cultural area, two books can be recommended:

K. G. Izikowitz, 'Lamet: hill peasants in French Indochina', *Etnologiska Studier*, no. 17, Göteborg, 1957.

Gordon O. Young, *The Hill Tribes of Northern Thailand*, United States Operational Mission for Thailand, Bangkok, 1961.

Annie Hubert-Schoumann

Food with the Yao

In the mountains that cover north Thailand, north Laos and north Vietnam live a number of different ethnic groups gathered under the vague term of 'hill tribes'. One of these, the Yao, have recently settled in this area, after a century-long, slow migration from the Ho Nan and Yunnan provinces of China. The Yao's real name is 'Mien'. Strong Chinese influences are evident: they use Chinese characters in writing their mythical history, their genealogies and much of their poetry. The Chinese influence is also felt in a certain 'refinement' of life that seems absent in the other groups living in the same mountains. It's also deliciously evident in their food.

The mountains in which they dwell are thickly covered with forests and no roads lead to them. They live in the heart of the notorious opium-growing 'Golden Triangle' (the Mien themselves are also opium-poppy growers), and to reach their villages one must travel on foot by steep mountain trails through magnificent landscapes. The villages are set in clearings in the forest which rise steeply on the hillside, and consist of ten to fifteen split bamboo or wooden houses which are covered by long thatch-covered roofs. The houses are large, to shelter extended families (grandparents, married sons and un-married daughters and grandchildren). The village area is carefully cleared of all vegetation, apart from a few orange trees, tea bushes and one or two fenced-in small herb gardens.

The Mien practise shifting cultivation: every two years each household picks a part of the surrounding forest, cuts down all the trees and bushes and sets them alight. The ash-covered, cleared ground (the swidden) is then planted with rice or maize. Opium fields are prepared in the same way, on or near hilltops. When, after one or two years, the ground has lost its fertility, the swidden is shifted further on. They later return to the same swidden, after allowing it to lie fallow for about ten years.

The staple crop is dry rice. Indeed, for the Mien, rice is synonymous with food as a general term. All care goes to the rice swidden which produces the best-tasting fragrant rice possible. In the swiddens are also planted a

Pounding rice

variety of vegetables such as mustard greens, cabbage, pumpkin, aubergine, peas, green beans, white radish, dill, coriander, ginger, tomatoes and chilli peppers. The immediate surrounding area is planted with banana and papaya trees, melons, water-melons and occasionally pineapple and sugarcane. The forest around the villages is another source of food: women gather edible plants there such as mushrooms and bamboo shoots, while the men hunt with their impressive home-made muzzle-loading rifles. They bring back deer, wild boar, civet cats or monkeys. Young boys hunt with crossbows for rats, birds or squirrels. But no matter how abundant the supply of meat or vegetables, if there is no rice the Mien are hungry. To them rice is the source of life and strength.

Pigs or chickens are killed only for sacrifices, so that meat is eaten only at irregular intervals. However, pork fat is much valued and preserved in large bamboo tubes, and is used generously in daily cooking.

Everyday meals consist of rice and vegetables. But it is by no means a dull or monotonous diet. The Mien like to eat, and they eat well. In their houses the kitchen is a large, well-equipped room. Occupying the whole left side of the house, it opens up onto the 'front room' where an open fire burns day and night. In the kitchen are set two clay stoves, a long, low one with holes which hold two pots, and a square one that holds a huge, round-bottomed cast-iron pan used to prepare pig food or to melt pork fat. On the floor against the wall there is a long rice-pounder, operated by foot. Bamboo shelves store china and kitchen-ware: bowls, chopsticks, knives, chopping-boards, mortar and pestle, frying-pans, pots, wooden spoons and so on.

The water room adjoins the kitchen. The Mien often have running water brought down from higher up in the hills in bamboo canal systems. These divide up in the villages and bring water to every house. It falls from the bamboo tube into a wooden trough in the water room, which is on a higher level, and overflows and falls into the ground below.

Meals usually take place three times a day: in the morning, at midday and in the evening after sunset. The women usually prepare the food, although occasionally, when women go to the swiddens, men take over the kitchen. The first thing to be cooked is rice. Freshly husked in the rice-pounder, it is then steamed in large cast-iron or aluminium pots. In refined households, rice is cooked twice a day, so as to be served fresh and hot at morning and evening meals. Just before a meal, a low wooden or rattan table is set between the kitchen and the front room. This is covered with fresh banana leaves (perfect throw-away tablecloths). On it are placed a bowl and a pair of chopsticks for each person and little saucers of soy sauce, crushed fresh chilli pepper and salt, fresh dill, coriander leaves and mustard relish. These are condiments to the daily food. The mustard relish is rather like sauerkraut. To prepare this, the green leaves are placed in a jar alternately with layers of salt, and then tightly covered. After a couple of weeks the relish is sour and ready. Bamboo shoots are treated in the same way.

When one of the women calls, 'Come and eat rice!', everyone takes up a low bamboo stool and sits around the table. A woman brings in one or two dishes of vegetables, and the head of the house fills each bowl with rice and all start eating. The vegetables are usually sautéd in pork fat, stewed with onions, or puréed, as in the aubergine recipe below. One takes up some vegetables with the chopsticks, brings them to one's bowl and eats them. The rice bowl is held in the left hand. Between mouthfuls of vegetables one can nibble some fresh coriander leaves dipped in soy sauce or in the crushed chilli pepper. This, together with the fragrant nut-tasting rice, is enough to make a delicious meal. No one drinks during the meal. Drinking follows the meal – usually in the form of tea, which is kept constantly warm on the front room fire. Dessert doesn't exist, and sweet food (fruit and sugarcane) is considered exclusively children's food, although occasionally women are supposed to crave it.

Grilled Aubergine (*Khia bua*)

6 medium aubergines
4 cloves garlic
2 limes or 3 lemons
salt

1 fresh red chilli pepper or ½ tsp chilli paste ('Sambal Gelete') or chilli pepper

Place the aubergines over a charcoal fire or in the fireplace (if you have neither, a very hot oven would do). When they feel soft if pierced with a fork, take them off the fire and let them cool. Split them open and scoop out the pulp with a spoon. In a mortar, pound to a paste the garlic and chilli pepper. Slowly add the aubergine pulp and keep pounding. When it has the consistency of a thick purée, add salt to taste and the juice of the limes (or lemons). It's best to use a real fire, for the finesse of this dish is its slight smoky taste.

When, for a small sacrifice a chicken is killed, it is usually eaten as a soup.

Sour Chicken Soup (*Tong ka sui*) (To serve 4–6)

half a chicken
1 tbsp crushed fresh ginger or ¼ tsp
  powdered ginger
2 cups chopped Chinese cabbage
  (*bak choy*) or mustard greens (use
  Swiss chard, celery or 'celery
  cabbage' if not available)

1 red chilli pepper or ½ tsp chilli paste
1 cup pickled* or tinned bamboo
  shoots (about 8 oz./220 grams)
2 limes or 3 lemons
1 stalk fresh lemon grass or 1 tsp
  'Sereh' powder
3 tbsp pork fat

Chop up the chicken in small pieces. Sauté it in pork fat. Add the crushed chilli, the crushed ginger, then the cabbage or mustard greens. When all is well coated with pork fat, add the bamboo shoots. Cover with water and simmer until the chicken is cooked. Before serving add salt to taste and the juice of the limes.

The soup is eaten directly from the serving bowl, with a 'Chinese' spoon. It should be thick.

Pork is eaten when there happens to be a sacrifice or for New Year (Chinese traditional calendar). It is always the occasion for a banquet. Men take over the kitchen, and women become mere helpers. The pig is sacrificed in the house, in front of the ancestors' altar. It is cleaned and cut up in the water room. All the fat is set aside to be melted and preserved for cooking. Some meat is preserved in salt in bamboo tube containers, but most of it is eaten immediately. The two most important dishes of a banquet (except at wedding banquets) are blood and chopped meat, both eaten raw. The blood is coagulated, salted and mixed with fresh herbs. It is passed around in a large bowl and spooned up by all the men invited. This, together with the raw meat, is considered to be men's food. Women are not supposed to like it. In fact, very few actually taste it.

If you cannot face the idea of eating raw pork, you can make the following recipe with beef. The Mien sometimes make it with venison.

* Chinese pickled vegetables, more easily available in western markets, are saltier and less sour than the Yao ones. If using Chinese, add a lot of water or else use the natural, unpickled ones.

Chopped Raw Meat (*O to tsua*) (To serve 4–6)

1 lb (450 grams) fresh meat (pork or beef)
2 tbsp rice
5 spring onions
1 handful fresh coriander leaves
1 sprig fresh dill
2 sprigs fresh mint
2 cloves garlic

½ stalk lemon grass or ½ tsp 'Sereh' powder
2 red chillis or 1 tsp chilli paste
1 tbsp ginger root (fresh) or scant ¼ tsp powdered ginger
1 lime or lemon
1 tbsp soy sauce

Grind the meat to a paste. In a frying-pan place the raw rice and grill it (without water) as if it were coffee-beans, until it becomes dark brown. Pound it to a powder in a mortar and add to meat. Chop all the other ingredients very finely and mix them with the meat paste. Salt to taste, add the lime juice and soy sauce. It is served on banana leaves, surrounded with raw cabbage leaves and coriander.

During banquets, men drink rice spirit and recite poems. Women and children eat in the kitchen or after the men. And when the feast is over, routine takes over the kitchen, alternating the vegetables through the seasons . . . And, with luck, their Prince of the Five Cereals will ensure that the Mien shall not go hungry.

Merete Aagard Henriksen

Some Recipes from Northern Thailand

The recipes are from the northern area. There are regional differences; moreover, dishes which might bear the same name in the north and the south may contain rather different ingredients.[1]

The following three dishes are served with rice, along with other dishes, for according to Thai tradition everything prepared for a meal is served at once, and the amount and variety is strictly according to individual preference.

Chicken and Mushroom Soup (*Kaeng chud kai kabhed*)

1 cup chopped chicken
2 cups sliced mushrooms*
  (8 oz./220 grams)
1½ cup minced or finely chopped spring
  onions or leek greens

2 tbsp *nampla*† (fish soy)
bunch coriander (preferably fresh)
freshly ground pepper
3 cloves garlic, fried
3 to 4 cups stock

Cut most of the meat off the bones of a medium-sized chicken and then cover the bones with water (about 3 cups), season with salt and boil for about an hour to make a chicken stock. Add the cut chicken meat and the fish soy and cook gently until tender. Then add the sliced mushrooms and allow them to cook for

* If using Chinese mushrooms (which are dried), soak them in warm water until soft, remove the hard skins and then slice. Use only about 6 to 8, since they are very strong tasting. Fresh Thai mushrooms (*hed-fang*) are different from the European variety, but I always use fresh European mushrooms in preference to the Chinese variety, which in Scandinavia are rather expensive and not quite appropriate for Thai cuisine.

† *Nampla* is not the same as Chinese fish soy. *Nampla* or fish water is made from small fish put in a jar with salt and water and allowed to ferment. Once fermented, it is ready for use, but it cannot be bought in Denmark as no preservative is added and therefore its importation is forbidden.

a few minutes. Add freshly ground pepper, fried garlic and garnish with coriander leaves. The latter have a wonderful taste and look particularly nice on top of the greyish soup.

Fish with Sweet and Sour Sauce (*Plakrapong pad priaw-wān*)

1½ lb (700 grams) flounder or other flat fish

10 tbsp sugar

½ cup vinegar

2 tbsp dark soy sauce (*kikkoman*). Do not use fish soy, as it is too salty.

2 tbsp cornstarch

1 cup water

2 tsp salt

½ cup flour

oil for deep frying

raisins (optional)

Clean the fish without removing head and tail. Make three deep cuts on each side, and sprinkle the fish with salt and let stand for 20 minutes.

Coat the fish with flour and deep fry until brown. Drain on absorbent paper.

To make sweet and sour sauce: mix sugar, vinegar, soy sauce, 1 tsp salt and water and bring to boil. Blend the cornstarch with a little cool water, add it to the boiling mixture and boil, stirring 30 seconds. Pour over the fish. Add an optional handful of raisins.

Mussulman Curry (*Kaeng Masaman*)

½ cup shallots or onions

5 cloves garlic

1 tsp allspice

1 tsp salt

½ tsp ginger or 2 tsp chopped green ginger

1 tsp Worcestershire sauce

⅓ tsp dried red pepper (crushed)

2½ lb (1–1·25 kilos) round steak

6 whole cloves

2 sticks cinnamon

2 tbsp cider vinegar or lemon juice

½ tbsp sugar

3 whole cardamon

¼ cup whole roasted peanuts

2 cups coconut cream (mixture of thick and thin)

2 tbsp oil

2 tsp cumin seeds

2 tbsp coriander

Slice the meat into cubes. Cook the meat covered in water until soft (about ¾ hr) or in a pressure cooker with a cup of water at 15 lb pressure for 5 minutes.

Mince the shallots and garlic very fine. Melt the oil in a pot, add the minced shallots and garlic and fry gently. Drain the cooked meat, reserving the broth. Add the coconut cream to the meat and stir. Add all the spices, fried shallots and garlic and the rest of the ingredients except the broth. Simmer for 1 hour or till the meat is tender, and then add the meat broth little by little.

Just before serving add 4 tbsps of very thinly sliced crisply fried shallots.

This dish is served with sliced cucumber, sliced bananas, pickled beetroots, raisins and extra peanuts. If prepared one day in advance, it is more tasty.

NOTE

1 See Rosemary Brissenden's excellent book, *South East Asian Food*, Penguin, 1969, for variations of the above recipes.

Rosemary Firth

Cooking in a Kelantan
Fishing Village, Malaya

When Raymond and I settled in a small village on the east coast of Kelantan in Malaya in 1939, to study the fishing economy, one of the things which seemed most to impress the local people was that we took all our meals, with the exception of a breakfast of toast and coffee, in Malay style. We had a house built for us of bamboo and palm thatch, facing the sea and adjacent to other village houses. It had a typical village-style kitchen at one corner of the house, with a sanded and raised platform for a wood fire, over which cooking-pots of iron rested on metal grids – while the smoke found its way out of a hole at the side of the roof. One prepared all the food, and ground the spices, squatting on the floor before a wooden board. The washing-up was done in a tin or enamel bowl filled with water drawn from an adjacent well, and stored in large cool pottery jars, filled daily. The house was built on stilts, with the floorboards laid loosely together, so that water and waste matter could fall under the house, where it was absorbed in the sand, or was disposed of by local chickens scratching for a precarious living. A separate place with its own water jar was reserved for personal washing, for the Malay villager has always been scrupulously clean in his personal affairs, as becomes a good Muslim. We had engaged a local Malay and his wife to look after us. Her cooking was varied and delectable; rice was cheap and easy to buy, and fresh fish was available from the beach every afternoon when the boats came in. Except of course on Fridays, the Sabbath, when nobody put to sea, and we killed a chicken or a duck, or used their eggs instead.

Malay cooking holds a high place in the estimation of outsiders who know it, and deservedly so, but it is not often found outside the country, for two reasons. The first is that the preparation of spices for flavouring traditional dishes is apt to be a laborious and time-consuming process; the second is that many Malay dishes depend for their special flavour on the use of fresh cream pressed from an unripe coconut, unobtainable in the west. Commercial coconut cream is made from the flesh of ripe nuts, and is only an imperfect substitute.

Cooking over a pit fire; man in background stirring pudding for feast

All Malay cooking has been subject to foreign influences, Chinese, Indian, Javanese and European, but it has maintained its essentially national character notwithstanding. It has strong emotional associations for emigrants, and at least until recently, Malay students and others would regularly arrive in England with a trunkful of spices and other local ingredients, to enable them to cook and eat meals in their own way as far as possible. Today, when it is much easier to buy oriental spices, as well as to find small restaurants catering for various overseas national tastes, true Malay cooking is still difficult to find in the west. I have found only a couple of restaurants in London, and one in Liverpool, that served genuine Malay dishes; but I have been privileged to sample the real thing cooked in Malay homes in London, which shows that it can be done.

The foundation of every Malay meal is a dish of rice, accompanied by various relishes, of which the number and variety will depend on the means of the individual. Every village housewife we knew could make a delicious curry if she could afford the ingredients, but an ordinary family in those days might only eat curry once a week, or less. The most common relish was fish, rubbed with salt or turmeric, inserted in a split bamboo and grilled over wood embers. In extreme poverty, or in the monsoon season, there might only be dried or salted fish, or a chilli or fishpaste sauce. But important as is the relish, rice is the symbol of nourishment and wellbeing, and as such occupies an important place in the social and ceremonial life of the fishermen, in addition to being the staple. The word for cooked rice, *nasi*, stands as the synonym for food. *Beras*, or husked raw rice, is brought to the host at a feast by women guests. It is given and exchanged on numerous ceremonial occasions, is offered to spirits, and scattered at a spirit seance by local *bomors*. Ground rice of a special kind is cooked with coconut cream and steamed in little three-cornered parcels of banana leaves, tied in little packages and taken round to guests whom one solicits to attend a wedding party, or to bring goodwill to friends on religious festivals. Sweet potatoes, bread or other cereals were occasionally eaten on special occasions; but one of the greatest hardships of the Japanese occupation, when food was scarce, was reported to us as being the necessity to eat potatoes every day, instead of rice.

During the year in which I made a detailed study of the housekeeping pattern of many differently situated Malay families, I collected recipes for everyday food and for special 'feasts'. A feast in Malay culture was not only an occasion for celebrating some important social event, it was also the means of collecting capital and of organizing loans, and repaying debts between persons with kinship or economic ties. The method was as follows. Women guests would bring rice or other small food contributions, carried proudly on the head, as they arrived during the afternoon. This food was to replace that used, and was not taken directly to the kitchens. After greeting their hostess, they would be served in groups of eight or ten, separately from their menfolk, who might come later in the day. After the men had eaten, and before departing, they would take ceremonial leave of the host, who sat with a scribe beside him, next to a large copper bowl. Into this bowl the guest would formally throw a number of silver coins, according to his means, and perhaps his obligations; and as each dollar rang in the dish, the scribe would call the name of the donor loudly, and the amount of his contribution. This would be written down by the scribe. Thus, 'Abdul bin Mohamat, one, two, three, four, five dollars', or whatever the sum. This money was a recorded loan to his host, and was repayable at some future date, when the roles of host and guest would be reversed. Thus, to give generously in this public way both showed support of the host and tied him to repay the loan when it should be required on another such occasion. Feasting, an apparently extravagant custom to the European, was thus an effective means of raising funds when needed. A large sum collected at the end of the day would be both a sign of faith in one's economic solvency, and also a corresponding future obligation. Thus the sum contributed, over and above the minimum of the single dollar gift, would depend not only on the wealth of the donor but also on his estimate of the likelihood of his receiving a similar return later on. The money was publicly given, and publicly recorded. This was the powerful social sanction that it would later be reciprocated.

At such a feast, varied dishes of curried beef, goat, chicken, fish and eggs and also vegetable dishes and some sweets were prepared some days previously, in variety and amount according to the means and the ambition of the host. On the following days, expenses and contributions would be cast up, to see if one had made a profit or a loss on the overall operation: if one was left with cash to spend or out-of-pocket.

Special foods were also cooked for specific religious occasions. A kind of scone served after funerals was made of cooked mashed sweet potato, mashed ripe banana, ground rice flour, palm sugar, ginger, peppercorns and coconut cream, stirred together and left to rise with yeast, then baked in little heavy iron pans, like egg-poaching dishes but with a lid, and which substituted for an oven. There was also a marvellous sticky sweetmeat made by stirring and beating over a fire for many hours a mixture of glutinous rice flour (*beras pulut*), palm sugar and coconut cream, which was one of the special foods offered to guests whom one wished to come to a feast where one hoped for monetary contributions. Most spectacular of all, perhaps, were the wedding cakes made with rice cooked with saffron and coconut cream, pressed into bowls and turned out upside down, like a Christmas pudding. The bright yellow shapes were then stuck with crimson-dyed hard-boiled eggs, and little decorative shiny paper flowers, and carried on the head on pewter platters in a procession through the village.

Girl carrying rice-cakes for a wedding

Another occasion for public cooking and celebration was the feast of *ashura* in Muhurram. This commemorates a time when Mohammed, being without food, is supposed to have thrown into one pot all the edible odds and ends he could lay hands on. Some time during this week, several people will announce their intention of organizing this event, and will invite other devout villagers to join them. The organizers may bear the brunt of the cost in time, trouble and perhaps cash, but material and labour is contributed by all those taking part, as is usual in all Malayan village celebrations. Several large iron cooking-pots, up to 3 feet in circumference, must be collected, together with firewood, cooking implements such as coconut graters, sieves, small mixing bowls and the like. Early in the morning of the chosen day, large holes will be dug in the ground, filled with wood and lit, to act as ovens. Women bring rice, coconuts, palm sugar, sweet potatoes, pumpkin, corn, onions, groundnuts, yams, spice, even goat or chicken flesh if available. Men usually organize the grating of coconuts, an onerous job, while women grind spices, cut and pound onions and nuts. The rice is then put into the huge containers filled with water along with cut-up pumpkin, potatoes, sweet corn and other vegetables, and all is boiled together during a whole morning. Later, coconut cream is added with the mixed pounded spice, and cooking and stirring go on without intermission. Men take turns to stir, and at about 10 o'clock a shade of sailcloth will be erected over the operation, and the laborious mixing goes on until well after noon. Last to be added is palm sugar; when all is ready, near 3 in the afternoon, everyone who has contributed ingredients brings his plate or bowl and all are spread out under the trees. When the pudding has been divided out, it is taken home to be eaten cold, although children are given small portions to eat at once, hot. The finished concoction somewhat resembles a Christmas pudding in appearance and taste, but it is thick and glutinous and should be dark in colour, sweet, spicy and nutty. Delicious it was to our palates, and a most impressive operation to watch all day.

On the occasion I recorded, the cost was about 6 Straits dollars (equal at that time to about £1 sterling); seventy people contributed, seventeen men assisted in the mixing and stirring, and a great many women also helped, not only with the main cooking but also with the provision of food for the cooks during the day's operation, which alone came to another dollar or so.

Recipes[1]

At a feast, several dishes of fish, beef, goat and vegetables cooked in various sauces will be served on a tray surrounding a dish of rice. This may be followed by various sweetmeats, made from rice flour, coconut cream, palm sugar, or from eggs and palm sugar, or from bananas, sweet potato, pumpkin and sweet corn, but their translation for westerners defies my ability. I give below a sample of sauces which I have tried myself in England, and which, while just missing the genuine flavour of our Kelantan experience, do seem to capture some of the characteristics of this excellent cuisine.

Amounts were naturally approximate (and would serve approximately 2 or 3 people). It is difficult to translate the amounts of coconut cream for western cooks. I have found that an ounce of commercial coconut cream cooked with a teacupful of water produces a reasonable cream, or less water or more coconut cream for a rich sauce. But it is worth noting that it thickens considerably when simmering. Cow's milk is a quite alien and inappropriate substitute.

Basic Curry Sauce (as used normally every day for fish or vegetables, not meat, since impoverished peasants would never eat meat except on special ritual occasions)

3 or 4 slices root ginger (this is fresh ginger – the nearest commonly available substitute seems to be ginger in syrup)

4 shallots
4 chillies
salt to taste

Pound all the washed spices together in a mortar with the shallots, and cook with 3 oz. coconut cream in 3 cups water till thick. This takes about 20 minutes. Then add raw fish or vegetables and simmer in the mixture.

The recipe is varied by the addition of turmeric, citronella, prawn paste, tamarind water and garlic.

White Curry for Fish*

1 piece fresh ginger, size of little
  finger, sliced fine
1 large tsp fennel seeds

1 tbsp leaf fennel, chopped
5 shallots, sliced
2 cloves garlic, sliced fine

None of the above is pounded, but put straight into coconut cream, at double strength – 1 oz. to half a cup of water. Lemon juice or prawn paste, if liked, is added at the end.

This sauce was for fresh fish, but I have found it good with western smoked haddock, flaked. Let fish cook for 5–7 minutes, when the sauce is bubbling.

Caramelized Prawns

Have large prawns, remove carapace but leave on head and whiskers, and cook whole in palm sugar (or brown sugar) until well coated and the sugar is slightly burnt. Eat cold, holding by the whiskers.

Rich Curry Sauce for Aubergines or Eggplants

1 piece cinnamon about ½ inch long
1 tsp black pepper
6 cloves

1 tsp nutmeg
1 tsp turmeric
1 tsp ginger

* The nearest common local fish is undoubtedly mackerel, a fish very nearly like the *kumbong* frequently caught by our village's fleet. But a good fat flat fish, like halibut or even sole, can also be used for grilling or with coconut cream.

1 piece mace, size of a bean
1 tsp coriander
1 tsp aniseed
1 tsp peppercorns, white

1 tsp caraway
1 pod cardamon
4 shallots
1 large clove garlic

Fry garlic and shallots together in coconut oil, pound all spice well in mortar, add and fry with 2 or 3 sliced aubergines, previously salted and left for an hour and then drained. Lastly add thick coconut cream, 3 oz. to 1½ cups water, and simmer till thick. The mixture should be rich, oily and a darkish fine green colour.

A Way with Green Vegetables and Fish

A green vegetable, such as spinach or kale, is first cooked in water, strained and chopped. It is then mixed with chopped onions and garlic, and shredded fish or prawns (or shrimps). Coconut cream is added and the whole simmered together.

Sati Sauce

1 tbsp coriander
1 tsp aniseed
1 tsp caraway
1 small piece mace
6 cloves
¼ of a nutmeg
10 black peppercorns
1-inch piece ginger or 2 little pieces
   crystallized ginger
1 stick cinnamon, about 1 inch long
2 shallots

4 cloves garlic
2 tbsp brown sugar (for palm sugar)
¾ oz. (20 grams) coconut cream to
   1½ cups water (for two or three
   coconuts)
1 small cup groundnuts (salted
   peanuts) chopped fine
½ lemon or lime, squeezed
red pepper or cayenne pepper, a good
   shake, to taste

Fry the chopped shallots and garlic, pound all spices in mortar and add to mixture, then add sugar, coconut cream and nuts and simmer slowly till thick and oily looking. This very rich, dark, thick sauce is used as a dip with small pieces of chicken grilled on a bamboo stick and basted with groundnut oil, and should be eaten with little cakes of ground glutinous rice flour (*pulut* rice). It is excellent as a sauce to eat on its own.

Note

1   All these recipes, with a good many others, are from my *Housekeeping among Malay Peasants*, LSE Monographs in Social Anthropology, no. 7, Athlone Press, 2nd ed., 1966. I have tried them myself, as have others, who have independently pronounced them good.

Foods of Bali

Balinese society is famed for its rich ceremonial life. There are the temple festivals when people bring splendid offerings and dance to the honour of the gods. And the life-cycle ceremonies, such as filing the teeth, weddings and, above all, cremations, are indeed happy and colourful occasions. Ceremonial events mean feasting, and involve beautiful, elaborate offerings, incense, flowers and holy water, and the eating of good food. People are seated in groups of eight, and eat communally from the same tray as a sign of friendship. The tray contains a big heap of rice which is constantly replenished, and a number of main side-dishes such as *ebatan*, consisting of a mixture of chopped vegetables, hot spices, blood and some meat, and *komoh*, which is blood mixed with spices and small pieces of liver. *Sate*, a preparation of roasted meat on bamboo sticks, is always served: the best-known type of *sate* is probably *sate asem*, pieces of barbecued meat; but another variety, seldom omitted, is *sate lembat*, the recipe for which is given below.

Golok, *the knife used by men at feasts*

The preparation of the meat dishes for traditional feasts is men's work. The night before the ceremony is to be held or early the same morning the male guests arrive, each armed with a *golok*, which is a huge knife with a curved wooden handle and a sharp, heavy blade, used only on ceremonial occasions for cutting meat and chopping up vegetables and spices. If it is to be a large feast, the male guests may spend all night preparing, interspersed with drinking coffee, palm wine (*tuak*) and rice wine (*berem*), chatting, joking and listening to recitations of palm-leaf manuscripts (*lontar*) in the classical language. It is an occasion for great enjoyment; the mood is happy and boisterous, while the sounds of chopping and pounding of spices blend with raucous voices and the laughter and crying of children. But the mood of the ceremony itself is somewhat more serious, albeit a far cry from the serenity of Christian church ceremonies.

It is possible to use any meat for traditional feasts, apart from beef, since the Balinese are Hindu. Nevertheless, beef is eaten on non-ritual occasions. What kind of animal to slaughter is partly an economic decision. If a man is poor, or for other reasons desires only a small ceremony, he may slaughter a hen or a duck. But if he is rich and wishes to enhance his status by holding a large feast, he may slaughter a water buffalo. (However, it is the pig which is the major ritual and sacrificial animal, so he is more likely to slaughter three pigs than one buffalo.) Unlike their Moslem neighbours, the Balinese seldom eat goat meat: this is largely due to the practical difficulties of raising goats while the lean and scabby dogs tend to overrun their villages.

Sate is not a dish exclusively reserved for festive occasions. Those who can afford it may eat *sate* every day. But the poorer people usually add only red pepper and salt to their daily rice dish; or even mix the more expensive and culturally highly valued rice with maize or sweet potatoes. The well-off Balinese usually have several dishes at each meal, all eaten at the same time and in no special order. Below I have provided a few recipes which are easy to prepare, which, together with the *sate*, constitute a 'complete' meal. Meat, fish and vegetables are generally well spiced and peppered. For example, when I slaughtered two pigs for a feast, 3 kilos of the very hot small red peppers were used in their preparation. Other spices are also used in large quantities, in this instance 6 kilos of garlic! But the food can be prepared with less pepper and every diner can add as much *sambal*, a peppery side-dish, as he desires to achieve the right amount of hotness. *Sambal* is usually eaten in very small quantities. Ready-made *sambal* can be bought, but home-made tastes much better.

The only 'exotic' ingredients are *santen* (coconut cream) and *terasi*. An artificial *santen* substitute can be bought in most big cities, to which hot water is added to provide a milky liquid. Failing that, *santen* can be made using

Grilling sate

grated coconut soaked in hot water, allowed to stand for ½ hour, then strained through muslin. *Terasi*, or shrimp paste, can be bought in most big cities. Though it has a distinctly unpleasant odour, it does enhance the flavour of the food, and provides its distinctly Balinese (or generally Indonesian) flavour.

The food may be served either hot or cold, so that meals may be prepared in advance. A Balinese eats with his right hand, since his left hand is considered unclean. I always found the food much tastier when I attempted to eat Balinese fashion, rather than with utensils!

Sate Lembat (To serve 4)

1 lb (450 grams) finely minced meat
1 cup (4 oz./113 grams) grated coconut (cocos)
1 to 3 red chilli peppers or ½–1½ tsp chilli powder
1 or 2 cloves garlic

½ teaspoon *terasi* or *blachan* (if not available, use shrimp paste or anchovy paste)
salt
a little white or black pepper
½ cup *santen* or creamed coconut

Grind the chilli, garlic, *terasi*, salt and pepper until it is like a porridge. Mix meat, spices, salt to taste, grated coconut and *santen* thoroughly and make small oblong meatballs. These can be put either on barbecue sticks and roasted over an open fire (the traditional Balinese way) or on an electric grill. They can also be fried in a frying-pan, without using any extra fat or oil if possible, since the oil of the coconut is probably enough.

If you leave out the grated coconut, you get a kind of *sate* called *sate pusut*

Kacang Goreng

2 cups shelled peanuts (1 lb/450 grams)
½ teaspoon *terasi*

salt
⅓ cup vegetable oil

Fry the peanuts in oil for about 1–2 minutes in a frying-pan *on low heat* with salt and *terasi*. Take care that the peanuts don't become darker than golden brown.

Sambal

3 or 4 red chilli peppers, preferably fresh
1 tsp *terasi*
¼ onion

1 or 2 cloves garlic (optional)
1 tomato (optional)
1 tsp vegetable oil

Grind all the ingredients until you get a 'pepper porridge'.

Dennis McGilvray

Pukkai

Sweetened milk-rice is one of the most common kinds of ritual food offerings in Sri Lanka, and it is also a sweet food which is cooked and eaten at home on special occasions. Milk-rice is known as *kiri bat* by the Sinhalese Buddhists and as *pukkai* by the Tamil Hindus and the Ceylon Moors (Muslims). Any anthropologist who proposes to do fieldwork in Sri Lanka must be prepared to consume vast quantities of it.

In the Tamil and Moorish region of eastern Sri Lanka where I have done research, the preparation of *pukkai* is a common element in formal religious rituals as well as a popular way to fulfil personal vows which have been made to supernatural beings. The Tamil Hindus prepare *pukkai* at the temple and offer it to the deity with fruit, betel leaf, areca nut and flowers. The hot milk-rice is scooped out of the pot and placed in large glistening heaps in front of the idol. After the priest has performed the formal rituals of worship (*puja*) and the god has finished eating the invisible parts of the *pukkai* (that is, the steam and aromatic vapours which waft upwards), the *pukkai* is distributed to the people who have come to attend the *puja*. All of the offerings which have been placed before the idol are believed to have been 'consumed' by the god, and what remains is the god's left-overs, a sort of blessed garbage which is shared among the worshippers. Throughout Sri Lanka and the neighbouring regions of south Asia, the public giving of cooked food from one person to another, and the refusal to accept food offered in return, places the giver of food in a clearly superior position. As an example, this is one of the ways in which a man of higher caste demonstrates his superiority to a person of lower caste. When the worshippers eat the god's *pukkai* and the other 'used offerings' after the *puja*, they are showing their inferiority as mere mortals in the presence of the deity. Of course, the *pukkai* and other offerings have to be prepared for the god by human hands, so elaborate measures are taken to prepare the *pukkai* in a pure and sacred manner.

One such ritualized way of preparing milk-rice among the Tamil Hindus is to conduct a *pongal*. The word *pongal* comes from the Tamil verb 'to

Freshly grated coconut is mixed with water and squeezed hard to extract coconut milk for making pukkai

bubble up and boil over'. A new clay pot is placed on an outdoor hearth in front of the temple or the household shrine room and is decorated with markings of sacred burnt cow dung, sandalwood paste, and vermilion powder. Sometimes also flower garlands are placed around the pot. The basic idea in a *pongal* is to heat the milk by itself over a brisk fire until it swells up and bubbles over the side of the pot in a messy but nevertheless auspicious and pleasing wave of white froth. One of the best times to do this is exactly at dawn, so that the heat of the fire can be adjusted to make the boiling of the milk coincide precisely with the first rays of the sun as they strike the side of the pot. Then, as the milk bubbles over, the rice is added to the pot, and the *pukkai* is cooked in the usual manner. This little ritual enhances the goodness of the *pukkai* by emphasizing the auspicious timing (sunrise) and the symbolic abundance of the overflowing milk. *Pongals* may be conducted at the house, at the temple, in the paddy field, at the threshing floor, or anywhere where health, prosperity and good fortune are particularly desired. At the annual Tamil festival of *tai pongal*, which is held in mid-January, the cooking of the milk-rice is carried out with the hope that the carefully prepared pot of *pukkai* will signal good luck and prosperity for the year ahead.

Pukkai is considered to be particularly suitable as an offering to gods because it is made from white substances (rice, milk) which are also very pure, noble and vegetarian. The rice may have been set aside from the very first threshing of the paddy harvest. The milk may be cow's milk (most sacred to the Hindus), water buffalo milk or coconut milk. Sweetening is provided by natural *jaggary* (brown palm sugar) or by white refined sugar, and this can be augmented by the addition of pieces of fruit such as dates, raisins and bananas. Sweet spices such as cinnamon and cardamon are also added sometimes to increase the fragrance of the *pukkai*. In fact the general idea is to make the *pukkai* as rich, sweet and fragrant as possible for the god and for the people who are eventually going to eat it.

At the same time, special restrictions apply to the preparation of the *pukkai* if it is to be offered in a religious context. No menstruating women should even come near to the place where the *pukkai* is being made. If *pukkai* is offered to a god, it must not contain any salt. Salt is recognized to be an absolute necessity of the human diet, a substance which epitomizes man's worldly dependence, while the gods, who exist on another plane, have no need for it. If *pukkai* is to be eaten merely for enjoyment at home, however, salt may be added.

According to local standards in Sri Lanka, *pukkai* should have a somewhat gummy or rubbery consistency. For this reason, people prefer to use rice which has not been par-boiled to remove the excess starch. It is advisable to use rice which cooks to a soft and mushy consistency if possible. However, the consistency of the *pukkai*, its degree of sweetness and the types of fruit and spices which are added are all a matter of personal preference and may be varied according to taste.

Milk-Rice (*Pukkai*) (To serve 10–14)

4 cups milk (cow's milk, buffalo milk, or coconut milk – preferably thick, rich and creamy)

1½ cups rice

¼ cup parched husked green gram* (2 oz./57 grams)

2 sticks cinnamon

3 cardamons (inner kernels only) or 18 to 24 cardamon seeds

½ cup chopped dates, raisins or other dried fruit (4 oz./113 grams)

1 large ripe banana, cut into pieces

¾ cup brown sugar

If you wish to receive the utmost metaphysical benefit from the milk-rice, then you are advised to proceed with a *pongal* ritual as outlined above. However, if

---

* Green gram is optional, but it adds a very nice flavour if it can be obtained. Its scientific name is *Phaseolus mungu*, and the Tamil term is *paccai payaru*. It is a small yellow-green pulse which is available at wholefood shops or at Asian food shops, unhusked, under the name *moong bean*. If the green gram has not yet been husked, place it in a dry frying-pan over medium heat and stir constantly until the gram just begins to turn brown and a nice aroma can be detected. Remove from the heat and spread to cool for a few minutes. Then crush the green gram between two layers of cloth with a rolling-pin or a mallet. Place in a winnowing basket (or a large, lightweight tray) and toss gently to separate the clean kernels from the powdered husk. Discard the husk. Half a cup of unhusked green gram yields about ⅓ cup of parched husked green gram.

you would rather not have to get up before dawn to make the *pukkai*, or if you would prefer not to have boiling milk cascade over your cooker and onto the kitchen floor, it is perfectly acceptable to modify the procedures and adopt a less intricate style.

Place the milk, rice, green gram, cinnamon and cardamon kernels in a large pan over medium heat. Bring to the boil, stirring frequently. Reduce heat and stir constantly as the mixture thickens. Add additional milk if necessary to produce a thick, uniform, pasty consistency, like stiff pudding. Turn off heat, cover the pan, and allow the rice to continue to absorb moisture for at least 20 minutes. Then, after all rice kernels are soft, fully cooked and the consistency of the mixture is quite gooey, add dates, raisins or dried fruit, banana pieces and sugar. If the sugar is added too soon the rice ceases to soften and remains slightly crunchy – something which Sri Lankans find appalling. Stir to mix, then cover and allow to stand for about 20 minutes to soften fruit and release flavour. *Pukkai* is best served while it is warm, fresh and moist, on banana leaves or, if necessary, on plates.

Naomichi Ishige

Oyakodonburi from Japan

In Europe and America it is common to make a snack by putting meat, fish, vegetables, cheese, etc., on or between slices of bread. In Japan, a thrifty meal consisting of various foods on top of hot rice, called *donburi*, is often eaten at lunchtime. Originally, *donburi* referred to a large earthenware bowl. In time, these bowls came to be used for various types of rice dishes. Just as putting different kinds of food between slices of bread came to be known as a 'sandwich', whether a 'ham sandwich' or 'cheese sandwich', so there are different types of *donburi*: *oyako-donburi* (chicken-and-egg *donburi*), *unagi-donburi* (eel *donburi*) and so on.

Katsudon is the name of a popular dish and is simply a shortened form of *katsu-donburi*. '*Katsu*' is the Japanese pronunciation of 'cutlet'. Since the cutlet originated in European cuisine I'm not sure whether it should be called exotic at all. However, it's something that ought to be tried, since cutlet cookery has been completely modified to suit Japanese taste and nothing quite like it exists in Europe.

Until about a century ago, when Japan's seclusion from the rest of the world ended, eating the meat of domesticated animals was, at least super-ficially, taboo. This was chiefly, though not entirely, due to the influence of the Buddhist prohibition against killing animals. When it did become possible for the Japanese to eat meat in public, they devised some original ways of cooking it, like *sukiyaki*, but most of the ideas about meat cookery were borrowed from Europe or China.

When one looks at the contemporary Japanese dining table one sees dishes that have originated in various countries, and at first glance the cuisine seems not to belong to any country at all. But in fact the 'foreign' food cooked in Japanese homes is not the same as food imported from foreign lands. This is because the food has been transformed – Japanized – so that it ought to be called something like 'Modern Japanese Cuisine'. The same thing has happened to cultural borrowings other than cooking. We Japanese have 2,000 years' experience in borrowing culture from the east Asian mainland

and changing it into something uniquely Japanese. Anyone who does not pay attention to these changes will have difficulty in understanding Japanese culture.

When food imported from Europe becomes a part of the daily menu of the Japanese, some general adaptations are made. First, since we eat with chopsticks rather than with a knife and fork, the food must be cut into edible portions before it is served. Next, the flavour must be modified in order to go with the plain boiled rice which the Japanese eat with every meal. So spices are used sparingly and the strong flavour of meat juices is to be avoided. So far as possible, there is a tendency to substitute a slight soy sauce flavour for the stronger flavour of meat juices or sauces when preparing the dish.

Transplanting rice seedlings

Katsudon (To serve 4)

Pork is generally used for the cutlet, the back roast (loin) if possible. But beef cutlets or chicken cutlets can be prepared in the same way. The Japanese feel that the taste of lamb is too strong to go with the soup.

4 pork or veal or chicken cutlets
1 cup oil
1½ cups stock (chicken or *dashi*)
⅓ cup sake
2 tbsp sugar

¼ cup soy sauce
1 onion
3 eggs
3–4 cups cooked rice

Prepare one cutlet for each person by seasoning with salt and pepper and dipping in beaten egg, then flour or breadcrumbs. These should be deep-fried in oil and never pan-fried. (Deep frying is influenced by the traditional Japanese method of cooking *tempura*; in fact, we like to eat *katsudon* with a crispy crust, which cannot be obtained by pan frying.) After frying, drain cutlet well and cut into edible-sized pieces, trying to retain the original shape of the cutlet. One slices the cutlet into bite-sized portions not only to make it easier to eat with chopsticks but also so that it will more easily absorb the soup.

The soup:
Bring to the boil in a saucepan the chicken or *dashi* stock (*dashi* is a stock made from dried bonito flakes*), sugar and sake (if you can obtain a sweet rice wine called *mirin*, you may omit the sugar, and dry sherry may be substituted for the Japanese sake), and soy sauce.

Put onion sliced into very thin 1-inch pieces into the boiled sauce and simmer for about 5 minutes. Transfer the fried cutlets into the pan on top of the onions, leaving them for one or two minutes until they are thoroughly heated. Pour the eggs, which have been vigorously beaten, in a separate bowl, into the soup, and heat for about 30 seconds, until it has the consistency of runny scrambled eggs. Put some hot rice into a bowl 5 inches across resembling a *donburi* – if you have one. If not, a soup-bowl will do. Place a cutlet on top of the rice and pour the well-mixed egg and onion soup over it and serve.

This dish is a good way to use last night's leftovers.

* This is obtainable at Japanese grocers.

The Pacific and Australia

Otaheite, 1777

On the 4th a party of us dined ashore with Omai who gave excellent fare, consisting of fish, fowls, pork and puddings. After dinner I attended Otoo, who had been one of the party, back to his house, where I found all his servants very busy getting a quantity of provisions ready for me. Amongst other articles there was a large hog, which they killed in my presence. There was also a large pudding, the whole process in making which I saw. It was composed of bread-fruit, ripe plantains, taro and palm or pandanus nuts, each rasped, scraped or beat up fine, and baked by itself. A quantity of juice, pressed from cocoa-nut kernels, was put into a large tray or wooden vessel. The other articles, hot from the oven, were deposited in this vessel, and a few hot stones were also put into make the contents simmer. Three or four men made use of sticks to stir the several ingredients till they were incorporated one with another, and the juice of the cocoa-nut was turned to oil, so that the whole mass at last became the consistency of a hashy-pudding. Some of these puddings are excellent, and few that we make in England equal them. Otoo's hog being baked, and the pudding which I have described being made, they, together with two living hogs and a quantity of bread-fruit and cocoa-nuts were put into a canoe and sent on board my ship, followed by myself and all the royal family. [. . .]

The times of eating at Otaheite are very frequent. Their first meal is about two o'clock in the morning, after which they go to sleep; and the next is at eight. At eleven they dine and again at two and at five, and sup at eight. The women have not only the mortification of having to eat by themselves, and in a different part of the house from the men, but by a strange kind of policy, are excluded from a share of most of the better sorts of food. The women generally serve up their own victuals, for they would certainly starve before any grown man would do them such an office . . . (*Captain Cook's Voyages of Discovery: Third Voyage*)

Naomichi Ishige

Roasting Dog (or a Substitute) in an Earth Oven: an Unusual Method of Preparation from Ponape

Ponape, one of the Caroline Islands, lies near the equator and has a year-round summer climate. With nothing but the sea to block it, the wind covers the island's highest peaks with clouds and rain falls throughout the year. Blessed with abundant water and a warm temperature, Ponape's climate is ideally suited to agriculture. Its main crops are breadfruit, taro, yam, banana and the coconut palm. These crops, plus shellfish and coral fish, make up the traditional daily fare of the Ponapeans. If you go to the mountain fields you can see these crops in abundance and if you go to the seashore you can see shellfish being caught. 'On Ponape nobody lacks food' is a popular saying among the islanders.

Like the other islands of Micronesia, Ponape experienced a thirty-year period of Japanese rule, during which time the islanders became accustomed to cooking rice and to using metal pots and pans. This completely changed their daily eating habits. Even today much rice is imported. Moreover, the simple daily food of the Ponapeans consists of canned fish poured on a plate of rice, for even though the sea is rich with fish they prefer the taste of canned fish.

However, when they hold a banquet, called *kamatep* in Ponapean, metal pans are not used. On these occasions they decide to cook in the old way, serving traditional food cooked in an earth oven.

Cooking in the earth oven is the men's job. The women's only responsibility is to eat what the men cook. And, since the traditional tableware is the banana or other type of leaf, there's no washing up after the banquet.

One evening a Ponapean friend invited me to a *kamatep*. The banquet, which brought her whole family together, was given for an old woman who was leaving the next day for Guam. More than twenty people gathered in the garden of the family holding the banquet. Women talked happily while the men were hard at work. In a small cook-house fitted with a tin roof, coconuts were roasted. Many small volcanic stones were placed on this fire to heat. These hot stones were then placed in a large, shallow hole about 6 feet wide which had been dug for the purpose.

Each member of the family contributed a share of the food to be cooked, which was laid out on banana leaves spread on the ground until it was needed. There were about twenty breadfruit, one taro and one freshly slaughtered pig which was to be the main course of the evening's feast. The taro was a giant which in three years had grown to a thickness of 1 foot and a length of 3 feet. It looked like a log. One side of it was planed flat with a knife and then, using wooden choppers, the men cut it into easy-to-eat bread-like slices. The pig was put on the hot stones to burn its hair off; then the belly was slit open and the inner organs taken out.

It was at this point that I suddenly heard a bark. A man appeared carrying a burlap grain sack on his back. Something was rustling around in the sack: it was a dog. The man put the sack on the ground and stepped firmly on its opening. Men standing near by raised wooden clubs over their heads and, aiming at what they thought to be the head, struck once, twice . . . When the howling stopped they dragged it out of the bag. It was brown with white spots, about 4 feet long. Two men took the dog by the legs and carried it over to the fire and put it on the hot stones. When all the hair had been singed, the belly was cut open and all the inner organs removed – except the liver which was left to be cooked. When this was done, all preparations were complete.

Since taro and breadfruit are tastier and spicier when charred, they were put directly on top of the hot stones. Over them were placed two or three layers of banana leaves. Then came the carcasses of the dog and the pig. Finally about twenty banana leaves were used to cover all the food and the hot stones. All that was left was to wait for the food to cook. As the hole was covered with banana leaves none of the heat escaped and the stones served as an oven. And as no water was used, none of the flavour of the food was lost. This is a method of cooking used by a culture that had no metal cooking implements or china tableware.

After an hour the banana leaves which covered the oven were taken off and the fragrance of charred breadfruit filled the air. The pork and dog were carved and placed on the banana leaves which served as plates, each person receiving a portion. None of the food was seasoned or salted.

The breadfruit tasted rather like a sweet potato though a little less sweet. The dog did not taste as bad as its smell would have led one to believe, though it was a bit tough and had to be chewed for a long time, almost like chewing gum. But chewing brought out the rather rich-tasting juices of the meat. The pork had a rather bland flavour by comparison.

There is a tradition of eating dog, not only in the Pacific Islands but in most of the countries of east Asia, including China, Japan and Korea. In areas where pastoralism or hunting has not been developed, the idea of a dog having a particularly close relationship to man ('man's best friend') like the Western European sheep-dog or hunting-dog, simply doesn't exist. And looked at through alien eyes, our attitudes can only seem to be a kind of fetishism.

Since there are not large wild animals to be hunted and, besides chicken, the only other traditional domesticated animal is dog (pigs were introduced by white men), roast dog is the most sumptuous of banquet fare in Ponape and the village elder must be invited to such a feast.

This particular *kamatep* lacked the boisterous gaiety which usually characterizes such events. I learned from the whispering that the guest of honour, the old woman who would fly to Guam the next day, was quite ill. A doctor at the Ponape hospital who had examined her found that she had only about six months to live, so he decided to transfer her to the better equipped hospital on Guam in the hope of prolonging her life. Thus everyone ate in silence.

For people who put more trust in dogs than in people and who have become accustomed to treating them as members of the family, the idea of eating dog is the same as eating human flesh (cannibalism). I can also recognize that it is something that can be considered disgusting. I don't want to advocate roasting dogs: I simply suggest that instead of taking pots and pans when you go on a picnic, bring a shovel and some canvas and enjoy the pleasure of using an earth oven.*

In place of the proper ingredients (taro and breadfruit) you can substitute unpeeled potatoes, sweet potatoes, squash and aubergine. Place these on the hot stones. As for meat, beef, pork or lamb, seasoned with salt and pepper and wrapped in cooking foil, will do. Fish similarly seasoned, with lemon slices added and wrapped in foil can also be used. You can either use fish fillets or whole river trout which have been gutted. When everything you want to cook has been placed in the hole, cover it with canvas and on top of this spread a good 3 inches of soil and wait an hour. The food will certainly be ready in 1 hour, but it can be left for 2 hours or so. Since the stones cool as the food cooks, there is no danger of overcooking.

* For precise instructions, see Paul Sillitoe's article.

Paul Sillitoe

The Earth Oven: an Alternative to the Barbecue from the Highlands of Papua New Guinea

This is less a recipe than a description of a way to cook. The aim is to describe how the Wola people of the Southern Highlands of Papua New Guinea cook in earth ovens,[1] and to offer suggestions, based on personal experience, as to how this may be modified to suit a suburban back garden and so advance it as an alternative to the barbecue.[2]

How to Prepare and Cook in an Earth Oven

The Wola build two kinds of earth oven, although they call both *nay saway* (lit: 'food earth oven cook'*). One kind is small and usually used to cook vegetables for a small number of people, such as a family, and the other kind is a long pit used to cook pork for many people at a pig kill or ritual.[3] In addition to their different sizes, these ovens vary in that pork requires a hotter pit than vegetables and takes longer to cook. This account deals mainly with the smaller kind of oven, although it interpolates some remarks about the larger one.

An earth oven requires the following:

(a) An area of garden where you can dig a hole and light a fire without causing too much damage.

(b) A number of stones. You need to exercise some care when collecting these and not use any, such as flint, which explode when heated. The Wola use pieces of limestone, but pieces of house brick, which are easier to come by, are quite suitable – for the oven outlined here you will need about forty bricks.

(c) Firewood to heat the stones – enough to build a solid platform 3 ft × 3 ft × 2 ft high.

* In Melanesian Pidgin, an earth oven is a *mumu*.

(d) Some large leaves (3 lb large cabbage leaves) and a roll of cooking foil (18 in. × 15 ft) to line the pit.

(e) The food which you wish to cook. The materials required vary, of course, with the size of the oven and the amount of food to be cooked. The size of oven outlined here can cook more than enough food for ten people, that is twenty strips of belly pork, ten sweet potatoes (3 lb), ten potatoes (2 lb), ten large spring onions, 3 lb spring greens, ten cooking bananas, ten carrots (2 lb), ½ lb mushrooms (at a squeeze it could probably accommodate twice this amount).

The Wola call oven pits *ongort*, and each house yard has a small one, which is simply cleaned of any rubbish and stones when people wish to use it. The trenches for large ovens on the other hand are situated on the park-like clearings where people stage important events, and as they are not often used men have to dig them out for each occasion. The oven described here follows the pattern of the small household one, which people also prepare when working in their gardens, and it requires a circular, saucer-shaped pit about 3 feet in diameter and 1 foot in depth at the centre (Fig. 1).

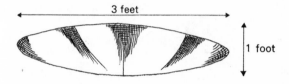

3 feet

1 foot

Near by, spread out on the ground some of the stones for the oven in a square about 3 ft × 3 ft, and on top of these build up a pyre-like platform, called by the Wola *haen tor bay* (lit: 'stone platform make'). First place four large pieces of wood around the edge of the stone square, and then lay a small fire in the centre using small pieces of wood. Next, build up a platform by placing large pieces of wood in layers first one way across the square and then at right angles on top – four or five layers are enough. Next, put the remainder of the stones on the top of this platform and then light the fire to heat them up (sometimes the Wola put another layer of wood on top of the stones, but this is not necessary (Fig. 2*)).

It will take about 45 minutes for the fire to burn down, and in this time prepare the pit to receive the hot stones. The Wola line their ovens with banana (*Musa* sp., in Wola *diya shor*) or palm lily leaves (*Cordyline fruticosa*, in Wola *aeguwp*), but neither of these is available in temperate regions and you will need to improvise. Any large leaves will suffice to line the pit, so long as they do not give off a strong flavour which will taint the food (be

---

* When heating stones for an oven to cook pork, the Wola build the fire over the trench to obtain the maximum heat.

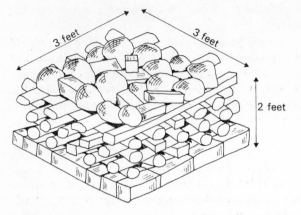

careful not to use toxic leaves, such as those of rhubarb) – large cabbage leaves and sheets of cooking foil are good substitutes. The Wola line the pit by placing the leaves in it so that they radiate out from the centre and stick out above the edge of the hole, and you can do likewise with kitchen foil (Fig. 3*).

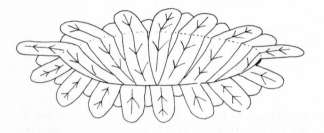

Also, while the stones are heating up, prepare the food to go in the oven. Any vegetable which you normally cook is suitable but, for those who wish to keep their oven authentic, Table 1 lists the foods which the Wola cook in this way; it also gives instructions on how to prepare them and indicates their places in the pit.[4] Although the Wola usually cook pork in a separate oven from vegetables because it requires longer to cook and greater heat, it is possible to cook them together if you cut the meat into small pieces – strips of belly pork are ideal.

When the fire has burnt itself down, you must act quickly before the stones cool off. First, take some stones and put them in the bottom of the pit on top of the lining. The Wola use rough tongs which they call *kopa* to handle the hot stones – they make these by splitting a 6-foot green sapling in two and then breaking the two pieces in the middle to make tongs; but if you still have an open fire, then coal tongs are excellent for the job. Blow the ash

---

* They line large trench ovens by placing leaves along the bottom, and then building up layers of hot stones and meat on top of these.

Common name	Latin name	Wola name	Preparation	Place in oven
Sweet potato	Ipomoea batatas	hokay	Scrape off skin	At bottom
Edible pit pit[a]	Setaria palmifolia	kot	Either as it is, or remove outer leaves	On top
Banana	Musa hort var.	diya	Remove skins, except for variety Wola call hond	On top
Gourd	Lagenaria siceraria	senaemiyl	Cut in half and remove seeds, but leave skin	Near top
Cucumber	Cucumbis sp.	laek	As it is, with skin on	On top
Various greens	e.g. Hibiscus manihot	komb	In bundles	On top with hot stone in middle of bundle
Taro	Colocasia esculenta Xanthsoma sp.[b]	ma	Scrape off skin, and cut up if large	At bottom
Beans	Dolichos lablab Phaseolus lunatus[b]	taeshaeniyl	Leave in pods	Near top
Pandanus nuts	Pandanus sp.	aenk	Cut up syncarp and remove core	Usually steamed in oven on their own, mesocarp either eaten or cooked drupes mixed with water to make thin sauce
Edible fungi	Several varieties	sez	Cut up if large	Near top
Pumpkin and young leaves[b]	Cucurbita sp.	pumpkin	Cut in sections and remove seeds, but leave skin	Put in after tubers with skin uppermost and a hot stone inside. Wrap leaves in bundle round hot stone and put near top
Maize[b]	Zea mays	keudiyl	Leave wrapped in outer leaves	In middle
Onions[b]	Large spring onion	umun	As they are, with roots cut off	On top
Cabbage[b]	Brassica sp.	cobaj	Cut in half	Near top
Potatoes[b]	Solanum tuberosum	asbus	Either scrape off skin or wash	At bottom with sweet potatoes
Pig	Sus scrofa papuensis	showmay	Singe off hair, and butcher into joints	Commonly cooked in large trench ovens with edible tree-fern fronds (Cyathea sp., in Wola henk) to soak up fat
Birds	Numerous species	sor	Pluck, remove stomach & intestines, dismember if large	Sometimes cooked on own in small oven
Marsupials	Several species	sab	Singe fur, remove stomach and intestines, dismember if large	Commonly cooked on own in small oven with edible fern-leaves to soak juices

a *pit pit* is a Pidgin word.　　b Crop introduced by Europeans.

off each stone before putting it in the oven, and be careful lest children try to help and burn themselves. Cover the layer of stones at the bottom of the hole with some leaves (the Wola crumple up banana leaves for this so that they fill all the odd-shaped gaps), and then fill the oven with food in the order indicated in Table 1. As you put the food in, place a few hot stones with it.

The Wola close an oven by packing earth round the outside edge of the pit against the banana leaves, so making them fold over the food; they call this ridge of earth *suw gob*. When they have sealed the oven with leaves in this way, they then place the remaining hot stones on top. Before sealing the oven they pour 4 or 5 pints of water over the food if they wish it to steam quickly. When they cook pork they increase the intensity of the heat by covering the stones with more leaves and a layer of earth. This is not necessary for vegetables, but if you think that your stones are not hot enough or you take some time filling and closing the oven, then you may wish to bury it and so increase the retention of heat (if you do this, put leaves over the stones first or else you will not be able to remove the soil without mixing some of it with the contents of the oven).

When the oven is closed it steams the food in a similar fashion to a pressure cooker. The time it takes varies with the size of the oven, but the one described here should be ready to open in 1½ hours (Fig. 4*).

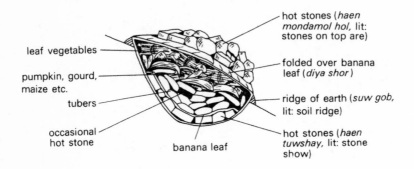

leaf vegetables

pumpkin, gourd, maize etc.

tubers

occasional hot stone

banana leaf

hot stones (*haen mondamol hol*, lit: stones on top are)

folded over banana leaf (*diya shor*)

ridge of earth (*suw gob*, lit: soil ridge)

hot stones (*haen tuwshay*, lit: stone show)

While food is steaming in an oven, the Wola cook small tit-bits over the embers, they roast small pieces of meat on the end of rough wood skewers, bake vegetables in the ashes and steam meat, greens and other soft vegetables in lengths of bamboo called *pay kuwla*. Many people congregate at events

* An earth oven takes some time to cook food, and people who wish to eat quickly sometimes prepare a small package of vegetables (not tubers, which require considerable heat) and a few hot stones wrapped in banana leaves. To cook in such a hot stone bundle is *ombuwgay*.

where men cook pork in large trench ovens and while they wait for it to steam they chatter and exchange gossip. But when the hosts open the oven (*kobay*, lit: 'open') and distribute the pork, the guests leave to eat their share at home. People who make a small vegetable oven, on the other hand, open it and eat the food quickly with no formality – they may not even share it out but sit round the pit and eat.

At a suburban dinner-party you will no doubt wish to depart from Wola ways and not see your guests gobble their food down and leave, or take it away to eat at home. But you may wish to eat your food with fingers off pieces of leaf as the Wola do. Also, like the Wola, you will probably wish to add salt to the food which, although it has a characteristic *mumu* flavour, tastes better with some condiment (salt is a scarce and valuable commodity for the Wola and they use it sparingly). Sauces and savoury dips for guests to add to their vegetables and meat, supplemented with bread rolls and butter, make tasty innovations. The Wola drink only water, which is good for washing down a stone oven meal; but your guests would probably frown on this alone, and any long drink goes well with it.

A Wola *Saway* and a Suburban Garden Party: Points of Difference

In many ways the Wola are similar to people reported from other areas of the Highlands. They are shifting cultivators and their staple crop is sweet potato, which they supplement with the other crops listed in Table 1. Men do the initial preparation of new gardens, and women most of the routine work. Men also do most of the work involved in keeping pigs, but, unlike vegetables, these are not simply a source of food: they are wealth. Other items of wealth include pearl- and cowrie-shells, crude salt, birds' feathers and stone axes, and the exchange of these things on specified occasions, such as at a marriage or at a death, is very important to the Wola, and men who excel at this achieve positions of renown. But, although their success earns them some influence, these men are not leaders of groups and their position does not give them control' over the actions of others.

The Wola live in named groups which they call big families. These occupy specific territories and have a genealogical connection, but they are not corporate bodies which unite for collective action. Temporary action-sets characterize group events in Wola society and these form when several men think that it is in their individual interests to join together for some activity. A belief in the value of the freedom of the individual to control his own actions, which is the ethos of Wola life, precludes the existence of permanent political groups which men are obliged to support. The exchange of wealth is highly valued, and successful men earn respect because, in the absence of other institutionalized mechanisms, it is this which ensures an ordered social life without interfering with the sovereignty of the individual.[5]

The daily eating habits of Wola adults, who do not often share a meal together, reflect the emphasis placed on individual action, and it is to balance this anarchic drift that their society places value on formal exchanges of wealth, because these bring people together and prompt them to co-operate socially. Pork is one of the valuables which they give to one another in these exchanges, and, as a result, when men cook several pigs at events analogous to garden parties, they emphasize the distribution of meat – not its eating: guests take home their share to eat. Even when they prepare an oven for vegetables, the mainstay of their diet, and come together over the meal, commensality is not important to them.

This is the reverse of our attitudes at a garden party, where it is sharing the meal which is important and expresses sociability. But the principle of exchange, on which Wola society has overtly developed, also underlies these occasions. All social interaction, including communal meals, involves exchange,[6] and in England, where many individual rights fall under state control, exchange still figures prominently at the level of interpersonal relations, and the reciprocation of food at a party, drinks in a pub, presents and cards at Christmas, and so on, play a significant part in maintaining social relations. So, while the outward appearance of a Wola *saway* mark it off from a suburban garden party, the same forces are at work in different guises.

As a final point of interest on a less academic plane, hosts may wish to exercise the imaginations of their guests by telling them that many cannibals in the South Seas cooked their meals of human flesh in earth ovens, and not in the iron cauldrons of comic strips.

NOTES

1   The earth oven is found throughout the Pacific and descriptions of it in Melanesia occur regularly, from early accounts through to present-day monographs – for example, see Codrington (1891, 320), Haddon (1912, 132), Blackwood (1935, 273), Pospisil (1963, 371–2) and Heider (1970, 47–8). A detailed description of this way of cooking in another part of the South Seas occurs in Firth's (1963, 95–103) account of Tikopia people.
2   I acknowledge a debt of gratitude to the Wola people of Haelaelinja who taught me how to cook in an earth oven, and to my wife and our neighbours, the Motherwells, who helped me to build an earth oven in our Cambridge back garden.
3   See Sillitoe (1975) for a description of such events.
4   Some of the more exotic vegetables are available in Asian food shops.
5   See Sillitoe (1975) for details of this interpretation of Wola society.
6   See Ekeh (1974) for a summary of sociological ideas relating to exchange.

REFERENCES

Blackwood, B., *Both Sides of Buka Passage*, Oxford: Clarendon Press, 1935.

Codrington, R. H., *The Melanesians*, Oxford: Clarendon Press, 1891.

Ekeh, P., *Social Exchange Theory*, London: Heinemann, 1974.

Firth, R., *We, the Tikopia*, Boston: Beacon Press, 1963.

Haddon, A. C., *Reports of the Cambridge Anthropological Expedition to Torres Straits*, Cambridge University Press, 1912.

Heider, K. G., *The Dugum Dani*, Viking Fund Publications in Anthropology no. 49, New York: Wenner–Gren Foundation, 1970.

Pospisil, L., *Kapauku Papuan Economy*, Yale University Publications in Anthropology, no. 67, New Haven, 1963.

Sillitoe, P., 'The Exchange of Wealth and Achievement of Renown in Wola Society', Cambridge: PhD dissertation, 1975.

Lindsay Verrier

Pacific Island Recipes

An Island Yeast (Rice and Seawater)

Take a clean 2-pint jar (it needn't have a tight lid) and in it put 3 tbsp flour, of sugar, and of dry uncooked rice. Then add rather more than a pint of half seawater and half freshwater. Leave it around the kitchen, with the lid off, for a few days, and it will soon ferment when a wandering yeast blows in with the wind. (A spoonful of a neighbour's successful yeast is a good starter.) When it is nicely bubbly, mix well, let the rice settle, and use (1¼ pt to 2 lb flour, or 850 ml to 1 kilo flour) when making bread, buns, and so on, by any usual method. Leave yeast-residue in the jar, with lid on.

When you next contemplate making bread, start the night before, making up the volume with half seawater and half freshwater, and stirring in 3 tbsp flour and 3 tbsp sugar. The rice, with these repeated operations, will gradually diminish and will need renewing.

Sometimes a dreadful-smelling yeast finds its way in, and you have to wash out and start again; but mostly it works well: I kept one brew going for more than a year at Tarawa in the Gilbert Islands. Of course the sea there is crystal clear.

Coconut Leaf Cookery

In 1962 Messrs Checchi and Company (USA), according to a report in the *Fiji Times* of Suva, made a survey of tourism in the islands, and among other measures advised that tourists be fed on local foods, such as 'fish baked in coconut leave'. This inspired the following.

The American advisers to the tourist trade have told us to offer people 'fish baked in coconut leaves'. This is an excellent dish (says an experimental cook) which is too seldom seen on our tables. One fish and two coconut leaves will be enough. There is no difficulty about the fish; but the leaves will require careful manipulation. It is not so much getting them into the oven as getting them into the kitchen. Those who lead with the feeble or wavy end of the leaf mostly fail. You should take the *thick* end – the part that was joined to the tree – clasp it tightly to your waist, and run smartly into the kitchen. The thin end follows, as do various ornaments, side-tables, and teacups collected on the way. The second leaf, however, will have a clear field of entry. Take the fish, and wrap the leaves carefully around it in all directions. Most fish seem to resent this and tend to slither away. A good plan is to take eight broomsticks, and stack them in the kitchen like bivouacked rifles, when the fish can be firmly wedged on top, and the wrapping undertaken with free hands. You should start wrapping *always* with the *thin* end of each leaf, so that most of the work will have been done when you come to the awful business of wrapping with the thick ends. Many people (writes Aunt Betsy) just forget about the last little inch or two, and leave them sticking out. Do not pause in the wrapping process, because coconut leaves are great unwrappers. When the fish is fully wrapped, you can tie the bundle with wire and carefully remove the broomsticks one by one. Then give the bundle a good *shake* in an *up-and-down* direction, when the fish will easily slide out and can be baked in a tin in the usual way.

Isobel White

'The Natives Live Well'

In all the world there cannot be any other people who so evidently enjoy eating as do Australian Aborigines. There are reports from early explorers and settlers that some European foods were at first rejected, particularly fat of salt meat, but now there are few of our foods that are not eaten with relish, particularly those that are sweet and rich. Since animals traditionally hunted tend to be lean, Aborigines still prefer lean mutton and beef to lamb and pork, and lean meat is without doubt their favourite food. This is not to imply that fat had not traditional use or significance. Human kidney fat was reputed to be eaten by sorcerers; and emu and goanna* fat had special ritual and magical significance: it was rubbed on wooden spears and spear-throwers to preserve and strengthen them and was also massaged into painful joints. The Western Desert word *ganbi* (fat) is used exactly as we use 'sweet', to refer to a charming person, particularly to describe a good child.

Enjoyment of food comes from the food itself and could never have been much affected by the method of cooking, since all food is cooked on the fire without benefit of pots or pans. Animals, birds and reptiles are gutted and cooked whole, small ones merely thrown onto the hot coals, larger ones in a firepit. For a kangaroo a pit is dug and filled with firewood, which is lighted and allowed to burn down to hot coals. Then the whole animal is put in the pit, covered with hot coals and allowed to cook for anything from half an hour to 2 hours, according to the patience of those to be fed. Since the normal human condition is to be hungry, seldom is the meat even half-way cooked; in fact the inside of a large kangaroo, weighing 60–70 lb, may be only warm. The meat is dark red, tough and strong-tasting, and dripping with blood. At first I used to dread being handed my hunk of meat, which only good manners and fear of giving offence made me eat. Soon I discovered that there was variation in taste among my companions, equivalent to that shown in a steak-house, where diners are asked whether they want their

* The large iguana of Australia – up to 6 feet long.

steaks rare, medium or well done. So I would join others of the party who put their portions back on the fire to cook some more and by the time it had become brown, crisp and well cooked I could eat it with some pleasure. Lizard and goanna I could never get to like; witchetty grubs have a curious nutty flavour, but I can easily live without them. However, my favourite native food is wombat, a large burrowing marsupial, common on the Nullarbor Plain bordering the Reserve where I have done most of my research. Wombat meat is white when cooked and has a delicate flavour somewhat between pork and veal.

If any kangaroo meat is left for the following day it may be put on the fire to re-cook. Nowadays if a frying-pan and some cooking fat are available, the meat is cut into slices and fried. Once, while this was in progress, I witnessed an acrimonious fight between two sisters, both in their early twenties, and usually the best of friends and companions. An Aboriginal camp naturally has its share of the famous Australian blowflies, and meat is always fly-blown by the second day. The older sister carefully scraped off the maggots from each piece before putting it into the pan; the younger sister did not take this amount of trouble. The older sister called the other by terms which could be translated as 'dirty slut' and 'lazy, shiftless good-for-nothing'. The younger countered with the equivalent of 'goody-goody' and 'tattle-tale'. It seemed to me that many years of resentment – and, as between any pair of siblings, there were causes for resentment on both sides – were touched off by this minor disagreement.

In traditional times the division of labour between men and women (as with many other societies) delegated the more exciting and ritually important tasks to the men while women worked longer hours at the more tedious tasks. Aboriginal men went hunting (but not necessarily every day) and the women had the daily task of foraging, digging for roots, collecting berries, nuts, seeds and small animals. On return to camp seeds had to be winnowed and laboriously ground and made into damper (native bread). In addition women were, and still are, responsible for the family's supply of water and firewood.

In the 1970s, hunting still continues, but more as a pastime than a necessity, to add variety to the diet rather than for subsistence, and guns and European breeds of hunting-dog are used instead of spears, spear-throwers and half-tamed dingoes. The anthropologist, who is likely to be in control of a four-wheel drive vehicle, can gain popularity and repay some of his debt to his informants by taking them hunting, away from the immediate surroundings of the camp from which all game has disappeared.

The women's traditional contribution to the food supply, on the other hand, has been almost totally replaced by store-bought bread, biscuits, processed cereals, fresh and canned fruit, butter, margarine, jam, golden syrup, powdered milk, potatoes and onions, and those great staples (so damaging to the formerly perfect Aboriginal teeth) tea, sugar and flour. White flour is preferred because it is said to make better damper, and is bought by the sack,

25 or 50 lb. This is carried from store to camp on the head of the purchaser and on arrival at camp is put with other foods in a fork of a tree to keep it from the ever-ravenous scrounging dogs, which outnumber humans in any camp.

Today a woman is judged by how well she makes damper and I give here a recipe, learned by watching a famous damper-maker (mine were never as good as hers).

Australian Aboriginal Damper

1 Retrieve your axe from whomever has borrowed it, collect plenty of firewood and make up the camp-fire, so that it is 3 or 4 feet in diameter and burning brightly. I suspect there are few firewoods in the world so hot and clear burning as some of the Australian acacias. Where I lived with Aborigines the firewood used was Western Myall (*Acacia sowdenii*). (This wood is used to make native artefacts, the main source of income for these Aborigines; they are famous for their careful craftsmanship, and their products are sold all over the world; this activity leaves much waste wood, which is used for fires when dry and seasoned.)

2 Find a large pan or dish. This may be the hardest task of all. In a society unused to such items there never seems any place to keep them in the native bough shelters. In any case no woman can refuse to lend hers to a neighbour or refuse to hand it to any young child who wants it to make play dampers of earth and water· Having found a pan and shaken off the sand or dirt put there by the child, put in some flour, some salt and some baking powder ('some' means about 5 lb (2·5 kilos) flour, a couple of tbsp baking powder (about 2 oz./60 grams) and the same of salt).

3 Go and get some water (if you can find a bucket – the same process may be necessary as for the pan). The one water-tank kept filled by the mission water-truck is probably two or three hundred yards away, so it might have been better to get it first of all. N.B. While away getting water, make quite sure that the pan of flour is out of reach of children and dogs, or you will have to start the whole process again (if you still have any flour left). It would be much better if you could persuade a younger woman or a girl to fetch the water. Don't ask a man or a boy, as it is demeaning for a male to carry water.

4 Now add enough water to the flour to make a stiff dough. Spread an old flour-sack on the ground, turn the dough on to it and knead well.

5 Shape into a cake about 2 inches thick and perfectly round, about the size of a large bicycle wheel. (My teacher could make them so symmetrical that they looked machine made.) N.B. Fend off dogs and children all the time. The

children will want to pinch off pieces of dough. One dog will take the lot. This anthropologist once lost the whole of her supper while her back was turned for seconds.

6 Pull the fire aside. It should by now have burned down to hot coals. Rake flat an area of hot ash and place the damper on it. Cover with more hot ash (about 1 inch thick) and leave for 20 or 30 minutes. Jets of steam can be seen breaking through the hot ash during the cooking, and when there is no more steam, the damper is done. Remove from ashes and brush off adhering charcoal, ash and sand. This damper is delicious eaten hot with butter and jam, syrup or honey. Some of my Aboriginal friends dunk it in very sweet tea.

Another staple in today's diet is *dinamead* (tin of meat), the most expensive being corned beef, as all campers know. The cheapest is 'camp pie', a seasoned mixture of mutton and cereal, mostly cereal, which Aborigines quite like. I would rather go hungry. However, one of my fellow anthropologists assures me that you can make a meal of it if you are hungry enough, if you eat it with a can of beetroot.

I have written about the desert people, the ones I know well. Those who have lived longer than I have with Aborigines in the tropical coastal regions of Northern Australia are enthusiastic about some of the foods, for example, dugong, turtle and various kinds of fish and shellfish. Since these ingredients are not readily available it is not much good giving a recipe. I will only mention that the late, incomparable writer and raconteur, Bill Harney (a white man who spent most of his life with Aborigines), describes with enthusiasm the joys of eating turtle, killed, gutted and laid on its back, in a firepit, so that the shell acts as a cooking vessel and a most powerful soup collects at the bottom of the shell.[1] He also has the following useful recipe for hot-weather campers anywhere in the world.[2]

The Whistling Steak

A fact discovered by the Aborigines, and useful to people who are hard-pressed for food, is that food soaked in water loses any poisonous content (as witness the treatment of cycad palm nuts). Anything that has 'gone off' is soaked by the Aborigines.

I remember a 10 lb piece of rump steak that was hanging so long that it swelled up and went perfectly green. In fact, it whistled when you passed it. I yelled out to one of the people to throw it away. He said, 'No, we'll take it to the camp and eat it. This is good tucker.'

This is what the locals did: they soaked that piece of steak for two days in running water, then they cooked it in the ground oven with leaves around it, as usual, to flavour it. After it was cooked and taken out, it looked so beautiful and smelled so good that I reckoned I would have a little bit of it. It was absolutely marvellous! It was tender and tasty, and provided that you could get over the fact that it had been green, it made a fine meal.

A veterinary friend later told me that it was quite safe to have eaten the 'whistling steak'. The bacilli that poison people, he said, are on the meat only when it *first* starts to go off. Once meat goes green *it is not poisonous*. The water and the fire destroyed both the bacilli and the smell.

NOTES

1   *Bill Harney's Cook Book*, Lansdowne Press, Melbourne, 1960, chapter 7.
2   ibid., p. 59.

Claude Lévi-Strauss

The Roast and the Boiled

Food presents itself to man in three main states: it may be raw, cooked or rotten. In relationship to culinary operations, the raw state constitutes the unmarked pole, whereas the other two are strongly marked, although in opposite directions: the cooked being a cultural transformation of the raw, and the rotten its natural transformation. Underlying the main triangle, there is, then, a double opposition between *processed/non-processed*, on the one hand, and *culture/nature*, on the other.

Considered in themselves, these categories are no more than empty forms which tell us nothing about the cooking methods of any particular society. What each society understands by 'raw', 'cooked' and 'rotten' can only be determined through ethnographical observation, and there is no reason why they should all be in agreement about the definitions. The recent increase in the number of Italian restaurants in France has given French people a taste for raw food in a much 'rawer' state than was traditional with us: the vegetables are simply washed and cut up, without being prepared with an oil and vinegar dressing, according to the usual French custom – except for radishes, which, however, are significantly felt to require a generous accompaniment of butter and salt. Through Italian influence we have, then, extended our category of the raw. Certain incidents which occurred after the Allied landings in 1944 show that American soldiers had a broader conception of the category of the rotten than the French; under the impression that the Normandy cheese dairies stank of corpses, they sometimes destroyed the buildings.

It follows that the triangle formed by the *raw*, the *cooked*, and the *rotten* defines a semantic field, but only from the outside. In all forms of cooking, the food is not just cooked; the process must be carried out in some particular way. Nor does there exist any pure state of the raw: only certain foodstuffs can be eaten raw, and even then only after having been washed, peeled, cut up, and frequently seasoned. Lastly, even those traditions which most readily accept rottenness, only tolerate it in certain spontaneous or controlled forms.

In *The Raw and the Cooked*, I deliberately ignored these shades of difference. On the basis of South American examples, my aim was to define the culinary triangle in its most general manifestation and to show how, in every culture, it could be used as a formal framework to express other oppositions, either cosmological or sociological. Having thus characterized it from the inside by the analysis of its internal properties, I proceeded, in *From Honey to Ashes*, to approach it from the outside and to study its 'neighbourhood'. Still keeping to the formal point of view, I sought to define the raw, the cooked and the rotten, considered no longer simply in themselves or from the angle of oppositional systems comparable to the one they constitute, but in relation to peripheral functions: the more-than-raw, that is honey, and the more-than-cooked, that is tobacco. Although certain modalities of the cooked, such as the roast and the boiled, were met with in the course of the enquiry (*From Honey to Ashes*, p. 339, n. 32), I deliberately refrained from discussing them.

The time has now come to do so, since the myths studied in this third volume [*The Origin of Table Manners*] go beyond oppositions between the raw, the cooked and the rotten to establish a deliberate contrast between the roast and the boiled, which, in a great many cultures, represent the basic modes of cooking. Along with other no less genuine oppositions, they figure in a French work of the twelfth century which deserves to be quoted at the beginning of this discussion. In a concentrated form, which gives a denser meaning to each term, it outlines the possibility of a structural analysis of the language of cooking: 'Others devote too much vain study to preparing meats, excogitating infinite kinds of decoctions, fryings and seasonings; craving, like women great with child, now soft, now hard, now cold, now hot, now boiled, now roast, now with pepper, now with garlic, now with cinnamon, now with savoury salt' (Hugues de Saint-Victor, *De Institutione novitiarum*, in Franklin, p. 157). This passage establishes a major opposition between food and seasoning; and it distinguishes between two extreme forms of the preparation of foods: boiling and frying, which in turn have several modalities classifiable in pairs: soft and hard, cold and hot, boiled and roast. Lastly, it also classifies seasonings in contrasted pairs: pepper and garlic on the one hand and cinnamon and salt on the other, by opposing – along one axis – pepper and what, a century later, were still called in French *les aigruns* (garlic, onions, shallots, etc.; see Améro, vol. 2, p. 92); and, along the other axis, sweet spices and salt.

What, then, constitutes the opposition between the roast and the boiled? Roasted food, being directly exposed to fire is in a relationship of *non-mediatized conjunction*, whereas boiled food is the product of a two-fold process of mediation: it is immersed in water and both food and water are contained within a receptacle.

So, on two counts, the roast can be placed on the side of nature, and the boiled on the side of culture. Literally, since boiled food necessitates the use of a receptacle, which is a cultural object; and symbolically, in the sense that culture mediates between man and the world, and boiling is also a mediation, by means of water, between the food which man ingests and that other element of the physical world: fire.

The simplest way of conceiving of the opposition postulates that the more primitive technique appeared first: 'In ancient times men roasted everything', was the Greek view, as expressed by Aristotle. He adds that, consequently, it is permissible to boil meat that has been previously roasted, but not to roast meat that has been previously boiled, since that would be to run counter to history (*Problemata*, III, 43; quoted by Reinach, vol. 5, p. 63). His conclusion is far from being universally accepted, but its premises are found among widely differing communities. The natives of New Caledonia who were acquainted with the use of pottery before the arrival of the French were all the more inclined for this reason to stress that, once upon a time, 'people only broiled or roasted, "burnt" as the natives say . . . The use of the cooking pot and the eating of boiled tubers are proudly considered . . . as proofs of . . . civilization' (Barrau, pp. 57–8). An Omaha origin myth (Fletcher and La Flesche, pp. 70–1) relates how men first invented fire and ate their meat roasted; but they grew tired of this daily diet and wondered how they could prepare meat differently. So they invented pottery, put water in the pot, meat in the water and the whole lot on the fire. In this way they learned to eat their meat boiled. The Micmac also harked back to primitive customs, but to justify their predilection for roast meat (Wallis, p. 404).

The opposition by virtue of which roast is on the side of nature and boiled on the side of culture and which is implicit in the preceding examples, is underlaid by another opposition between non-processed and processed food. It should, however, be recognized that this last opposition can take on very different values, since not all societies define the boiled and the roast in the same way.

The Plains Indians provide an excellent illustration of the divergencies. Some tribes cook their food for a long time, others only for a little while, or they may prescribe very different cooking times, according to whether the meat is to be boiled or roasted. The Assiniboine, for instance, preferred roast meat to boiled meat, but in either case they liked it underdone (Denig, pp. 581–2). Their neighbours, the Blackfoot, who cooked their meat for a long time when they roasted it, reduced boiling to what our cooks call blanching, that is, they plunged the meat into boiling water for a few seconds, until it lost its external colouring (Grinnell, n. 205). These two cooking styles contrasted with the method practised by the Kansa and Osage, who liked their food to be overcooked (Hunter, p. 348), as well as with the practice of the Ingalik of Alaska: they believed that fish should be eaten either well done or raw, or dried or rotten, but never half cooked, since fish, when half cooked, was not considered to be well prepared (Osgood, p. 165).

Turning finally to South America, we find that, according to Armentia (p. 11), the Cavina used to eat overboiled food which they allowed to cook slowly from 6 o'clock in the evening until 2 o'clock in the morning and then left to stand until daybreak, before serving. No doubt it was from the Indians that the settlers of Dutch Guiana got their recipe for the 'pepper-poy', kept going from day to day by putting the remains of the last meal into the pot, along with a little freshly-made sauce. This stew improved with age. One example is quoted of a stew – a prized domestic possession, like a certain famous French *cassoulet* – which lasted for thirty consecutive years without the pot ever being cleaned (Schomburgk, vol. 1, p. 96).

I would not maintain, then, that all societies must necessarily put the boiled into the category of the processed and the roast into the opposite category. It would be more accurate to say, in the first place, that the opposition between roast and boiled seems to be operative in all contexts, however diverse its empirical content may be, and second that this particular way of formulating it seems to be more frequent than the other way. As a matter of fact, in many societies a double affinity can be observed: that of the roast with the raw, i.e. the non-processed, and that of the boiled with the rotten, which is one of the two modes of the processed.

The affinity of the roast with the raw results from the fact that, more often than not, it is compatible with incomplete cooking, this incompleteness even being a sought-after effect in our West European societies. Incompleteness occurs whenever roast meat is unevenly cooked, either on one side or the other, or on the outside in relation to the inside. A Wyandot myth (Woodman, p. 8) emphasizes this paradoxal nature of roast meat: 'The Creator caused fire to gush forth and directed the first man to put a portion of the meat on a stick and to roast it before the fire. But the man was so ignorant that he let it stand until it was burnt on one side, while it was raw on the other.' The Pocomchi of Mexico regard roasting as a compromise between the raw and the burnt. After the universal conflagration (Mayers, p. 10), that which had escaped the fire became white, and that which had been burnt, black. That which had been merely singed became red. This explains the various colours of corn seeds and beans. Among the Waiwai of British Guiana, the shaman must never eat roast or fried meat. However, the Waiwai rarely resort to these methods of cooking and 'prefer to boil or cure their meat' (Fock, p. 132); nor must he come into contact with the colour red or with blood, a detail which also suggests an affinity between the roast and the raw. Aristotle rated boiling higher than roasting, on the grounds that it was more effective in destroying the rawness of meat: 'roast meat being rawer and drier than boiled meat' (quoted by Reinach).

The affinity between the boiled and the rotten is indicated in several European languages by expressions such as *pot-pourri* or *olla podrida*, which refer to different kinds of meat seasoned and cooked with vegetables; there is also the German expression *zu Brei zerkochtes Fleisch*, 'meat cooked until rotten'. Certain American languages indicate the same affinity, and it is significant that this should be so among the Sioux communities, neighbours of the Mandan, who were extremely fond of 'gamy' meat, to the point of preferring the flesh of a dead animal which had been a long time in the water to that of a freshly-killed buffalo. In the Dakota language, the verb *i-ku-ka* conveys both the idea of decomposition or deterioration caused by some external influence, and that of boiling food which has been cut into pieces and mixed with other ingredients (Riggs, p. 196). The Mandan verb *na'xerep* here, 'to boil', seems to imply prolonged cooking until the meat falls off the bones (Kennard, p. 12).

These distinctions by no means exhaust the complexities of the contrast between the roast and the boiled. Boiling takes place inside [a receptacle], whereas roasting is cooking from the outside: one suggests the concave, the other the convex. Thus, the boiled often belongs to what might be called 'endo-cooking', intended for private use and for a small closed group. This is most forcefully expressed in the Hidatsa language, where the same word *mi dá ksi* is used for the fence surrounding the village, the cooking-pot and the pan, since all three delimit an enclosed space (W. Matthews, p. 126). The roast, on the contrary, belongs to 'exo-cooking', the kind that is offered to strangers. In France in the old days, *la poule au pot* (boiled fowl) was a family supper dish, whereas roast meat was reserved for banquets, where it enjoyed pride of place. It always came after the boiled meat and herbs which were served at the beginning of the meal, and was accompanied by rare fruit, such as melons, oranges, olives and capers: 'The roast is set down on the table while the boiled food and the entrées are being cleared away . . . But the time to serve the fish is towards the end of the meat course, between the roast and the dessert' (Franklin, pp. 221–3).

The same opposition is found in non-European societies, although they do not formulate it in the same way. Among the Kaingang of southern Brazil, widows and widowers are forbidden to eat boiled meat, and so is someone who has killed an enemy (Henry, vol. 1, p. 184, and n. 15). Boiled meat could thus connote a strengthening of family and social ties, and roast meat a weakening of these ties.

The opposition between the roast and the boiled may occur on other levels too, not only in myths and ritual, but also in daily life. Several American tribes associate the roast with living in the bush and masculinity, the boiled with village life and femininity. The Amazonian Yagua boil or smoke their meat. The first process is carried out only by the women, but the smoking may be done by the men when they are out hunting, and in the village itself if the women are absent (Fejos, p. 44). Karsten explains (p. 115) that the Jivaro boil meat in an earthenware pot or roast it in front of the fire. They use the second method when they are camping away from the village to hunt, fish or perform other tasks, and it is the only method that a man may decently employ. In the village, boiling is carried out exclusively by the women; a man never boils anything apart from decoctions of tobacco and other magic plants. Goldman (p. 79) states that the Cubeo adopt 'the common tropical forest pattern: women boil, the men bake and broil'.* In Trumai villages, according to Murphy and Quain (p. 30), 'the men did all the roasting, although it was permissible for the women to help. However most foods were prepared by boiling, and the burden of cooking thus fell on the women'.

The Ingalik of the north-western part of the northern hemisphere divided foodstuffs into two categories, according to whether they had to be boiled or broiled: 'the boiling of food is the standard method of cooking when food is prepared in the house . . . and . . . broiling, except for certain fish, is limited to the travelling camp' (Osgood, pp. 276–7). On the other hand, the Tanana, their easterly neighbours, who ate almost all their food boiled, nevertheless made cooking a purely male task. This unusual practice was, it seems, shared by other northern Athapaskan tribes, such as the Ahtena, the Tanaina and certain Kutchin communities, although groups such as the Chandalar-Kutchin and the Loucheux, who were closely related to them in respect of habitat, language and culture, entrusted cooking to the women (McKennan, pp. 41–6). But among the Sahaptin of the Columbia River, it was the men who did the cooking (Garth, p. 52).

As was noted above, the Sioux-speaking Assiniboine reversed the usual connotations of the roast and the boiled in their culinary procedures. It is consequently all the more curious to find them adopting attitudes similar to those of the Athapaskan to which I have just referred: 'when the men were at war . . . they ate their food boiled. The women never used this method: their normal method consisted in roasting the meat on a spit tilted over the fire . . . formerly they used to make and cook with earthenware receptacles . . . but only the men used them' (Lowie, p. 12). A group of Menomini myths follows the same system: contrary to the real life practice, they present the women as roasting the meat, and the men as boiling it; but the women in these myths are ogresses. The attribution of boiling to men and of roasting to women also seems to occur in certain eastern European countries.

The existence of these deviant systems poses a problem. It suggests that the semantic field of recipes includes a greater number of dimensions than I indicated at the beginning of my discussion. No doubt, the communities among whom these inversions occur are thinking in terms of different oppositional axes. In this respect, I can make one or two tentative suggestions. For instance, boiling provides a method of preserving all the meat and its juices, whereas roasting involves destruction or loss. One suggests economy, the other waste; the second is aristocratic, the first plebeian. This aspect of the matter is obvious in societies which stress status differences between individuals or classes. Among the ancient Maori, a nobleman was allowed to

---

* However, the terms 'bake and broil' do not seem to be very consistent with 'the common tropical forest pattern', which is based rather on roasting and smoking.

roast his own food, but he avoided all contact with cooking utensils and baking-ovens, which were looked after by slaves and low-class women. To compare someone with a 'steaming oven' was, moreover, to proffer a deadly insult. Nothing, it was thought, was more likely than steam to spoil the physical and mental attributes of a highly born person, or of nature in its wild state: birds disappeared from the forests when people got into the habit of taking boiled food there. When white settlers introduced pots and pans into New Zealand, the natives believed that these were infected utensils, like the hot stones of their ovens (Prytz-Johansen, pp. 46, 89, 208–11). These attitudes represent a striking reversal of those already noted among the Kanaka of New Caledonia.

Similar observations can be made about European societies, in which attitudes towards the roast and the boiled have evolved in the course of time. The democratic spirit which inspired the compilers of the *Encyclopédie* in the eighteenth century is reflected in their vindication of boiled food: '. . . one of the most succulent and nourishing foods available to man . . . It might be said that the boiled is to other dishes as bread is to other kinds of food' (see under 'bouilli'). Fifty years later the dandy, Brillat-Savarin, was to take the opposite view (p. 73):

> Professors never eat *bouilli*, both out of respect for the principles of gastronomy and because they have often preached this undeniable truth to their pupils: *Bouilli* is meat without its juice. This truth is beginning to penetrate, and *bouilli* is no longer served by the self-respecting host; it has been replaced by a roast fillet, a turbot, or a *matelote*.

The reason why the Czechs look upon boiled meat as a man's food may be that their traditional society is more democratic in character than that of their Slovak or Polish neighbours. A similar interpretation might be suggested for the contrasting attitudes of the Romans, the Greeks and the Hebrews towards the roast and the boiled, which have been recently described by Professor Piganiol.

Elsewhere, the opposition may take a different form. Since boiled meat is prepared without loss of substance and within a closely confined space, it may seem a fitting symbol of cosmic totality. The Arawak of Guiana had a rule that the meat of animals killed in the hunt should be gently boiled in a pot without a lid, which had to be constantly watched in case it boiled over. Should it do so, all animals of that species would leave the area and could no longer be hunted (Roth, p. 295). At the other extremity of the continent, in the Great Lakes area of North America, the Fox observed the same rule for the cooking of ceremonial food: 'Should it boil over, then all life would all go outside.' There was also a rule that nothing must be dropped into the pot during cooking; while the contents were being eaten, not even the tiniest scrap could be left, or dropped (Michelson, pp. 249, 261).

Boiled food is life, roast food death. Folklore the world over offers countless examples of the cauldron of immortality; but there is no indication anywhere of a spit of immortality. A rite performed by the Cree Indians of Canada conveys very clearly the cosmic totality attributed to boiled food. The Cree believed that the Creator told humans that the first berries to be picked had to be boiled. Then the bowl had to be held first towards the sun, 'who was asked to ripen the berries, then towards the thunder who was asked for rain, and finally towards the earth, who was asked to bring forth her fruits' (Mandelbaum, p. 285). For the Ojibwa too, boiled meat had a relationship to the order of the universe; although they usually cooked squirrels by spitting the carcases and roasting them in the flames, they purposely boiled them when rain was needed (Speck, p. 80). In this case, the roast and the boiled are given differential functions and their combination constitutes a culinary universe, which is a miniature reflection of the cosmos. No doubt a similar interpretation would be appropriate for the extraordinary Welsh recipe which involved stuffing roast goose with boiled ox-tongue and then encasing it in a layer of forcemeat, inside a pastry crust; the dish was supposed to last all through Christmas week (Owen, p. 34).

Here we find a link-up with the symbolism of the most remote Indo-European past, as it has been reconstituted by Professor Dumézil (p. 60): 'To Mithra belongs that which breaks of its own accord, that which is steamed, that which is properly sacrificed, milk . . . and to Varuna that which is cut with an axe, that which is sealed in the naked flame, *soma*, the intoxicating liquid.' It is not a little surprising, but extremely significant, to find certain genial philosophers of cooking of the mid-nineteenth century showing the same awareness of the contrast between knowledge and inspiration, serenity and violence, moderation and excess, symbolized in like fashion by the opposition between the boiled and the roast: 'A man can become a cook, but he has to be born a rôtisseur' (Brillat-Savarin, p. 14, aphorism XV); 'Roasting is both nothing at all and absolutely everything' (Marquis de Cussy, *L'Art culinaire*, in Améro, vol. 1, p. 367).

REFERENCES

Améro, J., *Les Classiques de la table*, 2 vols, new ed., Paris, 1855.
Armentia, N., 'Arte y vocabulario de la Lengua Cavineña', *Revista del Museo de la Plata*, 13, 1906.
Barrau, J., *L'Agriculture vivrière autochtone de la Nouvelle-Calédonie* (Commission du Pacifique sud), Nouméa, 1956.
Brillat-Savarin, J.-A., *The Philosopher in the Kitchen*, Harmondsworth, 1970 (originally published as *La Physiologie du goût* in 1825).
Denig, E. T., 'Indian tribes of the upper Missouri', *46th Ann. Report Bureau Am. Ethnology* (1928-9), Washington, D.C., 1930.

Dumézil, G., *Les Dieux des Germains: Essai sur la formation de la religion scandinave*, Paris, 1959.

Fejos, P., 'Ethnography of the Yagua', *Viking Fund Publications in Anthropology*, vol. 1, New York, 1943.

Fletcher, A. C. and La Flesche, F., 'The Omaha tribe', *27th Ann. Report Bureau Am. Ethnology* (1905–6), Washington, D.C., 1911.

Fock, N., 'Waiwai: Religion and society of an Amazonian tribe', *National-museets skrifter: Ethnografisk Roekke*, 8, Copenhagen, 1963.

Franklin, A., *La Vie privée d'autrefois: Les repas*, Paris, 1889.

Garth, Th.R., 'Early nineteenth-century tribal relations in the Columbia Plateau', *Southwestern J. Anthrop.*, 20 (1), 1964.

Goldman, I., 'The Cubeo Indians of the northwest Amazon', *Illinois Stud. Anthrop.*, no. 2, Urbana, 1963.

Grinnell, G. B., 'Cheyenne woman customs', *Am. Anthrop.*, 4, 1902.

Henry, J., *Jungle People: a Kaingáng Tribe of the Highlands of Brazil*, New York, 1941.

Hunter, J. D., *Manners and Customs of Several Indian Tribes Located West of the Mississippi* (reprint), Minneapolis, 1957.

Karsten, R., 'The headhunters of western Amazonas', *Societas Scientiarum Fennica* (Helsingfors), 7 (1), 1935.

Kennard, E., 'Mandan grammar', *Int. J. Am. Linguistics*, 9 (1), 1936–8.

Lévi-Strauss, C., *From Honey to Ashes*, London, 1972.

Lowie, R. H., 'The Assiniboine', *Anthrop. Papers Am. Mus. Nat. Hist.*, 4 (1), New York, 1909.

McKennan, R. A., 'The upper Tanana Indians', *Yale Univ. Publ. Anthrop.*, 55, 1959.

Mandelbaum, D. G., 'The Plains Cree', *Anthrop. Publ. Am. Mus. Nat. Hist.*, 37 (2), New York, 1940.

Matthews, W., *Grammar and Dictionary of the Language of the Hidatsa*, New York, 1873.

Mayers, M., *Pocomchi Texts*, University of Oklahoma Press, 1958.

Michelson, T., 'The mythical origin of the white buffalo dance of the Fox Indians', *40th Ann. Report Bureau Am. Ethnology*, Washington, D.C., 1919.

Murphy, R. F. and Quain, B., 'The Trumaí Indians of central Brazil', *Monographs Am. Ethn. Soc.*, 24, New York, 1955.

Osgood, C., 'Ingalik social structure', *Yale Univ. Publ. Anthrop.*, 53, 1958.

Owen, Trefor M., *Welsh Folk Customs*, Cardiff, 1959.

Prytz-Johansen, J., *The Maori and his Religion*, Copenhagen, 1954.

Reinach, S., *Cultes, mythes et religions*, 5 vols, Paris, 1905–23.

Riggs, S. R., 'A Dakota-English dictionary', *Contrib. to N. Am. Ethn.*, 7, Washington, D.C., 1890.

Roth, W. E., 'An inquiry into the animism and folklore of the Guiana Indians', *30th Ann. Report Bureau Am. Ethnology* (1908–9), Washington, D.C., 1915.

Schomburgk, R., *Travels in British Guiana 1840–44*, 2 vols, Georgetown, 1922.

Speck, F. G., 'Myths and folk-lore of the Timiskaming Algonquin and Timagami Ojibwa', Canada Dept. of Mines, Geological Survey, *Memoirs*, Anthrop. Series, 71 (9), Ottawa, 1915.

Wallis, W. D., *The Micmac Indians of Eastern Canada*, Minneapolis, 1955.

Woodman, J. J., *Indian Legends and Tales of Captivity*, Boston, 1924.